THE FIGHTING TIGERS 1993-2008

Merry Christmas, Dad

Forever LSU!

Scott Rabalais

THE FIGHTING TIGERS 1993-2008

Into a New Century of LSU Football

SCOTT RABALAIS

With a Foreword by Peter Finney

 Louisiana State University Press
BATON ROUGE

Published by Louisiana State University Press
Copyright © 2008 by Louisiana State University Press
All rights reserved
Manufactured in China
First printing

Designer: Laura Roubique Gleason
Typefaces: Whitman and Myriad Pro
Printer and binder: Everbest Printing Co. through Four Colour Imports, Ltd., Louisville, Kentucky

Library of Congress Cataloging-in-Publication Data

Rabalais, Scott, 1966–
  The fighting Tigers, 1993–2008 : into a new century of LSU football / Scott Rabalais ; with a foreword by Peter Finney.
      p. cm.
  Includes index.
  ISBN 978-0-8071-3370-5 (cloth : alk. paper)
  1. Louisiana State University (Baton Rouge, La.)—Football—History. I. Title.
  GV958.L65R33 2008
  796.332'630976318—dc22

                                                2008007293

To Michell, my wife and best friend, and LSU fans
everywhere, who make Saturday nights in Tiger Stadium
one of the greatest spectacles in American sports.

CONTENTS

FOREWORD

When Paul Dietzel's 1958 LSU Tigers won a national championship, it had been fifty years since the 1908 Tigers, after smothering ten opponents behind the heroics of Doc Fenton, were acclaimed as the No. 1 team in the land by something called the National Championship Foundation.

I can remember a Tiger fan wondering, "Does it mean we'll have to wait another half century to do this again?"

Well, not exactly.

By the time another fifty years went by, a couple of LSU coaches, Nick Saban and Les Miles, were hoisting crystal footballs in the Superdome, sending purple-and-gold–painted crazies into mega-states of hysteria. Since the birth of the Bowl Championship Series in 1998, LSU became the first school crowned twice by the BCS, all of which triggered "dynasty" talk in some sections of Tiger Country.

Time out, Miles said. "When you're playing in the SEC," he cautioned in the afterglow of LSU's victory over Ohio State, "you don't think dynasty. You think only of your next opponent."

What can be said, as we enter another season of autumn madness, is that LSU football has never enjoyed a more sustained run of success than it has over the last five years: two conference and two national championships, and records of 13–1, 9–3, 11–2, 11–2, and 12–2.

In the ongoing history of the Fighting Tigers, I handed the torch to Scott Rabalais, and he has gone on to tie it all together, neatly and eloquently, for Tiger fans. The story of LSU digging its way out of its darkest period, six straight losing seasons, from the late 1980s into the '90s, followed by a steady, dramatic climb to the mountaintop.

It's all here, in words and pictures, in cheers and tears, in victories and defeats.

For me, the memories linger.

Gerry DiNardo had been fired as LSU coach ten days earlier and there he was, that evening in November 1999, sitting at a corner table in a Baton Rouge restaurant bearing his name. Between some storytelling, between sips of red wine, DiNardo occasionally looked up to steal a peek at Monday Night Football on the TV. The Patriots were playing the Jets, and it so happened that the highlight for losing New England was a kickoff return by Kevin Faulk, with the kind of explosive burst that once ignited magic inside Tiger Stadium.

Faulk was not only the first player DiNardo recruited. He was a freshman member of the 1995 LSU team that defeated Michigan State in the Independence Bowl, a team coached by the man who would succeed him, Nick Saban.

For his interview, at the Memphis home of his agent, Jimmy Sexton, Saban showed up with a legal pad full of questions. For the most part, he interviewed the search committee. He wanted to know why, with Louisiana such a rich recruiting territory, LSU had not been a consistent national contender. He talked details, facilities, academics. He made it clear that he could build a program to compete for an SEC championship in four years and a national championship shortly thereafter.

It wasn't long before LSU chancellor Mark Emmert spoke up: "We want you to be LSU's next football coach." On the flight home, Emmert told Athletic Director Joe Dean to ask Saban to name his price. It was $1.2 million. It wasn't long before Saban had his fourth LSU team in position to win its second SEC championship in three years. It wasn't long before Marcus Spears was roaring in to bury Georgia quarterback David Greene on the way to a 34–13 victory in the SEC championship game in the Georgia Dome. It wasn't long before the Tigers had climbed from No. 14 in week one of the 2003 season to No. 2 in the final BCS rankings, preparing to face No. 1 Oklahoma in the BCS championship game. And it wasn't long before Marquise Hill was putting relentless pressure on Sooners' Heisman Trophy quarterback Jason White, wasn't long before Spears was carrying an interception into the end zone for the winning points in a 21–14 victory.

On offense, freshman running back Justin Vincent followed an MVP performance against Georgia with another against Oklahoma. On defense, a bunch of Tiger speedsters were limiting an offense that averaged 461 yards to 154, a team that averaged 45 points to a couple of touchdowns, one on a 2-yard drive following a blocked punt.

Hysteria reigned.

A year later, hysteria would give way to anxiety. Nick Saban scratched an itch to become a head coach in the NFL, a day Athletic Director Skip Bertman knew would come. "I've always been driven by challenges," said Saban upon accepting the job to coach the Miami Dolphins. In stepped Les Miles, a fresh-faced 51-year-old who, at his first press conference, suggested there was a sense of humor lurking somewhere inside. "I'm relatively honest," he said, "but somewhat deceptive."

The most impressive part of the man coming in from Oklahoma State was breaking even in four games against Oklahoma at a time when the Sooners were national contenders. "The more I looked at Les," Bertman said, "the more he seemed like a perfect fit to follow someone like Nick. He's spent more than 30 years in coaching and there are no yellow flags in his background."

When his first press conference was over, a member of the media said, "He smiled more in 30 minutes than Saban smiled in five years." He talked like a man who knew about the high expectations, who knew he would be trying to fill some big shoes, who was anxious to take on a far greater challenge than he faced in his previous job. His first challenge was not football. It was Hurricane Katrina. As Paul Dietzel, talking as a onetime coach-turned-fan, put it: "Les proved what kind of person he is by the way he handled things after the hurricane turned everything inside out. Players had evacuees living in their homes. He's in a new job and games are switched and rescheduled. His team plays what's supposed to be the home opener in Arizona State. Through all the chaos, he kept everything together. To go on and have the kind of season he had was amazing."

It would be the first of back-to-back 11–2 seasons, followed by That Championship Season.

That would be a season after the team lost four first-round draft choices to the NFL, one of whom was the starting quarterback, JaMarcus Russell. A season when the starting quarterback was a fifth-year senior who had started one game in four seasons. A season LSU entered as the "must-win" No. 2 team in the country. A season that would send the Tigers to Alabama to play a team coached by the man Miles succeeded as LSU coach.

What a trip it would be. All those gambles. A faked punt and two faked field goals, one against South Carolina that saw Matt Flynn complete an over-the-shoulder pass to placekicker Colt David for six points instead of three. Five fourth-down conversions in a 28–24 comeback against Florida. The last-second touchdown pass to Demetrius Byrd to beat Auburn, 30–24. The fumble-forcing sack by Chad Jones to set up the win over Alabama. The pick by Jonathan Zenon to beat Tennessee for the SEC title. The field-goal block by Ricky Jean-Francois that lit the fire for an explosion against Ohio State, a night when Jacob Hester was always fighting for an extra yard while a healthy Glenn Dorsey was creating negative yardage for the Buckeyes. As Early Doucet liked to say, the philosophy of this championship team was simply, "When we need to, we do."

Once more, purple-and-gold hysteria reigned.

And there was Les Miles, with wife Kathy at his side, standing on a balcony on Bourbon Street, holding a crystal football overhead, engulfed in a Mardi Gras atmosphere.

The "Michigan man," whose coaching journey had taken him to a fork in the road, had made one of those lifetime decisions. Coaching the LSU Tigers is no stepping stone. Said Les Miles: "It's a destination."

Peter Finney
February 2008

PREFACE

The pharaohs built pyramids to honor themselves. Americans build stadiums to honor our teams.

There was perhaps no pharaoh as beloved by his people as the LSU Tigers are by the people of Louisiana. Every fall they come to pay homage, to root and weep and cheer and curse as their Tigers course their way through another football season. The place they come to is in Baton Rouge, not far from where the Mississippi River cuts a wide, silvery band through south Louisiana's flatlands. Indeed, the place the Tigers call home is on a piece of bottomland formerly part of a plantation known as Gartness. There generations of Tiger fans have come to giddiness and grief.

Tiger Stadium. What a monument it is.

As football season draws near, the place is stifling and still, the heat of summer having worked its way well into the concrete, the occasional sound echoing through the grandstands like the ghost of some old play. Billy Cannon's punt return. Bert Jones to Brad Davis. Tommy Hodson to Eddie Fuller. But like the nearby Gulf of Mexico, whose storms have through the years jarred and altered the course of LSU football seasons, its pent-up energy gets released come fall. A game in Tiger Stadium is not for the timid. They don't call it Death Valley for nothing. It can be a difficult place to play—on either side. "It's like walking into a volcano," Thomas Dunson, a much-vilified drop linebacker in the late 1990s, once said. "You never know if it's going to explode on you or the opposition. You've got people who are either going to fight for you or kill you. But it's more fun to play in that stadium than to not."

LSU football has over the years been many things—magnificent, heartbreaking, exhilarating, maddening—but it is never boring. In the pages that follow is the story of a program that over a span of fifteen years rose from the depths of its greatest despair to emerge in this new century as one of the premier college football powers in the nation. This is the story of the teams, players, and coaches who emerged from Death Valley to shake the college football world.

My first thanks go to Peter Finney, a great sportswriter and a greater friend and inspiration, who recommended me as his successor in chronicling the history of the LSU football program. Since I was a boy I have read and reread his *Fighting Tigers* books countless times. Following in his footsteps is a tremendous honor and a humbling experience, and I am in his debt.

The research necessary for writing this book had to be compiled in a relatively short period of time. It would not have been possible without the assistance of LSU senior associate athletic director Herb Vincent, LSU Sports Information director Michael Bonnette, and the Sports Information staff, especially Brianne Mickles, Ashley Bourdier, and Bill Martin. Bill unhesitatingly agreed to let me print his moving e-mail from the first few hours on the LSU campus after Hurricane Katrina.

Special thanks go to LSU Athletic Department photographer Steve Franz, who dropped what he was doing whenever I asked and willingly gave his time to help me track down most of the photos you see in this book. Thanks also to Southeastern Conference media relations director Charles Bloom, Alabama Sports Information director Doug Walker, and Margaret Hart and Catherine Kadair of LSU Press, who so patiently walked a first-time author through the publishing process.

I began covering LSU football in 1992 for *The Advocate* in Baton Rouge. Most of the information for this book was obtained from clip files from *The Advocate*, the *New Orleans Times-Picayune*, and the *Shreveport Times*. Other information came from new interviews I conducted in 2007 and 2008 with Joe Dean, Gerry DiNardo, Kevin Faulk, Matt Mauck, Kevin Mawae, Les Miles, Nick Saban, Marcus Spears, and Herb Vincent. The *ESPN College Football Encyclopedia*, published in 2005, was a useful and frequent reference guide on polls, bowls, teams, and coaches through the 2004 season.

Thanks, of course, to my wife Michell for her support, her prodding, and her proofreading skills, and to our children, Megan, Nicholas, and Katherine, for putting up with their dad's crazy hours and frequently grumpy moods while writing the bulk of this book.

And in response to all the people who for years have asked me, "When are you going to write a book?" I can say, Well, I finally did. What's your next question?

THE FIGHTING TIGERS 1993–2008

1

PIGS WILL FLY

1993–1994

It was billed as LSU's "Golden Century Weekend," a time for Tiger football greats and fans to gather and reflect on the program's one hundredth anniversary. A century of legendary players, stunning upsets, and championship teams. LSU fans picked their modern-day LSU team of the century, a list studded with all-time greats like Billy Cannon, Bert Jones, Tommy Casanova, and Charles Alexander. A media panel selected the pre-1936 team, made up of such players from LSU's sepia-toned past as G. E. "Doc" Fenton, Gaynell Tinsley, and Charles "Pinky" Rohm.

That weekend in April 1993 was a time not only to revel in long-ago glory but to forget the program's recent history. Simply put, LSU football at the turn of its golden century was a tarnished legacy. After claiming a share of the 1988 SEC championship to crown a brilliant five-year stretch under coaches Bill Arnsparger and Mike Archer—a 44–12–3 record, two SEC titles, and just the second run of five straight bowl appearances in school history— the Tigers had strung together four consecutive losing seasons.

The 1993 Tigers could have used a Cannon, an Alexander, or a Tinsley. Only 10 starters returned from the 1992 team that went a feeble 2–9, establishing dubious school records for overall losses, conference losses (LSU went 1–7 in the first year of the newly expanded 12-team SEC), and losing streaks (eight games). There was talent. Players like sophomore quarterback Jamie Howard, a backup to senior Chad Loup, who spent his summers pitching in the Atlanta Braves farm system; seniors Scott Ray (wide receiver) and Kevin Mawae (center); and sophomore cornerback Tory James. A former Tiger quarterback, Lynn Amedee, returned for his second stint as an LSU assistant, this time as offensive coordinator. But none of it was enough to keep the media from picking the Tigers to finish sixth in the SEC Western Division. Dead last.

The Tigers were entering their third year under head coach Hudson "Curley" Hallman, an Alabama native who played defensive back at Texas A&M under Gene Stallings. Hallman was picked for the LSU job after building a reputation as a giant-killer and a disciplinarian at Southern Mississippi. Yes, Hallman was strict and tough, which Archer supposedly was not, telling players to put their earrings in a box or "send them to your mama." But LSU was still starved for wins, the kind that Hallman teams at Southern Miss—which included a singular quarterback talent named Brett Favre—had delivered. Originally enamored with Hallman's get-tough approach, Tiger fans were naturally beginning to become a bit restless. "They thought if he was beating the teams he was beating at Southern Miss, why couldn't he do it here?" said Joe Dean, who hired Hallman in 1991 while LSU's athletic director.

Part of the problem was the schedule. LSU was in the midst of a 10-year home-and-home series with Texas A&M, a team LSU opened the season against eight times from 1986 through 1995. The Aggies were at the height of the powerhouse built by Jackie Sherrill and maintained by R. C. Slocum, and beginning with A&M rarely allowed LSU to get the season off to a good start.

The 1993 opener on September 4 in College Station was a continuation of the theme. LSU held the No. 5-ranked Aggies to a scoreless tie at half-time. Perhaps, though, that had something to do with Slocum's suspension of five players for the game, including tailback Greg Hill, who rushed for 212 yards against the Tigers in 1991. But A&M still had Rodney Thomas, who rushed 25 times for 201 yards—including an 80-yard sprint for a third-quarter touchdown—in a 24–0 A&M victory. It was the first shutout loss in a season opener for LSU since 1980. At Mississippi State on September 11, the Tigers avoided an 0–2 start by inches in a tense 18–16 win. Starting place-kicker Matt Huerkamp was 1 of 3 on field-goal attempts and was victimized by a botched extra-point snap before Hallman went with André Lafleur. The walk-on from Lafayette's Acadiana High had made two field goals in his entire prep career, the longest just 35 yards. Somehow, Hallman's faith in him was rewarded. Lafleur drilled field goals of 32 and 49 yards, then came on for a 26-yard try with 10 seconds remaining, the Tigers trailing 16–15. Lafleur pulled the ball just inside the left upright for a 26-yard game winner. "I looked up and said, 'Hmmm, that's ugly,'" he commented later. "But it doesn't matter. Points is points."

Auburn was 2–0 but an unknown commodity when it visited Tiger Stadium on September 18 under first-year coach Terry Bowden after slipping past Ole Miss 16–12 and handling Samford 35–7. After opening with a 10-yard touchdown pass from Howard to Scott Ray, LSU got buried under a 28-point Auburn avalanche. Quarterback Stan White sneaked over on a pair of 1-yard touchdown runs and threw for 282 yards as Auburn romped 34–10, outgaining LSU 554–245. "We've got to get it together," junior cornerback Rodney Young said. "We don't want another 2–9 season."

Unfortunately for the Tigers, they were beginning to follow a familiar pattern: play well early, even lead, then unravel. It was the same story the next week at Tennessee, where the Tigers made an overflow crowd of 95,931 in Neyland Stadium nervous early. LSU trailed Tennessee 14–6 midway through the second quarter and was driving when sophomore tailback Jay Johnson fumbled untouched. Ten plays later the Volunteers took a commanding 21–6 lead on an 8-yard touchdown pass from Heath Shuler to Cory Fleming and went on to a 42–20 win. Tennessee improved to 18–3–3 all-time against LSU and was on its way to a 9-win season and a berth in the Citrus Bowl. Hallman's team was on its way back to Baton Rouge, desperately searching for victories. The Tigers found one October 2, sending rent-a-win Utah State back to the Big West Conference with a 35–17 defeat. Howard hooked up with freshman flanker Eddie Kennison—a recruiting coup for Hallman, who lured the *Parade* All-American away from mighty Florida State—on a 74-yard pass-and-run to highlight the win.

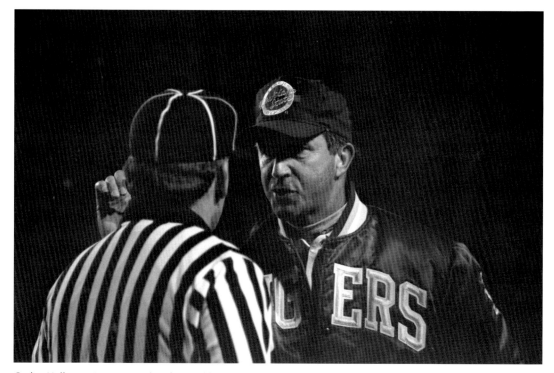

Curley Hallman: Arguing with referees, like his tenure, was a losing proposition.

STEVE FRANZ

But had the Tigers found the answers needed to avert another losing season? Fifth-ranked Florida provided a resounding, emphatic, definitive no. The 58–3 defeat on October 9 was LSU's worst ever. Almost comically, the Tigers scored first again on a 29-yard Lafleur field goal. Then three interceptions set up touchdowns for a Florida offense led for the first time by quarterback Danny Wuerffel. The freshman threw four touchdown passes, and ultimately three Florida quarterbacks racked up 352 yards through the air. Florida coach Steve Spurrier, who built his reputation on cocky quotes and sly jabs at the opposition, was actually apologetic. "I told Curley I was sorry it got out of hand," he said. LSU fans were once again second-guessing the decision to hire Archer instead of Spurrier in 1986. Now the defensive coordinator at Kentucky, Archer got the game ball from his players a week later when the Wildcats beat LSU 35–17 in Lexington. He called it his most difficult week since he was fired at LSU in 1990. "There's been a lot of anxiety," Archer admitted. While UK didn't embarrass LSU as Florida had done, the Wildcats scored the most points in Kentucky history against the Tigers.

At this juncture the Tigers (2–5 overall, 1–4 in the SEC) were in need of a little luck, and they got it in a Homecoming win over Ole Miss on October 30. LSU made its share of now-familiar mistakes—a bad punt snap setting up a Rebel touchdown, two interceptions, a fumble, and two missed extra-point kicks. LSU overcame it all to take a 19–17 lead with 11:51 remaining on a 4-yard run by Johnson before Lafleur's PAT misfired. The Rebels' Walter Grant then missed a 36-yard field-goal try wide left with 58 seconds remaining, allowing LSU to escape with the two-point victory.

It seemed the Tigers would need more than luck as they headed to Tuscaloosa on November 6 to take on No. 5-ranked Alabama, the reigning national champion. A 17–17 tie three weeks earlier against Tennessee had ended the Crimson Tide's 28-game winning streak, but Alabama's unbeaten streak was now at 31. Las Vegas oddsmakers installed the 7–0–1 Tide as a 25-point favorite. One Alabama newspaper viewed the game as a complete joke. TIDE COULD LOSE, PIGS MIGHT FLY, said the headline on sportswriter Jimmy Wigfield's column in that Saturday's *Mobile Register*. "Stallings will be merciful to his old pal Hallman. Alabama 30, LSU 7."

"They were 30–0–1 and coming off a national championship," Mawae recalled. "No one gave us a chance." But something told Mawae different. "I remember we were going through the walk-through on Friday and it was a gray, overcast kind of day. I called the team up without the coaches and I told them, 'This stadium is going to have a gray cloud hanging over it and the rest of their season if we win.'"

Saturday was cold and clear, with a wind chill in the mid thirties, and the game's opening minutes seemed to follow a script that would extend Alabama's unbeaten streak to 32. The Tigers went three downs and punt, giving the ball to Alabama near midfield. The Crimson Tide stomped toward LSU's end zone but finally had to settle for a 46-yard Michael Proctor field-goal attempt that banged off the right upright and fell into the end zone.

Eddie Kennison looks for yardage at Alabama, 1993.   BRAD MESSINA, LSU SPORTS INFORMATION

It was a sign of the frustration to come for Alabama. The Tigers' defense thrived on a string of big plays. Near the end of the first half, defensive end Gabe Northern shed a block and brought down Brian Bergdorf for a 6-yard loss at his 21, sending the teams off in a 0–0 halftime tie that gave the Tigers an emotional boost. It was the first time LSU had held Bama scoreless at the half since the Tigers' historic 20–10 upset in Birmingham in 1982. Another half remained to be played, though, and Alabama specialized in winning low-scoring defensive duels. But on Alabama's first possession of the third, Bergdorf was pressured and picked off by free safety Anthony Marshall, who stepped out at the Bama 38. In short order, Johnson smacked over from the 2 to put LSU up 7–0 with 10:41 left in the third quarter.

Defensive end Corey White drags down elusive Alabama star David Palmer.   STEVE FRANZ

Stallings refused to put in multitalented flanker David Palmer at quarterback as he had earlier in the season, turning instead to Freddie Kitchens to ignite the Crimson Tide offense. Kitchens couldn't get Bama going, but Crimson Tide punter Bryne Diehl did, running a fake 43 yards to the Tigers' 27. Again the LSU defense rose up, throwing Bama back before Ivory Hilliard picked off Kitchens at the Tigers' 24. A lateral to Tory James on the return and an Alabama penalty put the ball at the Tide 37. Five plays later, LSU went up 14–0 on a 2-yard run by Robert Toomer with 4:38 left in the third. Palmer finally took over at quarterback and promptly threw a 3-yard touchdown pass to fullback Tarrant Lynch with a quarter to go. A Rodney Young interception of Palmer led to a 36-yard Lafleur field goal with 4:22 remaining. But back came Palmer with a 22-yard touchdown pass to split end Kevin Lee with 2:41 left, making it 17–13. Palmer's run for two points came up short, but a successful onside kick could have put the ball back in his dangerous hands. It didn't happen. Alabama's Willie Gaston touched the ball before it went the required 10 yards, LSU's David Butler fell on it, and the Tigers ran out the clock before running onto the field in delirious, relieved celebration. "It's been a tough season," said Marshall, who came to LSU from Mobile, Alabama. "It was time for us to step up and be the men we are." In a span of four weeks, the Tigers had gone from suffering the worst defeat in the program's history to pulling off arguably its greatest upset. The tide had turned, indeed, especially for Hallman, who grew up across the Black Warrior River from the Alabama campus in Northport. "I love my hometown," said Hallman, who took his team the day before the game to a Tuscaloosa home for the mentally handicapped where his sister Marilyn spent the last eighteen years of her life. "I have a lot of ties here. When you play, you look over all these things."

The Tigers didn't see any flying pigs outside their chartered plane on the trip back to Baton Rouge that evening. But upon returning home they found a town reveling in the amazing victory. BELIEVE IT! blared the big, bold headline on the front of Sunday's *Advocate* sports section. "Pigs will fly" T-shirts were already turning a steady business. And officials from the Carquest Bowl in Miami held out the carrot of an invitation if the 4–5 Tigers could win their last two games of the season. LSU got to 5–5 with little difficulty the following week in Tiger Stadium with a workmanlike 24–10 victory over Tulane. The game plan seemed straight out of the leather helmet days as the Tigers played it safe with eight ball carriers combining for 247 yards rushing and two touchdowns on 44 attempts.

One more win, over Arkansas in Tiger Stadium the Friday after Thanksgiving, and the Tigers would have a winning season. Tied 14–14 at halftime, it appeared LSU had a good shot at basking in some Florida sun—but the Hogs wouldn't allow it. Three running backs rushed for over 100 yards: Oscar Malone (10 carries, 143 yards, two TDs), Carlton Calvin (14 carries, 123 yards, two TDs), and Marius Johnson (19 carries, 106 yards). In all, Arkansas rushed for 412 yards to run away with a 42–24 victory. As it turned out, pigs would

Flags will fly: Defensive end Mike Hewitt celebrates LSU's epic upset 17–13 at Alabama, 1993.   STEVE FRANZ

fly if LSU went to a bowl game. Instead, the 5–6 Tigers were home for the holidays again, while Virginia took LSU's place in the Carquest Bowl opposite Boston College.

In the postseason analysis, LSU's schedule was rated the nation's toughest. Three of its opponents won conference championships—Florida (SEC), Texas

Senior center Kevin Mawae leaves the field in dejection after losing to Arkansas in his last game, 1993.   STEVE FRANZ

A&M (Southwest Conference), and Utah State (Big West)—plus probation-bound Auburn went 11–0. Auburn, Florida, and A&M all finished in the Associated Press top 10. But 5–6 was still 5–6. LSU's string of losing seasons had now reached a record five straight.

LSU's Pick Six, Hallman Deep-Sixed

Could the Tigers win in 1994? It seemed Curley Hallman's job would depend on it. LSU at least had a chance with 13 returning starters, including Jamie Howard, Robert Toomer (moved from fullback to tailback), and a veteran secondary anchored by cornerbacks Tory James and Rodney Young and strong safety Ivory Hilliard, nephew of the great LSU tailback Dalton Hilliard. Still, with their track record, the Tigers were picked to finish fifth in the SEC West.

Ranked 15th but on NCAA probation, Texas A&M would wind up No. 8 with a 10–0–1 record marred only by a 21–21 tie with SMU. LSU would be one of A&M's more stubborn victims. The Tigers led 13–9 going into the fourth quarter on September 3 on a 24-yard interception return by James that had Tiger Stadium's 75,504 fans rocking. The Aggies closed to 13–12, then surged back in front to stay 18–13 when Leeland McElroy took off on a

59-yard touchdown bolt with 7:18 remaining. On his forty-seventh birthday, Hallman fell to 0–4 against his alma mater.

A week later LSU proved it was better than Mississippi State. Or, rather, Eddie Kennison proved he was better and faster than anyone the Bulldogs had. Midway through the fourth quarter Kennison fielded a punt on a bounce, grabbing the ball at the goal line. The first Bulldog down momentarily knocked Kennison back into his end zone, but Eddie kept his balance, zipped up the middle, and threw on the afterburners down the left sideline with a 100-yard punt return to cap a 44–24 win. It was just the sixth 100-yard punt return in NCAA history. "I picked it up and just tried to make something happen," Kennison said. "And it did."

A lot of things would happen when LSU visited Auburn on September 17. Almost all of them, from an LSU perspective, were horrendous. That LSU would lose 30–26 at No. 11 Auburn was not a surprise. How the two teams arrived at that final score was such an improbable script that any Hollywood studio would have turned it down. LSU outgained Auburn 407–165 and had 21 first downs to Auburn's 8. In the second half Auburn managed just 16 total yards and one first down. Its only scoring all day generated by its offense was a first-quarter field goal. "Little Bowden, Terry Bowden, can say what he wants," defensive coordinator Phil Bennett fumed afterward. "The best team didn't win today."

So how did LSU lose? In the most literal sense, the Tigers gave the game away. All of Auburn's touchdowns came on defense, starting with a Chris Shelling recovery of a Jermaine Sharp fumble in the LSU end zone. Still, LSU pushed its lead to 23–9 early in the fourth before it imploded. As fast as Howard could throw the ball, it seemed to find Auburn hands. And Auburn's defenders found the end zone.

- 12:14 remaining: Strong safety Ken Alvis returns a Howard pass 42 yards for a touchdown. LSU 23, Auburn 16.
- 11:08 remaining: Cornerback Fred Smith returns a Howard interception 32 yards for a touchdown. LSU 23, Auburn 23.
- 1:55 remaining: After a Lafleur field goal gives LSU a 26–23 lead, free safety Brian Robinson returns a Howard interception 41 yards for the winning score. Auburn 30, LSU 26.

The LSU coaches' decision to pass leading 26–23 when facing a third-and-4 at their 32 was highly criticized. Just over two minutes remained on the clock. Had LSU run but not made the first down, a successful punt would have left an Auburn team that hadn't driven the field all day needing to do so to win or at least make a field goal to force a tie. "Hindsight? Yeah, I would go back and run it," Hallman said grimly. Even after the last touchdown, the game wasn't

High plains dreadful: Auburn's Chris Shelling covers a fumble for a touchdown in 1994 next to Brian Robinson (20), who returned one of three interceptions for touchdowns.

BRAD MESSINA, LSU SPORTS INFORMATION

completely over. LSU still had almost two minutes to drive for the winning points, but Howard's confidence was completely spent. He threw yet another interception to Robinson, who fumbled the ball, recovered by LSU offensive tackle Marcus Price at the Auburn 46. Two plays later Howard threw *another* interception to Shelling, allowing Auburn to finally run the clock out. Howard's end: 18 of 41 passing, 280 yards, one touchdown, six interceptions. Auburn's three interception returns for scores tied an NCAA record. Teammates had to help a sobbing Howard into the locker room, where he stayed, refusing interview requests. Afterward, Bennett sat on a metal girder beneath Jordan-Hare Stadium and wept bitterly. "I've never experienced anything like it," Bennett said. "It makes you wonder why you're even in [coaching]."

The loss made a lot of people wonder how much longer Hallman and his staff would be coaching at LSU. After an open date, LSU returned to Tiger Stadium on October 1 to host 3–1 South Carolina. The game plan could be charitably called reactionary. "LSU wanted to keep its offense simple," *Advocate* sports editor Sam King wrote. "It succeeded. It was simple—simply awful." Howard threw an early 11-yard touchdown pass to Kennison but was just 7 of 16 passing for 53 yards with two interceptions and two fumbles, while the Tigers rushed 41 times for 156 yards, including a 130-yard effort from Sharp. It wasn't enough, though, as the Gamecocks' Stanley Pritchett blasted over on fourth-and-goal from the 1 with 12:52 left to play for an 18–17 South Carolina victory.

At 1–3, a road trip to face No. 1 Florida on October 8 wasn't the answer. The Gators jumped out to a 20–0 first-quarter lead that included an 88-yard interception return by Anthone Lott—this one off the hand of new quarterback Melvin Hill. He started instead of Howard, just the second black starting quarterback in LSU history after Carl Otis Trimble in 1974. Unfortunately, the freshman Hill met the same fate as Howard, intercepted three times in a 42–18 rout. Howard was back under center when LSU returned home October 15 to host Kentucky, but it was Hill who was productive in a 17–13 comeback victory. Hill tied the score 10–10 with a 6-yard touchdown pass to Brett Bech just before halftime and put LSU in front with a 34-yard pass to Kennison with 8:18 left in the third. An interception by linebacker Kimojha Brooks sealed the win with 1:02 remaining.

Hallman said he was happy with the win, but he was in the minority. LSU had squeaked by a 1–5 Kentucky team that ranked last in the SEC in offense and scoring defense. On October 29, the Tigers went to Oxford and were back to their self-destructive ways in a 34–21 loss to Ole Miss. LSU lost the handle on the ball seven times, fumbling four, with two of the fumbles leading to Rebel touchdowns. "Protecting the football," Hallman said, "has been our Achilles' tendon this season." Hallman's quote may have been a malaprop, but it was accurate. Turnovers were the Tigers' Achilles' heel, and at 2–5 they again had LSU teetering on the brink of a losing season. On November 5, Alabama pushed LSU over the edge. The Tigers fumbled seven times, losing just two, one of them returned 30 yards for a touchdown by Sam Shade. A blocked punt for a touchdown helped No. 6 Alabama race to a 28–3 halftime edge and cruise to a 35–17 victory. Hostility toward Hallman was mounting among the increasingly disenchanted LSU fan base. One sign in Tiger Stadium used the letters in ESPN (which televised the game) to connect the words WE SUPPORT DUMPIN' HALLMAN. Inside yet another somber LSU locker room, Bennett knew the score wasn't just 35–17. "I'm not a fool," Bennett said. "I know the situation we're in. No matter what happens, I'll be coaching somewhere next year."

Ironically, the final blow to Hallman's tottering tenure came from the program that made him look like such a good choice four years earlier. LSU's home finale against Southern Mississippi on November 12 drew an announced crowd of just 51,710 fans, the smallest attendance in Tiger Stadium in eighteen years. The 79,940-seat stadium looked only half full. Rarely, if ever, had Death Valley seemed more like a tomb, and LSU played like a team destined to lose again. After the Tigers rallied with a 15-point third quarter to take an 18–14 lead, Southern Miss kicker Chris Pierce drilled a 52-yard field goal for a 20–18 lead with two minutes remaining. Lafleur tried a 50-yarder with 15 seconds left, but USM's Michael Tobias tipped the ball enough to force it short and left.

Shortly after the Southern Miss game, Athletic Director Joe Dean and LSU chancellor William "Bud" Davis, himself a former football coach at Colorado, decided that nearly four seasons and a 14–28 record with Hallman was enough. On Monday, November 14, Dean left his sixth-floor office in LSU's new athletic administration building to meet with Hallman in his office on the second.

"Curley," Dean told him solemnly, "I don't want to lie to you, but I can't save you."

"You can't get me the extra year?" Hallman asked.

"I don't think so," Dean said. "I've got a lot of pressure on me from a lot of different directions."

Although word began to leak out regarding Hallman's dismissal Monday night, his firing wasn't announced until Tuesday. "It's time to move ahead," Dean said at a news conference alongside Davis. "We must become competitive on the football field." About 2½ hours after Dean and Davis spoke, Hallman held a news conference of his own to set the record straight. "I did not resign," he stressed. "This will be a great place again. I really believe that. Life is choice. They made the choice to go in a different direction. I understand

Frustrated holder Brett Bech stays on one knee after André Lafleur's field goal misses against Southern Miss in 1994, effectively ending the Hallman era. STEVE FRANZ

Assistants Lee Fobbs, *left,* and Phil Bennett look pensive as Curley Hallman addresses the media after being fired, 1994.　　　　STEVE FRANZ

my occupation." The announcement of Hallman's firing came four years to the day after Mike Archer stepped down, two very different men who met the same fate. Hallman's was sealed by fan dissension and apathy. The Tigers averaged just 65,124 fans per home game in 1994, after averaging just 60,535 in Tiger Stadium the season before. Hallman received a total annual package of $235,000 but was bought out for just $90,000, the base salary on the last year of his contract.

If Hallman's tenure before his firing had been like the last two weeks, he may never have been let go. The Tigers still made mistakes, but they and their coach seemed more relaxed. A meager crowd of 32,067 showed up at the Superdome to watch 2–7 LSU battle 1–9 Tulane on November 19. The Tigers' offense quickly took flight, as Howard hooked up with Kennison on a 43-yard touchdown pass. A 22-yard Rodney Young interception return in the second half helped LSU coast to a 49–25 victory. A dreary, overcast Saturday after Thanksgiving greeted the Tigers as they went to Little Rock for their finale under Hallman. Arkansas scored first on a 1-yard blast by Madre Hill, but Brandon Michel blocked the extra point and Tory James returned the ball 66 yards for a 6–2 first-quarter baseball score. The Tigers took a 9–6 halftime lead on a 1-yard run by Toomer and poured it on in the second half, Howard throwing a pair of touchdown passes to key a 30–12 victory.

Often surly in his four years at LSU, in the end Curley Hallman found it within himself to be magnanimous. "I'm very happy for the players, the coaching staff, and anyone associated with LSU," he said. "We made some things happen. We looked like a pretty good football team today." Hallman said it was hard for him to deal with the reality that his LSU career was over—a career that at 16–28 made him the only man to coach more than one season at LSU and leave with a losing record. One thing struck him, though: he wouldn't be criticized by the media again. "Just don't bash my ass anymore," he said with a laugh. "I'm not the head coach there anymore."

Curley Hallman and daughters Jessica, *left,* and Jennifer leave War Memorial Stadium in Little Rock after beating Arkansas in his final LSU game, 1994. STEVE FRANZ

2

BRING BACK THE MAGIC
1995–1997

hile Joe Dean watched the end of the Curley Hallman era play out from the press box in Little Rock's War Memorial Stadium, Sports Information director Herb Vincent kept handing him a stream of scoring updates from the Tennessee-Vanderbilt game in Nashville. A score that mounted against Dean's personal favorite candidate to become LSU's next football coach. "Joe liked Gerry DiNardo from some SEC meetings they had," Vincent said. "But he thought he would be a hard sell coming from Vanderbilt with no winning seasons." At 5–5, Vanderbilt had a shot at a winning record on that final day of the 1994 regular season before Tennessee pulverized those hopes 65–0. The next day, Dean still flew to Nashville and met with DiNardo at the airport Marriott.

"I'm surprised you showed up," DiNardo said. "One game doesn't mean anything to me," Dean assured him.

As the coaching search began, Dean worked on North Carolina coach and one-time LSU offensive coordinator Mack Brown through a third party, but his efforts went nowhere. Ohio State coach John Cooper interviewed, then signed a better deal with the Buckeyes. Dean also interviewed Hallman's defensive coordinator, Phil Bennett; Kansas State coach Bill Snyder; Ron Zook, then Florida's special teams coordinator; and two former LSU players—Texas A&M offensive coordinator Steve Ensminger and Washington Redskins receivers coach Terry Robiskie. By December, Dean had settled on two names: DiNardo and TCU coach Pat Sullivan. An SEC legend, Sullivan won the 1971 Heisman Trophy as Auburn's quarterback and had modest success with the longsuffering Horned Frogs. His team was 7–4 and preparing for an Independence Bowl meeting with Virginia, just TCU's third bowl appearance since 1960.

Sullivan interviewed at LSU on December 6, a Tuesday. DiNardo interviewed Wednesday. Dean had left Nashville wanting DiNardo as much as ever, but Sullivan was offered the job. "Perception sometimes plays a role in this," Dean said. "It didn't play a big role with me, but it did with the people

I respect, whose feelings and attitudes I had to honor." Informed of the decision, DiNardo announced Wednesday night through Vanderbilt's sports information office that he was no longer a candidate. The *Fort Worth Star-Telegram* quoted TCU wide receivers coach Tommie Robinson as saying, "It looks like we're going to LSU." An introductory news conference was planned for Thursday in Baton Rouge. "Unless there is something I don't know right now," Dean said Wednesday night, "and that's possible, I'd say we're probably through."

LSU's coaching search wasn't nearly through. Sullivan had a $400,000 buyout that he didn't think TCU would enforce, but the school held firm. Meanwhile, LSU was unwilling to pay more than $200,000 toward the buyout. If Sullivan had been Dean's first choice, would Dean have found a way to work a deal? Possibly. But he wasn't. After a Thursday of uncertainty, Sullivan withdrew his name. Dean announced the search was resuming, but he really had only one man in mind. DiNardo had just flown back to Nashville from a Vanderbilt recruiting trip when he heard on his car radio that Sullivan's news conference was canceled. A moment later, DiNardo's wife Terri rang his car phone.

"Gerry, you'll never guess who called."

"Yes, I will—Joe Dean!"

"How did you know?"

By that weekend, DiNardo was in Baton Rouge to accept the job. DiNardo had his own buyout, but he told Dean he would handle it personally (it was May 2000 before DiNardo and Vanderbilt finally agreed to an undisclosed settlement). Dean had a tougher selling job with DiNardo than Sullivan, and he knew it. An LSU Board of Supervisors meeting in New Orleans would be the final battleground. In a conference room shortly before the public board meeting, Dean made an impassioned plea on DiNardo's behalf. When he finished, Board of Supervisors chairman Milton Womack stood and solemnly told his fellow board members, "If Joe says it ought to be DiNovo, then it ought to be DiNovo." DiNovo? "Man," Vincent thought as he quietly observed the scene, "we're going to have a tough time selling this guy."

To everyone's surprise, "DiNovo" proved to be an exceptional salesman. The man who was known for being stubborn and difficult with the media in Nashville, who refused to call Tennessee by name (he referred to it as "that school in the east"), proved to be witty and eloquent. His first converts were LSU's players. December 11, the night before his introductory news conference, the Tigers held a players-only meeting that smelled of anarchy. Suddenly, Eddie Kennison emerged from Broussard Hall, announcing, "We're going to get him," and marched off to bring DiNardo from his office to talk. Once inside, DiNardo spied offensive tackle Trey Champagne, a Covington native who transferred to LSU from Vandy essentially to get away from Di-

Nardo. "Trey," DiNardo shouted out, "tell me this isn't your worst nightmare!" After several minutes, DiNardo had completely defused the situation, leaving the meeting laughing and joking with players.

Gerry DiNardo: The Magic Man meets the Louisiana media. STEVE FRANZ

DiNardo saved his best words for the next day. Before a packed news conference, the 42-year-old DiNardo made what is remembered as the best introductory speech ever by an LSU football coach. "It's my responsibility and our responsibility to bring the magic back to Tiger Stadium," DiNardo said. "We've got a lot of work to do, but we've got tremendous support. It's one of the truly, truly special places in college football."

The youngest of four sons of a New York City policeman, DiNardo grew up in a working-class section of Queens known as Howard Beach, though he was fond of playing up the fact that he was actually born in Brooklyn. "A guy from Brooklyn is head coach at LSU," DiNardo said. "Crazier things have happened." He also went to high school in Brooklyn at St. Francis Prep, an alma mater he shared with Vince Lombardi, taking the subway from home to school up to two hours each day. Larry DiNardo, Gerry's brother just ahead of him in age, was an All-American offensive guard at Notre Dame in 1969 and '70. Gerry followed in his footsteps, lettering for the Fighting Irish at guard from 1972 through 1974. Part of coaching legend Ara Parseghian's last three teams, DiNardo helped Notre Dame win the 1973 national championship, beating Alabama 24–23 in a Sugar Bowl thriller. As a senior he earned All-American honors himself, making Gerry and Larry the only consensus

All-American brothers in Notre Dame history. In 1971, Gerry was part of the last freshman class ineligible to play under NCAA rules. In his dorm room in South Bend he got his first real taste of LSU football, watching on TV as his teammates got steamrolled 28–8 in Tiger Stadium, one of LSU's greatest victories ever. "I could walk into that dorm room right now and show you where the TV was and where I was sitting," DiNardo said. "That was the defining moment for me regarding LSU."

DiNardo dived into coaching, heading to Maine and Eastern Michigan before going to Colorado in 1982 as part of Bill McCartney's first staff. He would stay nine years, during that time working alongside a former Michigan offensive lineman named Les Miles. They became friends, and when Miles and Kathy LaBarge got married in June 1993, DiNardo stood in their wedding. Gerry met his second wife, Terri, at Colorado. She was a trainer, and one day they decided to get married almost on a dare. "We didn't miss a meeting," Gerry said. DiNardo served as offensive coordinator on Colorado's 1990 national championship team—calling plays in the infamous Fifth Down victory over Missouri—but soon was pursued for his own head coaching job. He took over at Vanderbilt in 1991, and Curley Hallman's first LSU win came at the expense of DiNardo's Commodores, 16–14 in Tiger Stadium. DiNardo took Vanderbilt to records of 5–6, 4–7, and 4–7 his first three seasons, the best start for a Vandy coach since 1956. Now he was starting over at LSU, at an initial salary of $350,000 a year.

During his opening remarks at the news conference, DiNardo said he had to leave to make a recruiting visit, omitting the prospect's name because of NCAA rules. Everyone knew he meant Kevin Faulk, the *Parade* All-American from Carencro High and arguably the nation's top recruit. Landing Faulk would be the ultimate test of DiNardo's salesmanship. "It felt good that after he left his press conference he came to see me immediately," Faulk remembered. "It made an impression." A running quarterback at Carencro, Faulk rushed for 4,877 yards and 62 touchdowns in his high school career while throwing for 11 more scores and nearly 1,000 yards. He was the Class 5A player of the year as a junior and a senior, the first player twice honored as the best in Louisiana's top class since Joe Ferguson of Shreveport's Woodlawn High in the late 1960s. Pursued by Florida State, Miami, and Notre Dame, Faulk announced a commitment to LSU in a packed Lafayette sports bar a week before the national signing period began. LSU fans erupted as though the Tigers had just scored a touchdown. Indeed, DiNardo had his first big score as LSU's coach.

DiNardo's staff would include just two Hallman assistants: defensive ends coach Jerry Baldwin and administrative assistant Sam Nader, a fixture at LSU since 1975. DiNardo lured offensive coordinator Morris Watts, LSU's quarterbacks coach in 1983, from Michigan State despite the efforts of the new coach

LSU's white knight: DiNardo and the white-jerseyed Tigers.

there, Nick Saban, to keep him. Five assistants came from Vanderbilt: defensive coordinator Carl "Bull" Reese, defensive backs coach Ron Case, offensive line coach Hal Hunter, receivers coach Bob McConnell, and Bill Elias to coach tight ends and coordinate recruiting. DiNardo also tabbed a young Mike Haywood, who had played in Tiger Stadium for Notre Dame in 1984, as his running backs coach, and Mike Tolleson, fresh off the Southern Miss staff that beat the Tigers a season earlier, to coach defensive tackles.

Winning Again

LSU's premiere on September 2 at No. 3 Texas A&M, one of four preseason top-10 teams on LSU's schedule, provided a glimpse of the Tigers' mistake-filled past. A blocked field goal led to A&M's first touchdown, and a fumbled punt led to the second of three touchdowns by "Lectric" Leeland McElroy. He piled up a Southwest Conference–record 359 all-purpose yards, including 229 yards and three touchdowns rushing in a 33–17 win. Faulk had a decent debut against the Aggies, rushing for 73 yards on 14 carries. He was ready to erupt when the Tigers traveled to Mississippi State in their SEC opener the following Saturday. The Bulldogs scored on the first play from scrimmage, an 80-yard pass from Derrick Taite to Eric Moulds. Then Faulk took over, rushing for 171 yards and two touchdowns on 23 carries—the most yards by an LSU back in five years—as the Tigers won comfortably, 34–16.

A loss to Texas A&M. A win over Mississippi State. So far, the results showed there was little to distinguish the DiNardo era from the Hallman years, and the new coach knew it. "We've been here before," DiNardo said. "We need to challenge ourselves. I'm looking forward to the atmosphere at Tiger Stadium next Saturday." The September 16 game with No. 5 Auburn would be a night not seen in Tiger Stadium since the Earthquake Game against Auburn in 1988. Fans anticipating a classic—and knowing the game wasn't on TV—snapped up the remaining public tickets by Monday, September 11. The student section sold out Wednesday, but demand was so great that video screens were set up in the Pete Maravich Assembly Center. Fifteen hundred students showed up at the PMAC, while across the street 80,559 fans packed into Tiger Stadium, then the second-largest crowd ever for an LSU home game. Many of them wanted to see how Jamie Howard would

White Knight

It wasn't just the magic Gerry Di-Nardo would try to bring back to LSU, but that old white magic. In 1983, an NCAA rule mandated that home teams wear their dark or colored jerseys while visiting teams wore white. LSU's tradition of wearing white in almost every game from 1957 through 1982 was dismissed, and as the losses mounted, Tiger fans' belief that the purple jerseys were bad luck only grew. DiNardo went before the NCAA rules committee in February 1995 armed with white LSU jerseys with the committee members' names on the back. "As soon as they accepted the graft, I knew I had them," DiNardo said with a grin. The NCAA changed the jersey rule to say home teams may wear white if the visiting team agrees to wear its colors.

Kevin Faulk in his LSU debut at Texas A&M, 1995.

STEVE FRANZ

rebound after the six-interception nightmare he had at Auburn the year before. Howard, coming off a pair of solid, no-interception performances, was confident. "I've always said this can be the greatest place to play, or it can be the worst. This week it will be the greatest," he promised. Howard would do his part, completing 19 of 30 passes for 220 yards—and just one interception. A 4-yard touchdown pass to tight end Nicky Savoie gave LSU a 7–0 lead less than six minutes in. The Tigers then traded 41-yard field goals, but LSU pushed its lead to 12–3 seconds after André Lafleur's field goal with a safety by defensive end James Gillyard. Auburn's Matt Hawkins added a field goal in the third, setting up the end-game dramatics.

In a reverse image from the 1988 game, this time it was Auburn, down by six, driving toward Tiger Stadium's north end for a do-or-die touchdown. Taking over at their 29 with 2:19 remaining, the visiting Tigers worked their way to the LSU 11, where they faced fourth-and-3. With a stadium full of frenzied fans watching every move, Auburn quarterback Patrick Nix lofted a pass in the back right corner of the end zone for wide receiver Tyrone Goodson, locked in a one-on-one duel with Troy Twillie. Both leaped high into the air, but it was Twillie who came down with the ball as time expired. The sophomore cornerback challenged himself after being burned on Mississippi State's long touchdown pass the week before. "I was ready," said Twillie, who left the field still clutching the ball. "I was looking for it." Despite Twillie's heroics, much of the postgame adoration was showered on LSU's senior quarterback. Perhaps no other LSU athlete ever experienced the depth of redemption in the span of one year that Howard did, carried from the field conqueror-style by his teammates and straight into the locker room for a postgame news conference usually reserved for the head coach. It seemed like a rebirth for Howard—and LSU. "That marked a turnaround for the program," said Kevin Mawae, Howard's former center.

Troy Twillie vs. Auburn's Tyrone Goodson.   STEVE FRANZ

Jamie Howard leaves the field in triumph against Auburn, 1995.   STEVE FRANZ

At 2–1, LSU was above .500 for the first time since October 1990. The Associated Press ranked the Tigers No. 18, while the coaches in the *USA Today/CNN* poll had them at No. 20, LSU's first rankings since September 1989. "We've got to build on this," Howard said. "This is the step we've needed to make every year." Worries of a post-Auburn letdown quickly evaporated as LSU boiled Rice 52–7 on September 23, Howard throwing for 356 yards and a school record–tying four touchdowns. Now ranked 14th, the Tigers headed to Columbia, South Carolina, for the first time since 1973 to take on the 1–3 Gamecocks. South Carolina was last in the SEC in total, rushing, and scoring defense, but left LSU battered, bruised, and fortunate to come away with a 20–20 standoff on September 30. Freshman tailback Kendall Cleveland hurt his thigh, cornerback Raion Hill his neck. Howard left with a concussion and wearing a neck brace. Sheddrick Wilson sprained his knee and ankle but somehow hobbled back out to catch a 19-yard touchdown pass from Howard with 1:06 remaining. DiNardo kicked the extra point rather than risk all with a two-point try. "If I thought we could have gained three yards, I wouldn't have done it," he said. Because college football added overtime in 1996, it was the 47th and final tie in LSU history.

Walking wounded into an October 7 home game with No. 3 Florida wasn't the best way to play, especially since the Gators were revving up to full song under Spurrier. Florida gradually built a 21–0 lead on three rushing touchdowns by early in the second quarter. LSU responded with a 10-point outburst just before halftime that included the year's most entertaining play. LSU used freshman defensive tackle Anthony "Booger" McFarland at fullback, its version of the Chicago Bears' William "Refrigerator" Perry. With LSU camped at the Florida 3, Watts sent in McFarland with a pass play—for him. Howard said, "Booger, that's your play." "Man," McFarland replied, "I hope that's the right play." Booger's anxiety was heightened by the fact that he had dropped nine straight passes in practice that week. The tenth time was the charm, though, as he caught the touchdown pass and made the crowd of 80,583 love the endearing McFarland even more. Florida and Spurrier smirked, tacked on another score, and won 28–10.

Feeling his team needed a boost in the October 14 game at Kentucky, DiNardo decided to make another fashion statement: purple pants. Solid, deep purple with an LSU logo on the left thigh and missing the traditional striping down the leg, they were the Tigers' first departure from gold pants since 1948. They didn't help. With Howard sidelined by a shoulder injury and Faulk hampered by a thigh pull, LSU's offense again sputtered, unable to respond when Kentucky rallied for 17 fourth-quarter points to win 24–16. With Howard still shelved—and the purple pants banished for good—DiNardo gambled on starting Herb Tyler when the Tigers returned home on October 21 to face North Texas. A true freshman from O. P. Walker Senior High in New Orleans, Tyler didn't play a down in LSU's first seven games. But DiNardo was becoming desperate to move the football, so he decided to put his faith in this scout-team quarterback. "He wasn't as talented as he was well liked," DiNardo recalled. "He executed the game plan, he was coachable, had a presence. He had most everything you want in a quarterback." Tyler completed 19 of 26 for 208 yards, throwing for two touchdowns and rushing for another in a resounding 49–7 victory. "It just worked," DiNardo said. "No one could have predicted it."

Fashion misstatement: LSU's purple pants at Kentucky, 1995.

Howard was seaworthy enough to return to the starting lineup for LSU's November 4 trip to Alabama, but the game would mark the end of his college career. Howard reinjured his throwing shoulder after completing 10 of 23 passes for 127 yards. He also threw two interceptions, one of them to Alabama cornerback Deshea Townsend, setting up the winning touchdown by tailback Dennis Riddle six plays later in a 10–3 LSU defeat. One more loss would drop the 4–4–1 Tigers out of bowl contention and open them up to major criticism after the 3–1 start. Again, DiNardo picked Tyler to start as LSU hosted Ole Miss on November 11. And again LSU came up big with Tyler, Faulk, and Kennison doing the heavy lifting in a 38–9 rout. Tyler threw for two scores and ran for another, his nimble feet quickly becoming a trademark. Faulk caught a 56-yard touchdown pass from Tyler and rushed 23 times for 159 yards and another score. "It's easy to block for a guy like that," said freshman center Todd McClure, a product of Baton Rouge's Central High who went from being DiNardo's first recruit to All-American status as a senior. "He knows how to cut and hits the hole hard."

Veteran Tigers remembered being routed by Arkansas in 1993, robbing LSU of a winning season and a bowl bid. Now the 5–4–1 Tigers were in virtually the same position again on November 18, facing an 8–2 Arkansas team that had already clinched the SEC West. LSU focused six years of pain on the Razorbacks, inflicting an impressive 28–0 smackdown that paved the way for a trip to Shreveport's Independence Bowl to face Michigan State. The Tigers got all the points they needed on their first drive, an 80-yard march that chewed an incredible 9:55 off the clock before Tyler hit Wilson on a 9-yard touchdown pass. Cleveland rushed 24 times for 102 yards and LSU's last three touchdowns. "We gave Kendall an inch," senior guard Mark King said, "and he made a mile." "I don't see how they're only 6–4–1," said Arkansas quarterback Barry Lunney after being sacked five times. "That blows my mind that they're only that."

The Independence Bowl was an appealing matchup of up-and-coming programs under first-year coaches with identical records: Gerry DiNardo's 6–4–1 Tigers versus Nick Saban's 6–4–1 Spartans. Both teams were brimming with big-play potential: LSU with Faulk, Kennison, and Tyler, Michigan State with

Bowl bound: Gabe Northern (88), Joe Wesley (46), and James Gillyard after sacking Arkansas' quarterback Barry Lunney, 1995.   STEVE FRANZ

Muhsin Muhammad, Tony Banks, and Tony Mason. A crowd of 48,835 filled Independence Stadium on December 29 to see LSU's first game in Shreveport since 1975. They were barely in their seats before the Spartans hit the first big play: a 78-yard touchdown pass from Banks to Muhammad. The teams traded four touchdowns in a span of 1:33, leaving Michigan State with a 24–21 halftime lead. There were back-to-back kickoff returns—a 92-yarder by Kennison and a 100-yarder on the ensuing play by Mason. Then Faulk scored just over a minute later on a 51-yard run. In the Tigers' halftime locker room, Faulk told his teammate and cousin Derrick Beavers, "I'm going to cause a catastrophe with my feet." Faulk finished with an LSU bowl record of 234 yards rushing on 25 carries, scoring on a 5-yard run in a 45–26 victory. "LSU made the big plays," Saban said. "Our special teams gave up a score, our offense gave up a score. You have to be hard to score against." LSU finished 7–4–1 and ranked No. 25 in the coaches' poll, its first postseason victory since the 1987 Gator Bowl and first season-ending ranking since 1988.

Bengal Belles

In April 1996, Terry DiNardo, wife of then–LSU football coach Gerry DiNardo, approached a friend named Aimee Simon about starting a women's organization that would support and promote LSU football. Terri envisioned a group of 30 to 50 women when the Bengal Belles got their start, but she underestimated the passion of female LSU football fans. The first Bengal Belles luncheon drew about 250 members in September 1996, and the annual membership averages about 600. Over the years, the Belles have supported LSU athletics by donating $250,000 toward the construction of LSU's Cox Communications Academic Center for Student-Athletes; by hosting the "Toast the Tigers" event before the start of each sports year and the annual football banquet in December; and by organizing Football 101, a clinic before each football season to familiarize women with the inner workings of the game. Men are invited to join the organization as well—as Bengal Beaus.

Eddie Kennison in the 1995 Independence Bowl: Soon he would be off to the NFL.

STEVE FRANZ

See Kevin Run

The run-up to the 1996 season was like nothing LSU had experienced in eight years. In recruiting, LSU nabbed a top-10 class and kept more of the best players in state. Highlighting LSU's haul were New Iberia's Mark Roman, who signed after being committed to Mississippi State, and Leesville running back Cecil Collins, Louisiana's Mr. Football. There were key losses: Howard, Wilson, and Gabe Northern, an All-SEC defensive end, were graduating.

Kennison was going, too, forgoing his senior season to become the first Tiger football player to make an early entry into the NFL draft (he was selected 18th overall by St. Louis). But Tyler was 4–0 as a starting quarterback, and Faulk and McFarland, the SEC offensive and defensive freshmen of the year, were poised for bigger things as sophomores. At SEC Media Days in Birmingham, LSU was picked to finish second in the SEC West.

Texas A&M was finally off the schedule, but there were other challenges for No. 17 LSU. Six months before the season opener on September 7, Faulk was involved in a bar fight in Carencro, his status in limbo all summer. In August, Collins was declared academically ineligible. Two days before LSU faced Houston, DiNardo lifted Faulk's one-game suspension after his charges were dropped. "When Coach withdrew that suspension, I felt I had to do something special for the team and myself," Faulk said. If Faulk hadn't played, it's almost certain the Tigers would have lost. They tried anyhow. Five turnovers—the last a Faulk fumble returned 30 yards for a touchdown—gave the Cougars a 34–14 lead after three quarters. As soon as the teams changed ends, though, Faulk scored on a 78-yard punt return with 14:44 remaining. LSU rallied with the run, rushing for 433 yards. When redshirt freshman Rondell Mealey scored the game winner on a 36-yard run with 3:22 left, the Cougars were worn out to the point of being defenseless. Faulk, who earlier scored on runs of 3 and 80 yards, broke Charles Alexander's single-game school rushing record with 246 yards on 21 carries (Alexander ran for 237 against Oregon in 1977). Faulk finished with 376 all-purpose yards, the second-most in SEC history.

"That was one of the best performances I've ever seen in this stadium," Alexander said as he made his way through LSU's steamy locker room to congratulate Faulk. "They'd better get ready to put him in the Heisman race." Faulk was on his way to one of the best seasons ever for a Tiger back: 1,282

Rudy

A lot of players resented Dan "Rudy" Ruettiger's presence as a practice squad player on the Notre Dame football team. Gerry DiNardo wasn't one of them. "I'd get hit by him and he'd ask, 'Hey, Rudy, you all right?'" Ruettiger recalled. "Other guys said, 'Stay down.'" Ruettiger turned his life's story, and his battle to get into action in the last 27 seconds of the 1975 Notre Dame–Georgia Tech game, into a movie that came out in 1993. By 1996, Ruettiger had become a professional public speaker, and that April he was in Baton Rouge speaking at local Catholic schools. His old teammate DiNardo invited him to speak to the LSU team during spring practice. "Speak from the heart," Rudy said, "and people will tune in to that."

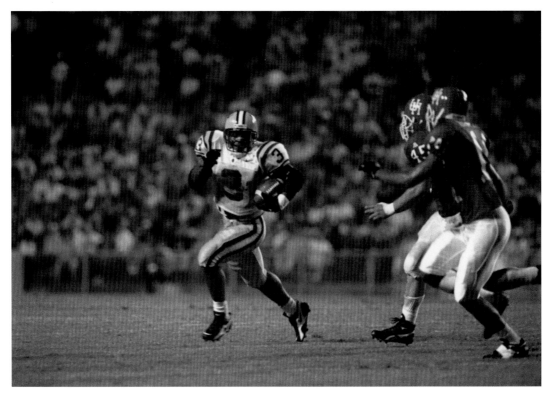

Kevin Faulk on his way to a record-breaking night against Houston, 1996.   STEVE FRANZ

yards rushing in 11 games (bowl stats didn't count then), second at LSU only to Alexander's 1,686 yards in 1977. Faulk earned AP All-American honors as an all-purpose player that year. He would rush for 1,144 yards in 1997 and 1,279 in 1998, the only Tiger ever with three 1,000-yard seasons.

How hot was the LSU-Auburn rivalry getting? Five of the last six games had been decided by six points or less, games that often carried nicknames. The Earthquake Game in 1988. The Interception Game in 1994. The Bring Back the Magic Game in 1995. But nothing would be as hot—or bizarre— as September 21, 1996: The Night the Barn Burned. The action on the field in LSU's 19–15 victory was exciting enough. But there was nothing stranger than the sight of flames climbing higher than Jordan-Hare Stadium's upper deck when Auburn's old wooden basketball arena was engulfed in an inferno. Fans weren't evacuated because fire didn't spread toward the football stadium—Jordan-Hare in relation to the old gym was comparable to the distance between Tiger Stadium and the original Alex Box Stadium.

As much as the Houston win belonged to Faulk, this one belonged to Raion Hill. The sophomore free safety returned a Jon Cooley interception 39 yards to put LSU up 17–9 with 7:19 remaining. After Auburn pulled within 17–15 on a 7-yard run by Rusty Williams with 38 seconds left, Hill intercepted

The Night the Barn Burned: Black smoke billows from a fire adjacent to Auburn's Jordan-Hare Stadium, 1996. STEVE FRANZ

Cooley's pass for two points and raced for two of his own as LSU won at Auburn for the first time since 1973. "When I caught it, I couldn't believe how far ahead I was," Hill said. "I had to turn around and look. I just couldn't believe it."

The weekend after Auburn, Mealey tied the LSU single-game mark with four rushing touchdowns as LSU routed hapless New Mexico State 63–7. Vanderbilt was next on October 5, typically an opponent that wouldn't have generated much talk at LSU. But Vanderbilt's roster was still dotted with players DiNardo had recruited, players he claimed Vanderbilt athletic director Paul Hoolahan (later executive director of the Sugar Bowl) never let him bid farewell after he took the LSU job. DiNardo and Vandy were still at odds over his buyout. And, the topper, new Vanderbilt coach Rod Dowhower refused to let LSU wear white jerseys. DiNardo responded by putting the Tigers in gold jerseys while most of the 80,142 in attendance (including LSU's coaches) wore white shirts to "white out" the Commodores. Faulk and Mealey each scored on 20-yard runs in the first quarter, and LSU's defense held winless Vandy to 207 total yards in a 35–0, um, whitewashing. Afterward DiNardo, wearing his hard feelings on his white sleeve, refused to shake Dowhower's hand. "I'm a lot of things, but I'm not a phony," DiNardo said. "If we're going to take that attitude going into the game, let's carry it right through." "They're a pretty darn good football team," Dowhower said. "I doubt the jerseys had much to do with that."

Now 4–0 and riding a seven-game winning streak, the No. 12 Tigers were eager to prove they were a top-flight program when they visited No. 1 Florida on October 12. "I feel we do have a good football team," DiNardo said, "and hopefully we'll bring that confidence with us." After Florida crushed LSU 56–13, one thing was clear: the Tigers might have been good and confident, but the Gators were great and expected to win. After "limiting" Florida to 321 total yards the year before, LSU defensive coordinator Carl Reese gave talks on stopping the Gators' "Fun-n-Gun" offense. When Spurrier heard of it, he went into attack mode. LSU was simply overwhelmed as Florida scored touchdowns on six of its first seven possessions to take a staggering 42–6 halftime lead. LSU netted just 28 yards rushing and was outgained 635–303. "It brings back memories," senior offensive tackle Ben Bordelon said. Bad ones.

While Florida was steamrolling toward a national championship, the 4–1 Tigers had to find their level. The Tigers restocked their confidence with a 41–14 victory over 1–5 Kentucky on October 19, Faulk rushing for 138 yards and two scores. Next came Mississippi State and a game memorable not for the play on the field, but the water. The old saying "It never rains in Tiger Stadium" was proven true. It wasn't rain that doused Death Valley on October 26; it was a monsoon, the worst in-game weather to hit Tiger Stadium since the 1988 Miami game. The first half was played on a relatively dry track with LSU taking a 28–14 halftime lead. Then came the rain, great gusting sheets of it, turning the saturated turf into a lake. "You needed a four-wheeler out there," junior cornerback Cedric Donaldson said. "It was nasty." The second half was a mud-splattered tug-of-war, with Faulk fumbling twice in LSU's half of the field, Tyler once. State could barely advance through the muck, though, settling for a pair of field goals as LSU survived 28–20.

Two weeks later, after LSU completely resodded its playing surface, the No. 11 Tigers hosted No. 10 Alabama, an inside track to the SEC championship game at stake. A crowd of 80,290 packed Tiger Stadium, while ESPN's College GameDay crew parked on the ramps of the Pete Maravich Assembly Center in the popular pregame show's first visit to Baton Rouge. In an added twist, Curley Hallman returned as Alabama's secondary coach, working from the press box. The game was reminiscent of the Hallman years as the Tigers were routed 26–0. Tyler bruised a nerve in his throwing arm late in the scoreless first quarter and could not continue, stagnating LSU's offense. LSU's defense couldn't stop Alabama redshirt freshman tailback Shaun Alexander, who rumbled for 291 yards and four touchdowns on 20 carries as Bama ran for 351 yards overall. "It hurts," LSU linebacker Allen Stansberry said. "It hurts real bad. This is my senior season. We want to get to the championship game. You want to have a chance to say you're champions. Now that's gone." Actually, it wasn't. While LSU was returning home from Oxford on November 16 after dispatching Ole Miss 39–7, Mississippi State upset Ala-

All-American offensive guard Alan Faneca makes a hole against Ole Miss, 1996.

bama 17–16. LSU could now reach the SEC championship game if it beat Arkansas and Auburn beat Alabama.

LSU's seniors bid farewell to Tiger Stadium with a November 23 home finale against traditional punching bag Tulane, though it wasn't quite so easy this time. LSU's only first-half score was on an 85-yard interception return by Roman, and when Tulane's Brad Palazzo kicked a 35-yard field goal, the Green Wave had a 10–7 lead early in the third quarter. LSU finally woke up, thanks to the nimble feet of its quarterback. Tyler threw for a touchdown and ran for two more in a 35–17 win, his seven rushing TDs tying a single-season school record for quarterbacks shared by David Woodley and Jeff Wickersham. Unfortunately for LSU, Alabama nipped Auburn 24–23 to clinch a berth in the SEC title game. The day after Thanksgiving, the Tigers hammered out a 17–7 victory over Arkansas in Little Rock to earn a hollow share of first place in the SEC West with Bama and a big prize. That prize was "The Boot," a brand-new, 200-pound, gold-plated trophy cast in the combined shape of Louisiana and Arkansas and valued at more than $10,000. Faulk and Tyler were again golden, Faulk rushing for 125 yards and a score, Tyler throwing for 191 yards with a 35-yard touchdown pass to Larry Foster.

Two days before Christmas, LSU traveled to Atlanta to begin preparations for a Peach Bowl appearance against 7–4 Clemson. Defense was dominant in the December 28 game. Trevor Pryce hit Tyler to force a fumble Clemson recovered at the 10, setting up a 5-yard touchdown run by Clemson quarterback Nealon Greene just before the first quarter ended. Tyler then led LSU on an 80-yard drive to tie the score 7–7 on a 3-yard touchdown run by Faulk. A 22-yard Wade Richey field goal with 4:35 left before halftime gave LSU the winning points, but the winning play was by Aaron Adams. He blocked Matt Padgett's 52-yard field-goal attempt with 1:10 remaining to secure the 10–7 LSU victory. "It was kind of typical of our year," DiNardo said. "We won ugly a lot this year." Ugly or not, LSU finished 10–2 and No. 12 in the final AP poll, the Tigers' most wins and highest ranking since 1987. It was just the fifth season of 10 wins or more in LSU history.

Knocking Off No. 1

From the start, 1997 was the year of the big tease for LSU. Amazing highs, awful disappointments, near misses, and plenty of what-might-have-beens. It started in January when the brothers Booty, Abram and Josh, arrived for spring semester classes. Abram was a blue-chip receiver prospect getting a jump start on college after graduating at mid-term from football factory Evangel in Shreveport. Josh was one of the nation's top quarterback prospects when he signed with LSU—in 1994. He also signed that year for $1.6 million with the Florida Marlins, an exclusive contract that ruled out football. By January 1997, though, Josh Booty was inventively trying to get out of the deal, offering the Marlins everything from $1 million to eliminate the baseball-only clause to $1.6 million from his first contract should he ever become an NFL quarterback. The team owned by Wayne Huizenga—a name that would haunt LSU years later—wouldn't yield. Within a month, Booty was in spring training, fielding grounders.

In February, LSU signed its second straight top-10 class, which besides Abram Booty included West Monroe fullback Tommy Banks, Crowley tight end Joe Domingeaux, Donaldsonville defensive end Jarvis Green, and a 6-foot-3, 220-pound quarterback from Hialeah, Florida, named Rohan Davey. Rated the nation's No. 2 quarterback prospect by *SuperPrep* magazine, Davey wavered because of Josh Booty's negotiations with the Marlins but picked LSU anyway, convinced DiNardo would give him a fair shot if Booty came.

Several of Louisiana's top prospects couldn't be swayed, though. All-American defensive tackle Thomas Pittman of East St. John High in Reserve signed with Auburn, Reggie Wayne of John Ehret High in Marrero with Miami.

Running back Travis Minor of Catholic High in Baton Rouge, the national player of the year, couldn't make up his mind. Fans at LSU's Bayou Recruiting Bash, the signing-day party begun by DiNardo the year before, were buzzing when the coach interrupted his talk on LSU's signees to take a call. Was it from Minor? No. His call eventually was to Florida State.

Any recruiting hangover was swept away by thoughts of what LSU had coming back. Eight offensive starters returned, including Faulk, Tyler, Foster, and All-SEC offensive guard Alan Faneca—who would earn All-American honors that year—plus Cecil Collins was finally going to play. Seven defensive starters were coming back, including All-SEC tackles McFarland and Chuck Wiley, Roman at free safety, and Donaldson at corner. Punter Chad Kessler would also be an All-American, the first man in NCAA history to average over 50 yards per punt for the entire season. It wasn't a surprise when LSU was for the first time picked to win the SEC West at SEC Media Days, or that the Tigers opened the season ranked No. 10.

LSU's September 6 season opener against traditional doormat Texas–El Paso was marked by exciting plays and disquieting mistakes. The Tigers rolled to a 55–3 victory despite losing three of six first-half fumbles. But Faulk scored three touchdowns, Tyler hooked up with Foster on a 32-yard TD pass, and Donaldson returned an interception 31 yards for a score. A week later in Starkville, Mississippi, Collins finally made his debut after starting the season with a one-week suspension. Nicknamed "the Diesel," Collins had rushed for 7,833 career yards and 99 touchdowns for Leesville High. With Faulk back in Baton Rouge resting a leg injury, Collins more than filled the void, rushing for 172 yards on 22 carries as the Tigers ground out a solid 24–9 victory.

Auburn visited Baton Rouge on September 20, a showdown for early supremacy in the SEC West that turned into a track meet. Auburn jumped on LSU 14–0 with a pair of Dameyune Craig touchdown passes before the Diesel went into overdrive, scoring on a 3-yard run and setting up a 1-yard Tyler keeper with a 48-yard run in which he broke two tackles. At halftime it was 21–21. Following an Auburn field goal in the third quarter, Collins counterpunched again, shaking a tackler on a 42-yard scoring run to give LSU its first lead, 28–24, with 13:34 remaining. With 3:12 left and 80 yards to go, Craig launched Auburn on a clutch drive. Peppering an injury-depleted LSU secondary for 69 yards on 5 of 8 passing, Craig handed off for the most crucial play, a 1-yard touchdown run by Rusty Williams with 30 seconds left to give Auburn the 31–28 win. "This was a big game, and both teams wanted to win very badly," Auburn coach Terry Bowden said. LSU couldn't win despite 232 yards rushing from Collins—the third-best total in school history—and 129 from Mealey.

After such a draining battle, the schedule provided another rent-a-win. LSU paid the Akron Zips from the Mid-American Conference $300,000

Cecil Collins: LSU's shooting star gains 232 yards against Auburn, 1997.   STEVE FRANZ

for the privilege of serving as fodder for a 56-zip Homecoming win on September 27. Several days later, during his weekly radio show, a caller wished DiNardo a big victory in his return to Vanderbilt on October 4. "Thanks," DiNardo replied, "but I'm preparing to win a one-point game at the end." DiNardo couldn't have known how prophetic he would be. On a sweep around left end during a scoreless first half, Collins, who entered the game second in the nation in rushing, broke his fibula and tore ankle ligaments, ending his season and as it turned out his LSU career. Late in the third quarter, Tyler hit Foster on a 13-yard scoring pass. Down 7–0, Vandy mounted a last-minute touchdown drive, Tavarus Hogans scoring on a 12-yard pass from Damian Allen with 12 seconds remaining. Vanderbilt coach Woody Widenhofer had already chosen to go for two points and the win, but the Commodores' bold decision never came off. Inexplicably, Vandy was hit with two consecutive delay-of-game penalties. Pushed back to the 13, Widenhofer was willing to settle for overtime and sent in his kicking team. That didn't work, either. Kenny Mixon blocked the kick for a shaky 7–6 win. "We have a lot of work to do," DiNardo said, "but I'd rather be doing it at 4–1."

A narrow escape over perennial SEC cellar-dweller Vanderbilt hardly seemed like the preamble to LSU's first victory ever against a No. 1-ranked

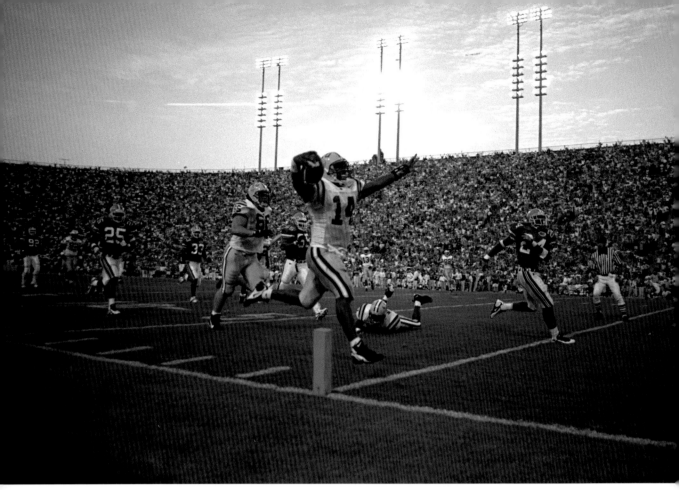

Herb Tyler's 40-yard keeper sparks an upset of No. 1 Florida, 1997.　　　STEVE FRANZ

Cornerback Cedric Donaldson holds an interception high on his way to the end zone against Florida, 1997.　　　LSU SPORTS INFORMATION

team. Especially since that team was Florida, the program that had run roughshod over the Tigers and the rest of the SEC for most of the decade. Even without Danny Wuerffel, Florida still had a potent offense led by Doug Johnson and a seemingly impenetrable defense. The week before playing LSU on October 11, Florida held Arkansas to minus 56 yards rushing in a 56–7 rout, the Gators' 25th straight SEC win that left them just two short of tying Alabama's record. But LSU had a plan, a link to the days when the Tigers were ranked No. 1: The Bandits were coming back on defense. "Sometime during the week Gerry told me about Carl Reese's plan to bring back the Bandits, to blitz them," Herb Vincent recalled, "but he told me not to tell anyone until the game starts." Reese's plan was to sub out eight defenders at a time in passing situations, coming at Florida with fresh legs out of a 3–3–5 alignment.

LSU had never beaten a No. 1 team in eight tries: 0–7–1, including a 56–13 rout in Gainesville a year earlier. Things would be different this time. Tyler set Tiger Stadium's second-largest crowd ever (80,677) rocking with 8:42 left in the first quarter when he took a keeper around right end and sped 40 yards for the touchdown. On the Gators' ensuing possession, Donaldson intercepted Johnson at the Florida 25 and returned the ball to the 7, setting up a scoring dive by "Touchdown" Tommy Banks to put LSU up 14–0 at the 7:44 mark. Florida, however, was hardly finished. Two 80-yard touchdown drives left the game tied 14–14 early in the third quarter. Johnson completed 32 of 57 passes for 346 yards but had no touchdowns—for his team. He was picked off four times, with one interception returned by Donaldson 31 yards for a touchdown with 13:13 remaining. After Tyler scored untouched on an 11-yard keeper to make it 28–14, the Gators pulled within 28–21 on Fred Taylor's second touchdown. But that's where the score would stay as Raion Hill intercepted Johnson to end Florida's final bid. "We had some bad plays we don't usually have," said Spurrier after his first loss to LSU in 11 games as a Florida quarterback and coach. "When those happen, you lose the game to a good team. LSU is a good team, and they just outplayed us." As the final seconds ticked away, thousands swarmed the field, pulling down the goalposts. It would be an hour before LSU Police, walking shoulder to shoulder from one end zone to the other, could clear the field. "Other than getting a bill from Joe Dean for the goalposts," DiNardo quipped, "it was a great night."

"Now," one LSU fan said, "I can die happy."

DiNardo wanted his now No. 8-ranked Tigers to build on what they had accomplished. He brought a list to his news conference before the Ole Miss game of great LSU victories followed by humbling defeats. "I hope we don't repeat history," DiNardo said. "This game tells us if we can handle success." Fans showed up in Tiger Stadium for an October 18 day game wearing coolie hats, backing the Bandits just as 1950s LSU fans did. Instead of beating the

"Now I can die happy." LSU fans dance away with a goalpost after toppling No. 1 Florida, 1997.

Gerry DiNardo, *left,* visits with ESPN College GameDay's Chris Fowler, Lee Corso, and Kirk Herbstreit after upsetting No. 1 Florida.

JENNIFER ABELSON, LSU SPORTS INFORMATION

Rebels in a big game like the Tigers did back then, however, LSU crumbled as DiNardo feared it would, 36–21. "Ole Miss did to us exactly what we did to Florida," he said. Not even Faulk could rescue the Tigers from themselves this time. He rushed for 172 yards and a touchdown, the first time LSU lost when he rushed for over 100 yards. LSU led 21–14 at halftime but was buried under a turnover-fueled surge in the second half. "This victory is bigger than life itself," Ole Miss tailback John Avery said.

After a week off, the Tigers headed to Lexington for a November 1 showdown between the SEC's top-ranked rushing team, LSU, and the conference's top passing team, Kentucky. Rushing won out as the Tigers rolled up a 63–28 victory, setting a school record for points scored in an SEC game. Faulk rushed for 212 yards and an LSU-record five touchdowns—four of them as LSU outscored UK 43–7 in a second-half onslaught—while Mealey added 131 yards and two scores. LSU's 600th all-time victory surprisingly thrust the Tigers back into the SEC West race as Mississippi State shocked Auburn 20–0, putting LSU and Auburn at 4–2 in the West with State just behind at 3–2.

To reach the SEC championship game, LSU needed to win out and have Auburn lose again because it held the tiebreaker. Winning out meant winning first at 4–4 Alabama. The November 8 game was nearly a 180-degree reversal of what happened in Tiger Stadium in 1996, with LSU winning 27–0 as defense set the tone. Wiley recovered a first-quarter fumble by Alabama quarterback Lance Tucker at his goal line for a touchdown as the Tigers limited the Tide to 93 yards passing and 250 yards overall. Then the running game tenderized the Tide, Faulk pounding for 168 yards and two scores.

Now 7–2 after two impressive back-to-back road wins, the No. 11-ranked Tigers returned home on November 15 to face Notre Dame for the first time since 1986 in the start of a scheduled home-and-home series. Outlined against a low, gray November sky with temperatures in the forties, weather more suited to the visitors from South Bend than south Louisiana, the 5–5 Fighting Irish rode to victory just the way LSU wanted to: with a dominant running game. Autry Denson and Clement Stokes each rushed for 92 yards and combined for three touchdowns as the Irish dominated 24–6. For the first time ever, Notre Dame completed a game without committing a turnover or a penalty. LSU had its troubles, though, as Tyler threw a career-high three interceptions. "Here's the scenario," defensive end Mike Sutton said. "We beat Florida, we lose to Ole Miss. We win last week, we lose [to Notre Dame]. I don't know what's going on around here."

For the second year in a row, the team that had to win the Iron Bowl for LSU to have a chance at the SEC championship game lost by a point—this time it was Alabama, 18–17, on November 22 while LSU was idle. Once again, LSU would be playing the Arkansas game for pride and a share of first place in the SEC West. The first half on November 28 was a wild back-and-

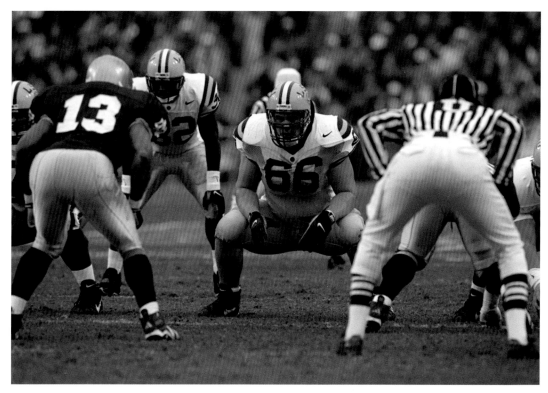

Alan Faneca against Notre Dame, 1997: The Irish prevail in round one. STEVE FRANZ

forth tussle with Faulk rushing for 138 yards and two scores, Mealey 55 yards and a touchdown, as the Tigers led 24–21 at halftime. Cleveland's 3-yard pass from Tyler, who was 15 of 23 for 171 yards, completed the scoring in a 31–21 LSU victory.

The 8–3 Tigers were headed back to the Independence Bowl but had to wait on an opponent. Notre Dame had doors shut to the Sun and Gator bowls, and accepted an LSU rematch after turning down the fledgling Motor City Bowl. Maybe December in Detroit would have been a better idea. As dominant as the Irish were in Baton Rouge, they were dominated that much and more on December 28 before a sold-out Independence Stadium crowd of 50,459. DiNardo played fashion designer once again, dressing the Tigers in previously unseen white helmets with gold jerseys and white pants. Notre Dame's biggest problem wasn't uniforms: It was its inability to stop Rondell Mealey. When Faulk left the game with an injury in the second quarter, Mealey stepped into his slot and never slowed down. Mealey rushed 34 times for 222 yards and two touchdowns in his team's 27–9 victory, including a 78-yard run to the Notre Dame 2 early in the fourth, the longest run in LSU postseason and Independence Bowl history. Mealey had enough breath left to score on the next play, then added a 1-yard touchdown run late in the game to earn offensive MVP honors. The Tiger defense switched from the 4–2–5 formation it had used most of the season to a five-man front, limiting Notre Dame to 243 total yards, including 66 yards on 8 of 18 passing by Ron Powlus in his final game. LSU finished 9–3 and No. 13 in the polls. "You have to give LSU credit," Notre Dame defensive end Melvin Dansby said. "They have a great team. The sun shined on them this time."

Three straight winning seasons, all capped by bowl victories and top 25 rankings. It seemed as if the sun wouldn't set on the LSU football program again for a long time.

Unusual uniforms, classic performance: Rondell Mealey rushes for some of his 222 yards vs. Notre Dame in the 1997 Independence Bowl. STEVE FRANZ

3

IS IT OVER?

1998–1999

As the new year beckoned, there was every reason to believe the Tigers were back, and ready to scale even greater heights.

With a 26–9–1 record the previous three seasons, LSU was winning consistently again. Recruiting was strong. Although some top prospects like Travis Minor and Thomas Pittman had slipped away, others such as Kevin Faulk and Cecil Collins had stayed home. At the top of it all was Gerry DiNardo, now entrenched as LSU football's leader and comfortable enough to put down roots. In the off-season months of 1998, he opened an Italian restaurant in south Baton Rouge that bore his name. He spent time, though not as much as some critics later thought, making a series of TV commercials for a local bank.

But even as LSU fans basked in the afterglow of defeating Notre Dame in the Independence Bowl and excitement for the new season built month by month, there were troubling clouds on the horizon. Before the bowl, defensive coordinator Carl Reese left for a similar position at Texas, ending a seven-year coaching run with DiNardo. Their working relationship had cooled when DiNardo took a more hands-on approach to the defense after the 36–21 upset loss to Ole Miss in 1997. Whoever was in charge, LSU had led the SEC in scoring defense for the second time in the last three seasons. To replace Reese, DiNardo hired Lou Tepper, dismissed as head coach at Illinois in 1996 after his third nonwinning season in five with the Illini. They had coached together in Colorado, and DiNardo was eager to fit a familiar hand into his program. He had a vision of doing things the LSU way.

"I didn't want this to be a coordinator-based program," DiNardo explained. "I wanted it to be the LSU offense and the LSU defense. Whether it was Carl Reese or Lou Tepper or Morris Watts, I wanted to be facilitator.

"Was it the right decision? Maybe not. But it wasn't a whim. It was the opposite of ego driven. I said, 'Let's make this about LSU.'"

Tepper may have been brought in to run the LSU defense the LSU way, but he had changes in mind. During his coaching exile after leaving Illinois, he wrote a book called *Complete Linebacking*. In it, he described a position that would become infamous to LSU fans: the drop linebacker. A utility position designed to stop the pass, support the run, press the tight end, and guard the flats near the sideline, it accomplished none of those objectives well at LSU. At the time, though, it was part of Tepper's plan to switch LSU from Reese's 4–2–5 to a 3–4 base formation. The change would require more linebackers, drop or otherwise. "We will find some linebackers," Tepper promised.

During Independence Bowl week, word came that Faulk was considering leaving school to turn pro. He wrestled with his decision for a couple more weeks before announcing he would return to LSU. "It's just that I wasn't ready to leave," Faulk said the day he made his announcement. "I love it here." LSU fans everywhere rejoiced, many glossing over the fact that Faulk was losing his best blocker—All-American guard Alan Faneca—who was leaving early for the draft. But senior quarterback Herb Tyler, 23–5 as a starter, was also returning. So were running back Rondell Mealey; Larry Foster and Abram Booty at receiver; Anthony McFarland, Mark Roman, and Raion Hill on defense. And then there was talented, star-crossed tailback Cecil Collins, healed from the broken leg and dislodged ankle ligaments that sidelined him in the 1997 Vanderbilt game.

Physically, Collins may have recovered, but there was plenty of heartache ahead. In June 1998, Collins was arrested for forcing his way into an apartment near the campus and fondling a 17-year-old woman who was there visiting her 18-year-old female friend. The next day, DiNardo dismissed him from the team. In July, Collins was arrested on a similar charge. "He challenges what the game is supposed to be about," DiNardo said. "Every coach has a breaking point. I went as far as I could." Collins transferred to McNeese State, where he played two games before failing a drug test, getting kicked off the team, and landing in jail. He eventually was drafted in the fifth round in 1999 by the Miami Dolphins. Again a rising star, Collins suffered another broken leg, then was arrested for illegally entering a neighbor's South Florida apartment and was sentenced to fifteen years in prison.

"He was high maintenance from the beginning," DiNardo said. "He was the opposite of Kevin Faulk. Drug tests, high school problems, a relationship with his mother that showed a lack of respect. We knew what we were getting into. But does the head coach at LSU turn down the best prospect in the state? Lose him in a recruiting battle and you're called a bad recruiter. Don't recruit him and you're dumb."

The Chinese calendar said 1998 was the Year of the Tiger. Instead, 1998 felt a lot like 1986, the year encapsulated by the *Sports Illustrated* headline "Crazy Days at LSU." Not only was Collins dismissed, but so was teammate Chris Beard for violating unspecified team rules. Track coach Pat Henry accused DiNardo of making sprinter and wide receiver Chris Cummings participate in spring practice with an injured knee. DiNardo didn't address the charge, but left the impression that he who provides the scholarship (DiNardo) makes the rules. Away from football, an NCAA investigation into allegations of wrongdoing in Lester Earl's recruitment would eventually land the men's basketball program on three years' probation. And in May, softball coach Cathy Compton was fired abruptly, her relationship with her players called into question.

And yet nothing was expected to derail the LSU football express. When the preseason polls were released, LSU started at No. 9, and the SEC football media again installed the Tigers as the favorite to win the SEC West.

The Tigers were the last of the 112 NCAA Division I-A teams to open the 1998 season when they hosted Arkansas State the night of September 12. The Tigers had already climbed to No. 7 in the polls and looked every bit the part with a comfortable 42–6 win. Faulk rushed for 180 yards and two touchdowns, and Tyler threw for a score and ran for another. Three turnovers and nine penalties could easily be explained as first-game rust. "We'll make improvements before next week," DiNardo promised.

LSU went to Auburn on September 19 and pounced on a pair of scoring opportunities on Auburn's first two snaps. First, strong safety Clarence LeBlanc made a one-handed interception of a Ben Leard pass and raced 21

Clarence LeBlanc runs back an interception for a touchdown three minutes into the 1998 Auburn game. STEVE FRANZ, LSU SPORTS INFORMATION

Kevin Faulk returned for his senior year in 1998, but couldn't help the Tigers have a winning season. STEVE FRANZ, LSU SPORTS INFORMATION

yards for a touchdown just three minutes in. On Auburn's first play after the kickoff, tailback Michael Burks of Kenner was stripped by linebacker Aaron Adams, and LSU's Thomas Dunson recovered at the 26. Five plays later, Tyler zigzagged his way into the end zone. Danny Boyd's extra point was blocked, but LSU still led 13–0 at the 9:34 mark. Auburn rallied to pull within 19–17 at halftime, but Tyler threw two second-half touchdown passes as LSU prevailed 31–19. "You're supposed to save your best for the big games," said Tyler, his throwing hand bandaged after striking a helmet. "We came out on top."

On September 20, LSU rose to No. 6 in both the Associated Press and coaches' polls, its highest ranking of the DiNardo regime. Flexing its muscle against Idaho in a 53–20 win on September 26 didn't prove to be that enjoyable, though. Hurricane Georges was spinning in the gulf, two days away from landfall in Biloxi. And while Faulk had 178 yards rushing and three touchdowns on just 13 carries, the Tigers committed three fumbles. LSU's defense was gashed for 192 yards rushing, much of it right up the middle, and 410 yards overall. "I'm glad we won," DiNardo said. "But we'll struggle the next six weeks if we play like that." DiNardo didn't know how right he was.

Still No. 6, LSU next hosted No. 12 Georgia on October 3, a showdown that looked like a preview of the SEC championship game. Georgia quarterback Quincy Carter passed and ran the Tigers silly, completing 27 of 34 passes for 218 yards and leading his team with 41 rushing yards. Trailing 28–21, LSU closed within 28–27 with two Christian Chauvin field goals. The second, with 5:08 remaining, gave the Tigers time to get a defensive stop and have a chance to win. On third-and-6 from the Georgia 24 with just over four minutes left, McFarland broke through and planted Carter in the turf. But not before he let go of the ball, a floater that led Champ Bailey perfectly for a 21-yard gain and allowed Georgia to run out the clock. "Quincy Carter was on fire tonight," Bailey said. It was the Tigers who felt burned.

"We can mope the rest of the season, or we can try to come back," DiNardo said. Now ranked No. 11, LSU hit the road for a game with No. 6 Florida on October 10. Neither team played brilliantly, combining for 22 penalties. But it was LSU that broke down at crucial times, watching a 10–6 halftime lead boil away into a 22–10 Gator victory. A week later LSU, clinging to the No. 21 spot in the AP poll, hosted Kentucky. Tyler threw for 268 yards and two touchdowns, and ran for three more. Kentucky's Tim Couch was 37 of 50 for 391 yards and three scores. Despite all the fireworks, the game would be remembered for a defensive play—or rather a lack of one—that to LSU fans epitomized all that was wrong with Tepper's defense. With overtime looming, UK faced third-and-12 at its 24. Wide receiver Quentin McCord swung out on a reverse, and as he did so, drop linebacker Jamal Hill committed inside to the tight end. McCord ran 38 yards to the LSU 33, a 5-yard face mask penalty putting the ball at the Tigers' 28. Three players later, Seth Hanson delivered on a 33-yard field goal as time expired, kicking LSU in the teeth with a 39–36 loss. Asked to describe the play, Hill gruffly replied, "If I could describe it, I would have stopped it."

The Tigers' stunning fall from 3–0 and No. 6 to 3–3 three weeks later perhaps shocked DiNardo more than anyone. For 3½ years he had all, or at least most, of the answers. Now the season, and possibly his LSU career, was spinning out of his grasp. "Sitting in his office after the loss to Kentucky, he said, 'Can you believe this is happening?'" LSU Sports Information director Herb Vincent recalled. "He could see it." The mood in Baton Rouge had swiftly gone from sunny to surly. Callers to local radio talk shows wanted Tepper's head, or better yet his and DiNardo's in a package deal. Suddenly, there was a break in the darkness, a game that was a reminder of how good the Tigers were supposed to be. SEC West–leading Mississippi State visited Tiger Stadium on October 24 with a 5–1 overall record and 3–0 SEC mark. It left looking like a team on a three-game skid, as LSU hammered the soon-to-be SEC West champs 41–6. "Everything fell our way tonight," Abram Booty said. "Everything." The LSU-career rushing record fell to Faulk, his 123 yards giving him 4,079 overall, eclipsing Dalton Hilliard's 4,050 yards from 1982 through 1985.

After one last feel-good moment, the rest of LSU's season would be an extended nightmare of four straight losses, each painful in its own way.

- October 31, Ole Miss 37, LSU 31 (OT): The Tigers rallied from a 31–10 deficit to force overtime with a 1-yard touchdown pass from Tyler to Mealey with two seconds left in regulation. In overtime the Rebels scored, then tipped away a Tyler pass intended for Foster in the end zone.
- November 7, Alabama 22, LSU 16: The Tigers surrendered two touchdowns in the final three minutes, making Alabama 14–0–1 in Tiger Stadium since its last loss there in 1969. "We've got a saying," Alabama wide receiver Quincy Jackson commented. "The Tide don't lose in Baton Rouge."
- November 21, Notre Dame 39, LSU 36: Despite Faulk's 88-yard kickoff return for a touchdown—LSU's first since 1981—the rest of the Tiger kicking game fell apart. LSU botched two extra-point tries and Boyd missed a 42-yard field goal just before the Irish launched their winning touchdown drive. "It tears your guts out," DiNardo said of the loss to his alma mater, but really speaking about the entire season. "It's not fun, for sure. It's a killer."
- November 27, Arkansas 41, LSU 14: Tyler pulled a hamstring trying to make a tackle after throwing an interception at Notre Dame, effectively ending his career and forcing Craig Nall to start. Nall and the Tigers couldn't keep pace with an Arkansas team that threw for 334 yards and piled up 509 yards overall. "We knew we could throw the ball against them," Arkansas coach Houston Nutt said, "because teams have been doing that all year."

Defensive coordinator Lou Tepper.

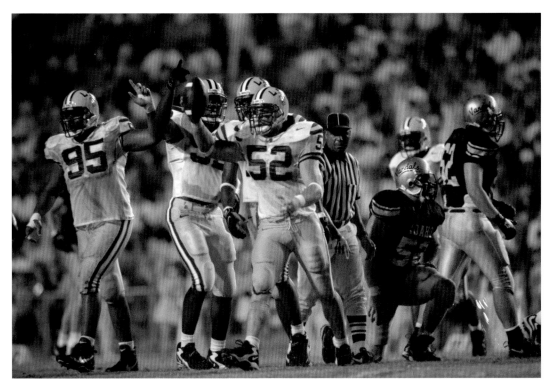

Drop linebacker Thomas Dunson (52): He became the focal point of LSU fans' frustration with the Tepper defense. STEVE FRANZ, LSU SPORTS INFORMATION

DiNardo's Demise

The Tepper defense was an unquestioned failure. The team that led the SEC in points allowed two of the previous three years under Reese gave up 25.4 points per game and set school records for yards per game (408.7) and yards per game passing (275.8) allowed.

Although stunned and dismayed by the year's 4–7 record, and personally hurt by the way LSU fans had turned on him after three popular (and winning) seasons, DiNardo was determined to get the program back on course. Past flirtations with the Dallas Cowboys and Notre Dame were long over now. The football world waited to see DiNardo prove himself again. Perhaps he didn't see much choice. "He was bound and determined to get it back," Vincent said. "By '99 he said, 'Every school could line up outside this door and I'm not leaving until I get this thing turned around.'"

One thing was certain: They would see DiNardo do it his way. Instead of searching far and wide for coaching talent, DiNardo seemed to be drawing the circle tighter around himself. When offensive coordinator Morris Watts left to return to Michigan State to work for Nick Saban—he was able to retire in the Michigan system with a better pension because of his previous years at the school—DiNardo quickly promoted receivers coach Bob McConnell, his assistant since 1991 at Vanderbilt. When DiNardo hired Charlie Coiner from Tennessee–Chattanooga as special teams coach and recruiting coordinator, his statement was, "Perhaps as important as anything, we have worked together in the past." Why, critics wanted to know, was that an overriding factor? What outsiders didn't know was how much responsibility DiNardo was placing on his own shoulders for all aspects of the program. "When Carl Reese left, he figured he could fix it himself," Vincent said. "When Morris Watts left, he figured he could fix it himself."

Athletic Director Joe Dean saw a problem when Reese interviewed at Texas. "I'm in New York at the College Football Hall of Fame banquet," Dean said. "We're trying to check out of the hotel and Herb [Vincent] said, 'DiNardo is trying to reach you.' I called Gerry and he said, 'Bull is going to interview at Texas.' I said, 'Gerry, let him go. I will keep him for you. I'll match whatever they offer.' He said, 'If he goes [to interview] I don't want him back. He's disloyal.' I said, 'Gerry, you can't look at it like that.' Hardheaded. Then he hired the wrong defensive coordinator [Tepper]. One of the nicest people. Quality human being. Good family. Just wasn't the right fit. Then when the offensive coordinator left, he turns around and hires Bob McConnell. The other assistants under him had no respect for Bob—not as a person, but as a coordinator.

"So the whole thing just blew up, offense and defense. It was just terrible. Then he tries to get in there and run it all."

DiNardo maintained he had his reasons for his choice of hires. "I wanted to stabilize an unstable program," he said. The Tigers lost only seven starters, but they included Faulk, Tyler, linebacker Joe Wesley, and a pair of All-American linemen, Anthony McFarland and Todd McClure. Rondell Mealey was back for his senior season, now the primary tailback. Larry Foster and Abram Booty were the starting receivers, while the defense was built around defensive end Jarvis Green and a seasoned secondary that included seniors Mark Roman and Damien Woods at corners and Clarence LeBlanc at strong safety. One positive in the wake of '98: Josh Booty was finally granted his release by the Marlins in January 1999 after he agreed to pay back an undisclosed part of his $1.6 million signing bonus. He enrolled at LSU and took part in spring practice, a 24-year-old sophomore happily zipping passes to younger brother Abram, now a junior. Josh's arrival turned the quarterback duel into a three-cornered battle with Nall and Rohan Davey that carried through preseason practice.

After all the changes, DiNardo was optimistic. "I hope to be standing here a year from now with a much different result," DiNardo told reporters at SEC Media Days in Birmingham. Few were convinced. LSU was picked to finish fifth in the SEC West. A crowd of 76,753 filed into Tiger Stadium on September 4, curious as to how their Tigers would fare against four-touchdown underdog San José State. LSU won 29–21, but gave up 377 total yards, was just 2 of 9 on third-down conversions, committed four turnovers, missed two extra points, and had a punt blocked. Leading 23–21, it took a 40-yard Davey-to–Jerel Myers pass on third-and-5 to launch LSU off its 14 to a safety-cushion touchdown.

One of LSU's problems was a quarterback controversy. Nall started but struggled. Davey wasn't dazzling but made the big play when it counted. And there was Josh Booty. Asked who would start against North Texas on September 11, DiNardo sighed and said, "Let me have some pasta and watch the tape in the morning." DiNardo picked Davey to start against the Mean Green, though all three quarterbacks played in a 52–0 romp. Davey was perfect (6 of 6 for 66 yards) and Booty solid (9 of 14, 86 yards), but Nall (1 of 5, 12 yards) was already losing ground. LSU scored on its first five possessions, reason for optimism with Auburn approaching. "Come Saturday we'll be ready," free safety Ryan Clark said.

First came shocking news. Foster, a senior and the team captain, was arrested September 14 for purse snatching and was charged with writing worthless checks. He wouldn't play another down for LSU, which went into the September 18 Auburn game a nine-point favorite but suffered a complete offensive, defensive, and special teams meltdown in a 41–7 debacle. LSU committed six turnovers and Auburn led 17–0 before the home team managed a first down. Auburn's first touchdown came on a 1-yard run by kicker Damon Duval, scoring untouched after a no-look flip from holder Jacob Allen on a superb fake. "If it had been fourth-and-5, we had it covered," DiNardo said. When it was over, Auburn coach Tommy Tuberville led his Tigers in a round of victory cigars that burned in the memory of LSU fans for years. It was already getting ugly in Tigertown, and the home team was still 2–1. "I didn't expect this at all," DiNardo said, quoted in the *Baton Rouge Advocate* over a picture of him throwing up his hands. No one could have known at the time, but DiNardo had won his last game as LSU's coach. The Tigers were heading down a dark path untraveled even in the leanest of years under Curley Hallman or Mike Archer: an eight-game losing streak, the longest in school history.

Not to say the Tigers wouldn't come achingly close to victory more than once. After Auburn, DiNardo named Josh Booty as the starter for LSU's October 2 game at No. 10 Georgia. With the Tigers trailing 23–16, Booty scrambled on fourth-and-10 from the Georgia 39 when he found wide receiver Reggie Robinson in the end zone with 18 seconds left. DiNardo immediately went for two and the win. Booty rolled right, then threw back across the field where Tommy Banks and Mealey appeared open, but at the last second Georgia linebacker Will Weatherspoon raced over to tip it away and preserve a

23–22 victory. "Maybe if I had thrown the ball three inches higher we would have won," Booty lamented. LSU returned home to sloppy, soggy Tiger Stadium and lost a sloppy, soggy game the next weekend to No. 8 Florida, 31–10. Steve Spurrier, who improved to 67–0 against unranked teams, lamented his 5–1 team's lack of discipline after committing seven penalties and four turnovers. DiNardo must have wished he had such problems. LSU's running game sank into the mud, netting minus 7 yards on 37 carries while Booty threw for 172 yards with three interceptions. The Tigers were now 10–12 since beating No. 1 Florida two years earlier. It seemed longer ago than that. Then, on October 16, after scoring 63 points on its last trip to Lexington in 1997, LSU couldn't even find the end zone in a 31–5 loss. A first-quarter safety on a blocked punt by Green was one of the few highlights.

Even LSU's traditional SEC victim, Mississippi State, piled on. The No. 12 Bulldogs would go 7–0 for the first time ever, but 2–4 LSU pushed them to the limit in a controversial 17–16 loss on October 23. On third-and-goal from the 6, Bulldog fullback Rod Gibson appeared to fumble a pass from Wayne Madkin at the 1 but was called down. On fourth-and-goal, Gibson slipped as he smashed off left tackle but was ruled to have scored with 1:39 left. Did Gibson think he scored? "I can't answer that question," he said, having been dazed on the third-down play. Gibson's teammates had to tell him about his touchdown. DiNardo was emotional in defeat. "I was really pleased with how hard they played," he said. "They just don't get rewarded for it." Nor would they. The Tigers clinched a losing season—their eighth in the last eleven years—on October 30 against Ole Miss. Future New Orleans Saints running back Deuce McAllister rushed for 140 yards and two touchdowns and Joe Gunn added 135 yards and two more scores as the Rebels rushed for 323 yards in a 42–23 victory. "There were some really huge holes," McAllister said.

The hits kept coming for LSU off the field, too. The following Wednesday, LeBlanc and Roman were declared ineligible after an investigation determined they had had contact with sports agent Randall "Banks" Menard, an NCAA violation. There were also allegations that several players made unauthorized long-distance phone calls with a university access card. Perhaps November 6 was the right time for a road trip, particularly to No. 12 Alabama, where the Tigers had won six of the last eight times. LSU was down 23–7 late in the third when defensive tackle Johnny Mitchell tipped an Andrew Zow pass at the line, grabbed it, and rumbled 66 yards for a touchdown. A John Corbello field goal in the fourth pulled LSU within 23–17, and then the Tigers mounted one last drive. On first-and-goal at the 1, LSU called Pass 56. As Booty rolled right, tight end Joe Domingeaux appeared to break open in the end zone. Instead of throwing, Booty tried to bulldoze his way over three Alabama defenders, got spun into the air, and landed just short of the goal line.

Denied: Quarterback Josh Booty tries to go over three Bama defenders in the end zone, but he and LSU come up short 23–17. STEVE FRANZ, LSU SPORTS INFORMATION

With no time-outs remaining, the Tigers were unable to get a play off before the last nine seconds expired in another excruciating defeat.

Then there was the 20–7 loss to Houston on November 13. The Tigers scored first on a 34-yard run by Mealey, then seemed to deflate as the Cougars built a 17–7 halftime lead. All the air had gone out of the once-promising Di-Nardo era. Fans who once believed he was the man to bring back the magic to the LSU program now went to Tiger Stadium wearing bags over their heads and T-shirts that proclaimed, "DiNardeaux must geaux!"

The following Monday, DiNardo met secretly with Joe Dean and new chancellor Mark Emmert at LSU's Lod Cook Alumni Center, where they told him he was through. "He became very emotional," Dean said. "There were tears. He was hurt." As with Hallman and Archer, DiNardo's firing was made public on November 15. Unlike his predecessors, DiNardo declined an offer to finish the season. "It's just not in me to be a lame duck coach," he said. "It would have gone against everything I have tried to stand for." DiNardo, whose final record at LSU was 32–24–1, still had four years left on his latest contract, which was paying him about $800,000 per year. LSU bought him out for $600,000, the equivalent of four years of his $150,000 base salary.

A Brave Face

As defeat piled upon defeat, Gerry DiNardo still managed to keep the dry wit that helped make him popular when he was winning. After yet another loss at home, DiNardo settled into the coaches' lounge for his customary postgame radio interview while Herb Vincent slipped next door to supervise player interviews. When Vincent returned, he was surprised to find that DiNardo's interview had already ended.

"Is it over?" Vincent asked.

"Do you mean the radio show?" DiNardo sarcastically shot back.

Chancellor Mark Emmert and Athletic Director Joe Dean announce Gerry DiNardo's firing on November 15, 1999.　　　　　　　　　　　　　　　　STEVE FRANZ, LSU SPORTS INFORMATION

"Success in LSU football is essential for the success of Louisiana State University," Emmert said upon announcing DiNardo's firing that afternoon. He promised that the university would have an "SEC caliber" coach, but more immediately, LSU needed a coach for the Arkansas game on November 26. It tabbed assistant head coach and offensive line coach Hal Hunter, the school's first interim football coach since 1916. The forty-year-old Hunter had been with DiNardo since his first season at Vanderbilt in 1991. Now, with an open date before the season finale, it was his difficult task to get the team through the Arkansas game, then lead the transition to the new head coach. Hunter made it plain that coach wouldn't be him. "You're like a migrant farm worker," he said. "You jump in the back of that pickup truck, go to that field, and pick those crops somewhere else." Hunter said he wouldn't tell fellow coaches who to start or play. In fact, he had just two directives: have fun and have enthusiasm.

Not surprisingly, Hunter's velvet touch paid off. A team burdened all season by the future of its coaching staff played fast and loose with Arkansas and routed the Razorbacks 35–10. Davey took over from Booty in the second quarter and proceeded to complete 10 of 12 passes for 224 yards and three touchdowns, including a 67-yard strike to Reggie Robinson. "I knew Monday we were going to win the game just from the attitude," Davey said. "The attitude was up because of Hunter and the whole coaching staff."

Not that the two losing seasons helped his cause, but DiNardo believed he didn't have Emmert's backing from the time he took over at LSU. "He was the team owner and I was the coach when he bought the team," said DiNardo, who went into broadcasting after head coaching stints in the XFL and at Indiana. "Emmert wanted to do something different. He had another agenda." In time, some of the bitterness faded over his dismissal. "It was the best job I ever had," DiNardo said. "I can't blame anyone but myself for losing that job. Whatever happened, I still had enough control to make those last two years better than they were."

When times were good for DiNardo and LSU, they were very good, days he remembered fondly. "It was a great place," he said. "I miss not being there. I go to bed every night wishing I had done a better job." LSU fans may not have believed it as the 1999 season ended, but better days lay just ahead. In fact, they would be the best days ever for the LSU football program.

Interim coach Hal Hunter prepares to lead the Tigers against Arkansas, 1999.

STEVE FRANZ, LSU SPORTS INFORMATION

4

SUGAR AND MIRACLES

2000–2002

I f LSU football fans couldn't have what they wanted most—a championship team—they got what some would say was the next best thing: a coaching search and all the accompanying excitement and intrigue. A large pool of names collected even before DiNardo was fired, including a bevy of college head coaches: Butch Davis, Miami; Dennis Erickson, Oregon State; Bob Pruett, Marshall; Glen Mason, Minnesota; Steve Logan, East Carolina; Hal Mumme, Kentucky; and even cigar-smoking Tommy Tuberville of Auburn.

Davis refused to budge, his eye on the NFL. Erickson, who had won a national title at Miami and coached the Seattle Seahawks, was a popular name, but LSU chancellor Mark Emmert was leery of his reputation from his days with the renegade Hurricanes program. LSU contacted Pruett, a former defensive coordinator at Tulane and Florida, but little came of it. On Monday, November 22, LSU officials flew to Chicago to interview Mason, but eventually Erickson, Pruett, and Mason all signed new deals with their current schools. As with the last search, LSU was making a lot of coaches richer but was no closer to landing one of its own.

A day after the Mason interview, Athletic Director Joe Dean got a call from his friend Sean Touhy, who played basketball at Ole Miss in the early 1980s. "Have you hired anybody?" Touhy asked. When Dean said he hadn't, Touhy replied, "I think the guy at Michigan State, Nick Saban, might be interested." Touhy had been in some business deals with Jimmy Sexton, Saban's agent in Memphis. Sexton asked Touhy to call Dean and gauge LSU's interest. Moments after Touhy and Dean hung up, Sexton called Dean. A meeting was arranged for that weekend at Sexton's home.

Saban first became intrigued by the LSU job during his NFL days, when a study the league commissioned said Louisiana was traditionally among the top five states per capita in pro players produced. "Everyone thought when I was at Michigan State that I was looking to go to the pros," Saban said. "I really wasn't looking at all. But I think we're always wanting to go someplace where you think you have a chance to win it all."

Waiting for Saban at Sexton's home were Emmert, Dean, and other members of LSU's search committee. Saban wanted to know what was wrong at a place like LSU that it could have had losing seasons eight of the last eleven years. Dean told him it was about finding the right person, like successful LSU baseball coach Skip Bertman. "Are you the right person?" Dean asked. As a condition of accepting the job, Saban wanted improved facilities—a football operations complex, an academic center for athletes, and better living conditions for his players. Before the LSU contingent returned to Baton Rouge, Emmert promised all would be done.

The only thing left was money. DiNardo made about $850,000 per year at the end, Saban just under $700,000 at Michigan State. Sexton proposed a contract of $1.2 million per year, a staggering sum then, with incentives that could push Saban's compensation to $1.5 million. It would instantly make him the nation's third-highest-paid coach behind only Florida's Steve Spurrier ($1.9 million) and Florida State's Bobby Bowden ($1.5 million). Emmert hastily agreed over Dean's objections. "I called Mark Emmert at his home and said, 'Here's where we are,'" Dean recalled. "He said, 'Go ahead and pay him $1.2 million, we might lose him.' I said, 'Mark, we're not going to lose him, he wants the job.' But he said, 'Let's pay him $1.2 million.' That's kind of how it happened."

Despite the intense negotiations, Saban had not been to Baton Rouge himself. As one last insurance policy, Saban dispatched his wife, Terry, to check things out. After DeLaine Emmert showed her the campus and around town, Terry reported back. "I think it's a diamond in the rough, Nick," she said. "If you're looking for a new challenge, I really think you can get it done there." Terry's appraisal of the LSU job was crucial to Saban's decision process. "I was trying to make a decision in the blind," he recalled. "I think her opinion of what the potential was and the quality of the people I met when I talked to them were probably the key factors in making the decision. Really, that's all I had to go on."

Saban accepted the job Monday evening, November 29, but spent a sleepless night plagued by self-doubt. It wasn't much different on Tuesday, when he flew to Baton Rouge for his introductory news conference. "We walked

> ## The Lunch Hunch
>
> As the search to find Gerry DiNardo's replacement wore on, T. J. Ribs, the popular, LSU-rabid restaurant near campus, erected a board and tallied customers' votes on candidates for the new coach. Monday, November 29, two women sat down to lunch there, dining in relative anonymity. First they scanned the board for one particular name. "Nick's not on there," said Terry Saban to her lunch companion, DeLaine Emmert, wife of LSU chancellor Mark Emmert. "Vote for me," their waiter, Tommy Mendoza, requested. "I'm going to be the next coach." They voted for Nick Saban, the first two of only three votes he got, and quietly left.

Nick Saban addresses the media at his first LSU news conference as Joe Dean, Mark Emmert, and members of LSU's search committee look on.

back to my office and I could tell everything was happening so fast for him," LSU Sports Information director Herb Vincent said. "He put his face in his hands, he seemed so stressed out. We were starting to get calls from people in Michigan that he wanted to go back. There were all these rumors." Saban overcame his misgivings, and Emmert exulted in what he was sure was an excellent hire. "You want big fish, you fish in deep water," Emmert said. "That's what we did here."

Nick Lou Saban was born on Halloween Day 1951 in Fairmont, West Virginia. He was named for his father and a cousin, Lou Saban, who became a legendary NFL coach. Nick grew up in nearby Monongah, a small town in the heart of West Virginia's coal-mining country, where the Sabans owned a restaurant and a gas station. Nick, or Brother as he was called, pumped gas while older sister Dene worked in the restaurant. Though neither Nick nor Mary Saban went to college, they were determined their children would, particularly so Brother wouldn't have to work in the coal mines. A high school quarterback, Saban earned a scholarship to Kent State.

The spring of his freshman year, Saban became enmeshed in one of the darkest days in American history. It was the height of the Vietnam War, and protests were touching down on one Ohio campus after another. "Everybody was looking for a cause," Saban remembered. The National Guard was sent to Kent State, which in the first week of May 1970 was in the grip of massive demonstrations. A rally on May 4 drew between 2,000 and 3,000 people to the university commons area. One of Saban's teammates, a linebacker named Phil Weatherspoon, wanted to watch. Nick persuaded him to go to lunch first. By the time they reached the protest site, they found a scene of chaos and blood. Thirteen students—some demonstrators, some simply walking to class—had been shot by the National Guardsmen about five minutes earlier. Four students died. One of them, a coed named Allison Krause, was a student in Saban's English class. "It was shocking," Saban said. "I don't know how many people have actually seen somebody dying or shot, but it has an effect on you. It really does."

When Nick called Terry, his girlfriend since grade school, she could hear helicopters in the background. "I'm coming home," he told her. "They're mailing me my grades." Kent State closed for the semester. There was talk it would never reopen but it did, and over the next three years Saban would letter as a defensive back and baseball infielder for the Golden Flashes. Nick and Terry married in December 1971, and after he graduated in 1973 he stayed on at Kent State part-time under his old head coach, Don James. When James left for Washington in 1975, Saban became a full-time assistant, but by 1977 he was ready to leave. He made the first of the frequent moves that have marked his and many coaches' careers, going to Syracuse to coach outside linebackers. Over the next twelve years he would coach at West Virginia, Ohio State, Navy, and Michigan State before serving as secondary coach with the Houston Oilers. The University of Toledo made Saban its head coach in 1990, where he led the Rockets to a 9–2 record. But after one season he was off again, serving as the Cleveland Browns' defensive coordinator under Bill Belichick before heading back to Michigan State in 1995. His first Spartans team went 6–5–1 and lost to LSU in the 1995 Independence Bowl. After years of 6–6, 7–5, and 6–6, the program finally blossomed in 1999, going 9–2 before Saban stepped down to go to LSU, never having spent more than five seasons in any one job.

The entire Michigan State coaching staff, including former LSU offensive coordinator Morris Watts, stayed behind in East Lansing when Saban left. He said it was because Michigan State's administration made their solidarity a condition of promoting assistant Bobby Williams to head coach. Others said it was because Saban drove his staff so hard that to a man they didn't want to coach for him anymore. Either way, when a plane was sent to Michigan State to bring back any coaches who wanted to join Saban at LSU, no one climbed aboard.

Saban was starting almost from scratch. He kept running backs coach Mike Haywood and administrative assistant Sam Nader from DiNardo's

The new east upper deck raised Tiger Stadium's capacity to 91,600 by 2000.

STEVE FRANZ, LSU SPORTS INFORMATION

Bigger and Better

As the Nick Saban era began, the finishing touches were being made to the first major expansion of Tiger Stadium since the west upper deck was added in 1978. Joe Dean wanted to build a new deck on Tiger Stadium's east side, to be paid for by two levels of private suites layered between the old bowl and the new seats above. The price tag: $50 million, the debt paid by the Tiger Athletic Foundation, LSU's athletic fundraising organization. The suites were called Tiger Dens, and by 2000 there would be 70 of them, renting for $34,000 to $95,000 per year depending on location. The addition raised Tiger Stadium's seating capacity from 80,000 to 91,600. Despite the last two losing seasons, all 70 Tiger Dens were snapped up before the 2000 season began, and a waiting list was established.

LSU began tearing down the old west upper deck immediately after the end of the 2004 season, the plan to rebuild the upper west side with a deck that would include a new press box and 3,200 club seats. With an asking price of $2,000 to $2,800 per seat, the club seats were all taken within a month and would generate $7.3 million annually. Construction delays and cost overruns, most of them the result of Hurricanes Katrina and Rita, meant that the $75 million project expected to be completed for the 2005 season wasn't entirely finished until 2006. The new deck raised Tiger Stadium's seating capacity to 92,400, making it at the time the nation's sixth-largest on-campus stadium.

staff. New offensive coordinator Jimbo Fisher was from Cincinnati, defensive coordinator Phil Elmassian from Wisconsin. Derek Dooley, son of legendary Georgia coach Vince Dooley, was named tight ends coach and recruiting coordinator. In a popular move with the LSU fan base, Saban enticed Pete Jenkins, twice LSU's defensive coordinator during the 1980s, to come out of retirement to coach the defensive line.

Brook Trout and Big Wins

While the players returning for LSU in 2000—nine starters on offense, eight on defense—brought a lot of experience with them, the question for the Tigers was, is it a positive to bring back almost every starter from a 3–8 team? Apparently many reporters didn't think so. Saban didn't vow to bring any magic back, and observers were skeptical that there would be any. For the first time since 1993, LSU was picked to finish last in the SEC West.

Saban didn't like depth charts, and that was probably a good thing when it came to the quarterback position in 2000. Josh Booty would start 10 of LSU's 12 games and earn a share of All-SEC honors at his position, but fellow junior Rohan Davey would push him all season. A crowd of 87,188—below Tiger Stadium's new capacity but still the largest ever to see a football game in Louisiana—watched Booty and Davey take turns riddling Western Carolina in a 58–0 debut on September 2. Booty was 12 of 15 passing for 291 yards and two touchdowns. Davey was a flawless 11 of 11 for 194 yards and three scores. "Well, obviously Nick didn't walk into a situation with a team that doesn't have any talent," Western Carolina coach Bill Bleil said.

The Tigers got off to a swift start on September 9 against Houston, leading 21–0 at halftime. But as in 1996, LSU found itself fighting for victory at the end against the Cougars. His team's lead cut to 21–13 in the final four minutes, sophomore cornerback Damien James intercepted one pass in the end zone and returned another pick 56 yards for the clinching score in a 28–13 win. "It was a good thing for our team in a way," Saban said. "We had to overcome adversity."

LSU couldn't overcome 2–0 Auburn the following week, unable to keep pace in a 34–17 defeat. Shining through, however, was the first big performance by the Tigers' next great wide receiver. A year earlier, Booty had suggested to DiNardo that Josh Reed move from running back to wideout. The 5–11, 200-pound Reed was a natural at using just enough of his hands and body to create space without drawing penalties, and was exceptional at running after the catch. Against Auburn, Reed had a game-high eight catches for 167 yards, including touchdown receptions of 75 and 45 yards. He would finish the season with 65 catches for 1,127 yards and 10 touchdowns to earn All-SEC honors.

Nick Saban coaching in his first LSU game, against Western Carolina in 2000.

LSU's early-season momentum came to a screeching halt when the Tigers hosted the University of Alabama–Birmingham on September 23. LSU committed six turnovers, had a like number of dropped passes, and was flagged 13 times for 113 yards. With 33 seconds left and the ball at his 29, Booty audibled to something that wasn't in the LSU playbook, resulting in an interception that led to UAB's game-winning field goal as time expired, 13–10. Saban did not hold back his anger. "There's no way an out route should have been thrown," he said.

Free-falling from 2–0 to 2–2, the Tigers were suddenly in crisis with No. 11 Tennessee coming in for a September 30 showdown. That week, sportswriter Gary Lundy wrote in the *Knoxville News-Sentinel* that Tiger Stadium's status as a fearsome place to play was now a myth. Lundy got 700 e-mails from angry LSU fans in the days leading up to the game. That Saturday night, Tiger Stadium lived up to the legend. Sold out for the first time in its new configuration, the stadium roared with the oppressive sound of the 91,682 fans in attendance. "I could feel it trembling in my hands it was so loud," LSU cornerback Fred Booker said. "I couldn't hear anything. I was just watching the receivers and playing off their motions." Saban decided to start Davey, but didn't tell him until just before kickoff. Despite the pain of an injured left knee and right ankle, Davey completed 23 of 35 passes for 318 yards and four touchdowns. Two of them to Reed covered 16 and 31 yards, staking LSU to a 24–6 halftime lead. Tennessee roared back to tie the game 31–31 on a 16-yard pass from A.J. Suggs to Cedrick Wilson with 1:30 left. In overtime, LSU went straight for the end zone, Davey lofting a 25-yard pass to tight end Robert Royal behind two Vol defenders. Tennessee moved to the LSU 4, but on fourth down Damien James broke up one last pass, bringing a flood of fans onto the field to rip down the goalposts in celebration of the Tigers' 38–31 victory. "I won't ever forget this game," said LSU linebacker Bradie James, hit but not hurt by a falling goalpost as he tried to get into the locker room. "Not for fifty years."

Robert Royal hangs on to a 25-yard Rohan Davey pass to beat Tennessee in overtime, 2000.
STEVE FRANZ, LSU SPORTS INFORMATION

LSU fans cart another goalpost through the crowd after beating Tennessee in overtime.

STEVE FRANZ, LSU SPORTS INFORMATION

The Tigers' effort a week later in a 41–9 loss at No. 9 Florida pleased their new coach not at all. "We had too many guys out there today that had 'the look,'" Saban said. "I call it the 'brook trout look.' You catch a fish, then you look at it. It gives you that blank stare. We had some blank stares out there today." Davey started but looked rattled, giving way to Booty after completing just 4 of 12 passes for 65 yards and an interception. The starter the rest of the season, Booty completed 15 of 24 for 184 yards and LSU's only touchdown but threw three more interceptions.

Instead of the "brook trout look," LSU gave the appearance of a team of strong swimmers when it beat visiting Kentucky 34–0 on October 14. "This was a pivotal game in our season," said Bradie James, who led LSU with 17 tackles.

One week later Tiger Stadium was rocking again for another thrilling LSU overtime victory, this one a 45–38 win over No. 13 Mississippi State. As the decibels piled up, ESPN analyst Bill Curry, the former Alabama and Kentucky coach and Georgia Tech player, essentially refuted what Gary Lundy had written about the place. "I've been here as a player in the early '60s," Curry said. "I've been here as a coach in the '80s. When the crowd is with it, there is no place like this in all of college football. I might add there is no place like it in the NFL. These [LSU fans] make a difference with their squad. It's tough to play them when they get like this." Down 31–17 entering the fourth, LSU rallied for a 38–31 lead on a pair of 3-yard touchdown runs by Domanick Davis bracketing a 20-yard Booty-to-Reed pass. In overtime the Tigers again scored quickly on a 13-yard run by LaBrandon Toefield, the capper on a 220-yard night against State's No. 1-ranked rushing defense. On fourth-and-2 at the 17, linebackers Treverance Faulk and Jeremy Lawrence forced Bulldogs quarterback Wayne Madkin out of bounds for no gain to end it.

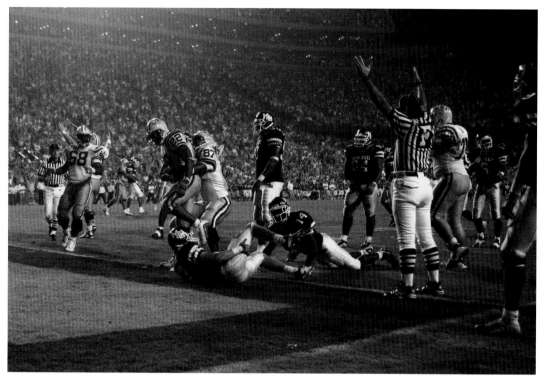

LaBrandon Toefield steps into the end zone to beat Mississippi State in overtime, 2000.

STEVE FRANZ, LSU SPORTS INFORMATION

Now 3–2 in the SEC, the 5–3 Tigers found themselves in a first-place SEC West tie with Auburn and Alabama. Auburn held the tiebreaker on LSU because of its win in September. Alabama held a jinx over LSU because it hadn't lost in Tiger Stadium since 1969. Quincy Jackson's mocking quote from two years earlier, "The Tide don't lose in Baton Rouge," still haunted LSU. The Tigers would finally prevail on November 4, but it took what may have been the first "instant replay" in college football history to secure it.

Leading 23–21 with 7:06 left in the fourth quarter, Davis lost the handle on a punt when Bama's Shontua Ray slammed into him. LSU's Erin Damond recovered at the LSU 14, but referees were so intent on deciding whether Ray had committed interference that they somehow forgot it was LSU's ball, signaling an Alabama first down after waving off a penalty flag against Ray. LSU's defense and Alabama's offense ran onto the field, but the Tigers were protesting all the way. Finally, Booker saw one official peek up at the giant video screen on the scoreboard behind the south end zone. Michael Bon-nette, who succeeded Herb Vincent as director of LSU Sports Information before the 2000 season, told electronic media coordinator Kevin Wagner to keep replaying the video showing Damond's recovery. After several anxious moments, LSU was properly awarded the ball at its 14. Catching Alabama flustered, Booty immediately launched a 50-yard pass to Royal, setting up a 16-yard touchdown toss to Royal three plays later in a 30–28 win. "The last time we beat them [here] man walked on the moon," strong safety Lio-nel Thomas said. "We'll be able to tell our kids we were part of history." In the end, the Alabama jinx proved to be no match for modern technology. "The player of the game is the JumboTron operator," Saban said. Wagner got a game ball for his office.

Upon further review: LSU players surround referees as they point to a Tiger Stadium replay screen during the Alabama game, 2000.   STEVE FRANZ, LSU SPORTS INFORMATION

LSU kept its championship game hopes alive with a 20–9 win at Ole Miss on November 11, its defense shutting down Ole Miss's potent offense on four red-zone trips. Once again, though, LSU was foiled in its bid for the SEC championship game as Auburn clinched with a 9–0 Iron Bowl victory over Alabama. LSU could have still earned a share of first place in the Western Di-vision and probably an invitation to the Cotton Bowl, but the Tigers stumbled and fumbled both away with a rain-soaked 14–3 loss to Arkansas on November 24 in Little Rock. "It's unfortunate things turned out the way they did," Saban said. "But I think we can be excited about what we accomplished."

While the Cotton Bowl invited 8–3 Tennessee, LSU accepted a bid to the Chick-fil-A Peach Bowl, though neither side was particularly thrilled about it. LSU was making its second trip to Atlanta in five seasons. The Peach Bowl was worried about LSU's reputation for soft bowl-ticket sales. At Saban's urging, Tiger fans snapped up their entire allotment of tickets, 21,000—the same as LSU's opponent, 9–2 Georgia Tech. A Peach Bowl–record crowd of

Rohan Davey came off the bench to earn MVP honors in the 2000 Peach Bowl.

STEVE FRANZ, LSU SPORTS INFORMATION

73,614 filled the Georgia Dome on December 29, and the hometown fans saw the Yellow Jackets surge to a 14–3 halftime lead. His offense stuck in neutral, Saban went with Davey in the second half. Although he hadn't taken a snap in a game since October 7, Davey was ready, leading LSU to 25 unanswered second-half points in a 28–14 victory. "It was no pressure," Davey said. "All you've got to do is play ball." Davey completed 17 of 25 passes for 174 yards and three touchdowns, a pair of them to fullback Tommy Banks in his senior finale. The LSU defense held Georgia Tech to just 100 yards over the final two quarters.

Tigers Take the Title

Winners of five of their last six games, the 8–4 Tigers finished No. 22 in the final Associated Press poll. "We weren't a great team that first year," Saban said. "But winning eight games and a bowl game was a real key to developing." The off-season months included a search for LSU's new athletic director to succeed the retiring Joe Dean. Eventually the university settled on outgoing baseball coach Skip Bertman. Meanwhile, expectations for football only grew. And why not? Although Josh Booty had left for the NFL, Rohan Davey was back for his senior campaign. And he would still have Josh Reed and Jerel Myers to throw to, LaBrandon Toefield and Domanick Davis to hand off to, and Robert Royal at tight end. Defensively, cousins Jarvis and Howard Green anchored the line, while Trev Faulk and Bradie James formed one of LSU's most talented linebacker tandems ever.

The best Baton Rouge duo to sign with the Tigers since Billy Cannon and Johnny Robinson in 1956 highlighted a stellar 2001 signing class: wide receiver Michael Clayton from Christian Life Academy and tight end Marcus Spears from Southern Lab. They signed along with Ben Wilkerson from Hemphill, Texas, who would become the Tigers' starting center that season; offensive tackle Andrew Whitworth from West Monroe; defensive end Marquise Hill from De La Salle in New Orleans; and highly regarded quarterback Rick Clausen from Woodland Hills, California. Saban convinced Spears he had a brighter future at defensive end—and that a bright future was ahead for the Tigers. "I didn't know much about LSU," Spears said. "Coming out of high school, you thought about Florida, Florida State, Miami. That's where the top recruits were going." As Spears and Clayton took several recruiting trips together, something dawned on them. "We realized that all of these guys who were winning national championships were from the state of Florida and were going to Florida schools," Spears said. "We realized with the players we had in Louisiana starting that year we could probably be pretty good."

The Tigers were picked to win the SEC West in 2001 and opened at No. 14 in the preseason AP top 25. It would end up being one of LSU's greatest seasons ever, but with unexpected and unprecedented twists and turns along the way. No season could open with a better omen than Toefield's score on a 28-yard run on the Tigers' first play in their September 1 game against Tulane. He would score twice more and Reed would roll up 135 yards on just six catches as LSU crushed the Green Wave 48–17. A week later it was the Toefield show again. He rushed for 183 yards on 27 carries and a career-high four touchdowns, scoring every time LSU crossed the goal line in a 31–14 romp over Utah State.

Monday, September 10, the focus in Baton Rouge was on Saturday's home game with Auburn for early SEC West supremacy. One day later, it was hard to imagine that a football game had seemed so important. The September 11 terrorist attacks left schools everywhere scrambling to decide what to do with the weekend's schedule. Wednesday, the SEC said it would play. By Thursday, September 13, one conference after another was postponing games. Indiana informed Kentucky that their game was off, and Bowling Green called South Carolina to say it wasn't coming. Although an SEC game like LSU-Auburn could have been played, SEC commissioner Roy Kramer decided the conference should be unified. "We would like to have played because we thought it was the right thing to do," Emmert said. "But we will stand with the SEC." September 15 games were moved to December 1, pushing the SEC championship game to December 8.

When the No. 14 Tigers and No. 7 Volunteers hooked up on September 29 in Neyland Stadium, the massive crowd of 108,472 had to endure extra security checks to get through the gates. Bands from both schools shared the field, playing the National Anthem, then "God Bless America." Once the game began, fans were treated to an All-American performance from Vol wide receiver Kelley Washington. His 11 catches for a Tennessee-record 256 yards and a touchdown helped stake Tennessee to a 26–7 fourth-quarter lead. "We just couldn't get Washington covered," Saban lamented. "We tried about every way you could try." LSU had a glimmer of hope after pulling within 26–18 in the final minutes, but Davey's 43-yard desperation heave into the end zone fell incomplete as time expired.

No. 18-ranked LSU returned home to be riddled again by No. 2 Florida on October 6. Rex Grossman was the king of Tiger Stadium, throwing for 464 yards and five touchdowns in a 44–15 rout. "I ain't got nothing to say but they kicked our tails," free safety Ryan Clark commented, "plain and simple, up and down the field. They whipped us." Making things worse for LSU, Davey went down with a strained left knee on a sack late in the second quarter. Matt Mauck, a 21-year-old freshman, filled in the rest of the way. He threw two interceptions in his first football game in five years. A native of Jasper, Indiana, Mauck signed to play football for Saban at Michigan State. Soon after, Mauck was a sixth-round draft pick by the Chicago Cubs. He would spend the next 3½ years in the minors before deciding to give football another try—at LSU. "Coach Saban kept in contact with me," Mauck said. "When I heard he was going to LSU, I jumped at the opportunity."

LSU fans, many of whom still viewed Saban as a 6–5 coach from Michigan State, were ready to jump off his bandwagon with the Tigers at 2–2 and 0–2 in SEC play. Dropped from the top 25, the Tigers had no easy task going to play at Kentucky on October 13. Davey returned to action and filled the air with passes, completing 27 of 38 for 383 yards, but LSU would need one crucial pass to save its season. On third-and-goal at the 6, Davey went over the middle to Clayton for a touchdown with 13 seconds left to produce a 29–25 victory. "We knew this game would make us or break us," Clayton said. A second straight road game on October 20, this one against the Mississippi State team that took LSU to overtime in 2000, looked like another difficult assignment. Instead, the Bulldogs were completely outmatched by LSU in a 42–0 Tiger runaway. Davey threw for 255 yards and three scores, Reed caught 10 passes for 146 yards and two touchdowns, and the LSU defense forced four turnovers in the Tigers' most lopsided SEC victory in fifteen years.

The Tigers lost to Ole Miss at home on October 27, by a score of 35–24.

Freshman wide receiver Michael Clayton gives thanks after pulling in the game-winning touchdown pass to beat Kentucky, 2001.   STEVE FRANZ, LSU SPORTS INFORMATION

In a case of déjà vu, the source of LSU's frustration was named Manning. In 1968, Archie Manning quarterbacked a 27–24 victory in Tiger Stadium as a sophomore. In 2001 his son, sophomore Eli Manning, rallied the Rebels from a 24–21 fourth-quarter deficit with two touchdown passes to Doug Ziegler in the final 6½ minutes with dad and older brother Peyton watching. As much as a Manning may have been Public Enemy No. 1 at LSU once again, the Tigers had themselves to blame. An LSU interception, blocked punt, and fumble all led to Ole Miss touchdowns. The Rebels' fourth-quarter scoring drives only had to cover 35 and 58 yards. On the way home, the Sabans' car radio practically melted with calls to LSU's postgame show from fans livid with the Tigers—and with their multi-million-dollar coach. "Daddy," young Kristen Saban wanted to know, "are we going to have to move again?"

Just when their season appeared over, the Tigers (4–3, 2–3 in the SEC) came up with a signature performance at Alabama on November 3. "We went into this game looking at it as if it were a character test," Rohan Davey said. He and Josh Reed were character personified. Playing pitch and catch like they were the only two men on the field, Reed and Davey rewrote sizable chunks of the SEC and LSU record books in a critical 35–21 victory. Reed caught 19 passes for 293 yards, both SEC records, and set a school record with his fourteenth 100-yard receiving game. Davey set school records for completions and yards, going 35 of 44 for 528 yards. "They played a lot of zone," Reed said. "We worked all week on getting to the open areas and just letting Ro make the reads." The Tigers' 35 points were the most they had ever scored in 65 games against Alabama, and LSU's 611 yards were the most the proud Crimson Tide had ever surrendered.

A 30–14 nonconference win over Middle Tennessee State on November 10 marked the time leading up to LSU's crucial SEC games with Arkansas and Auburn. A fan at the Arkansas game on November 23 brought a sign that read, ALL I WANT FOR CHRISTMAS IS AN SEC CHAMPIONSHIP! Over the next sixty minutes, the Tigers almost Scrooged themselves. LSU committed five turnovers—Davey threw four interceptions along with his 359 yards and three touchdowns—but managed to hold on for a wild 41–38 victory. "I think LSU realizes they're lucky," Arkansas coach Houston Nutt groused. "They deserved to win. But they were fortunate today." LSU rallied from a 19–14 second-quarter deficit to take a 20–19 halftime lead when Reed tipped a Davey pass to himself on a 20-yard scoring pass. He had seven catches for 183 yards—including a 38-yard touchdown reception in the fourth—while Toefield ran for 173 yards and three scores, one of which was a 62-yard touchdown run.

LSU's long-awaited home game with Auburn on December 1 would settle everything. No Iron Bowl upset was required. After this matchup the Tigers were going to the SEC championship game—either No. 22 LSU or No. 25 Au-

Josh Reed: Josh Booty's suggestion that he move to wide receiver made him an LSU legend.

burn. The game started on a bizarre note even before the biggest crowd of the season—92,141—was completely seated. Auburn received a 15-yard unsportsmanlike-conduct penalty before the kickoff when some of its players stomped up and down on LSU's "Eye of the Tiger" logo at midfield. Kicking off from the 50, Saban decided to add injury to Auburn's insult by calling for an onside kick, which Clayton recovered at the Auburn 36. Six plays later, LSU led 7–0 on a 2-yard run by Toefield on its way to a 21–7 halftime edge. In the second half, LSU tacked on a pair of John Corbello field goals and Auburn managed just one touchdown as LSU celebrated its first SEC championship game berth with a 27–14 victory.

A bigger game awaited, of course, against a team that had already proved it could beat LSU. While LSU was subduing Auburn, Tennessee went to Florida a 17-point underdog and came out with a stunning 34–32 upset, vaulting to No. 2 in the Bowl Championship Series standings. Another victory over No. 21 LSU would send the Vols to the Rose Bowl to play Miami in the BCS championship game. Davey, always a loose and laid-back competitor, heaped all the pressure on Tennessee's orange shoulders. "They're trying to play for the national championship," he said. "We're trying to raise the bar so we can say this is what our program is going to be in the years to come."

Tennessee fans, some clutching orange roses, outnumbered LSU fans in the Georgia Dome the night of December 8, anticipating the win that would send the Vols off to Pasadena. But maybe someone was looking out for the Tigers. No matter what happened, no matter what went wrong, on this night they simply couldn't lose. First, Davey went down with a hard shot to the ribs on the sideline and was carted away from the Georgia Dome in an ambulance. Mauck, who hadn't played since mop-up duty at Mississippi State on October 20, took over at quarterback and marched the Tigers to a 7–0 lead with 8:14 left in the first quarter on a 4-yard draw play. In the second quarter, Toefield exited the game with a torn knee ligament and LSU's offense bogged down as Tennessee seized a 14–7 lead. LSU got the ball back and faced fourth and an inch at its 29. Saban shocked even himself by deciding to go for it.

"It's 14–7 and momentum is going to hell in a handbasket," Saban explained. "I said, 'If we punt it back to them again and they score, it's over.'" LSU didn't make it, and immediately Saban kicked himself. "It was probably the dumbest decision," he said. "Even Terry told me that. She said, 'That was the dumbest thing I've ever seen you do in all the time you've been coaching.'

> ## A Loss Before Winning
>
> The Thursday before the Tennessee game, LSU lost a link to its glorious past. Charles McClendon, the beloved "Charlie Mac" who coached the Tigers from 1962 through 1979, died at seventy-eight after a lengthy battle with cancer. LSU equipment managers spent the morning before the game affixing stickers with the words "Coach Mac" to the back of the Tigers' helmets. "A lot of schools have a great tradition that will never die," Saban said Friday at his pregame news conference. "Coach McClendon was that at LSU. I'm very sad that Coach McClendon won't be with us to see us through the game."

Rohan Davey is helped off the field after a first-half injury in the 2001 SEC championship game vs. Tennessee. STEVE FRANZ, LSU SPORTS INFORMATION

But the defense went in there and we sacked them. They still ended up kicking a field goal, but we moved them back a little bit and it was our best series, probably. We went in [at halftime] down 17–7."

In the press box, Bertman was lobbying Outback Bowl executive director Jim McVay, trying to persuade him to invite what seemed likely to be an 8–4 LSU team. After thirty more minutes of football, though, the Tigers had sweeter bowl prospects. The LSU defense stiffened, allowing Tennessee just one more field goal the rest of the way. And Tennessee's defense was confounded by Mauck's shiftiness when they had prepared for Davey the drop-back passer. "We did a nice job featuring our personnel," Saban said. "Matt is a different type of quarterback, a good athlete, a runner. It actually worked in our favor. We did some formation things they weren't ready for. It neutralized their defense." LSU chipped into Tennessee's lead with a pair of Corbello field goals in the third. Early in the fourth quarter, defensive tackle Byron Dawson recovered a fumble at the UT 39. Five plays later, Mauck scored on a 13-yard draw to put LSU up 24–17 after a two-point pass to Reed. Leading 24–20 with 6:04 left, Saban again disdained the field goal and went for it on fourth-and-goal. Davis leaped over from the 1 to complete LSU's improbable 31–20 upset. Mauck, who completed just 5 of 15 passes for 67 yards but ran for 43 yards and two scores, was the MVP. "They played great," Tennessee defensive end Will Overstreet said of Mauck and Davis. "They lost two of their big players [Davey and Toefield] but they just seemed to play better."

Former minor-leaguer Matt Mauck earned MVP honors in relief against Tennessee, 2001.

STEVE FRANZ, LSU SPORTS INFORMATION

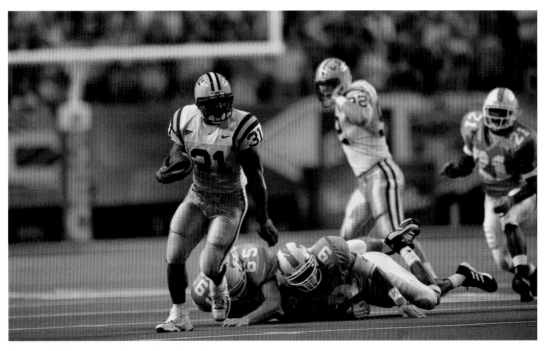

Domanick Davis looks for yards against Tennessee.

STEVE FRANZ, LSU SPORTS INFORMATION

Offensive guard Dwayne Pierce celebrates with a sign of the times, 2001.

LSU players celebrate winning the SEC championship—and bashing Tennessee's Rose Bowl hopes, 2001. STEVE FRANZ, LSU SPORTS INFORMATION

Now 9–3 and ranked No. 12, the Tigers didn't have to depend on the generosity of the Outback Bowl. While Tennessee was relegated to the Florida Citrus Bowl to play Michigan, the Tigers automatically qualified for the Nokia Sugar Bowl to play No. 7-ranked Illinois. The Fighting Illini—who gave football immortals like Dick Butkus and Harold "Red" Grange—had swept to just their second outright Big Ten title since 1963 with a 10–1 record, a 45–20 loss to the Michigan Wolverines the only blemish. The Illini were pleased to be in their first New Year's Day bowl in ten years, but a little disappointed that the BCS title game dislodged them from the Big Ten champ's traditional Rose Bowl slot. In fact, there was grumbling in Champaign, Illinois, as to why Illinois wasn't playing Miami for the national championship instead of a one-loss Nebraska team that didn't even qualify for the Big 12 championship game. Before January 1 ended, the Illini were probably wishing they were anywhere but in New Orleans.

The final score—LSU 47, Illinois 34—was misleading. The Illini were no match for LSU's overall team speed, as the Tigers sprinted to a 34–7 halftime lead on three touchdown runs by Davis—he finished with 122 yards and four touchdowns—and two Davey scoring passes. Davey would earn MVP honors, completing 31 of 53 passes for 444 yards, with 14 throws going to Reed for 239 yards. When it was over, the Tigers finished in the top 10 at No. 7 for the first time since 1987, had their first Sugar Bowl win since the 1967 season, and set or had a hand in 11 Sugar Bowl records and 13 LSU bowl records. It was a marvelous farewell for the gregarious Davey, who set yet another single-season school record with 3,347 yards passing. "As a group," Davey said, "we wanted to be remembered as the team that thrust LSU into the top 10, that thrust LSU into the national spotlight."

With Sugar on top: Davey goes out as the Sugar Bowl MVP, throwing for 444 yards against Illinois.   STEVE FRANZ, LSU SPORTS INFORMATION

After the Catch

They're called YAC—yards after the catch. And perhaps no LSU wide receiver was better at gaining them than Josh Reed. In just two full seasons as a receiver—as a freshman he was a running back, and he gave up his senior year to turn pro—Reed rapidly rewrote the LSU and SEC record books. By the time he was done, he was first in SEC history in receiving yards for a single season (1,740 in 2001) and career receiving yards (3,001). Following the 2001 season he received the Biletnikoff Award, given each year to the nation's best receiver. It was the first major individual award won by a Tiger since Billy Cannon won the Heisman Trophy in 1959.

Josh Reed on the run after one of 14 catches vs. Illinois in the 2002 Nokia Sugar Bowl.

Josh Reed accepts the 2001 Biletnikoff Award. Pictured, *from left,* are Don Shula; Josh's mother, Margaret Reed; Josh; LSU receivers coach Stan Hixon; and Fred Biletnikoff.

Dash Right 93 Berlin

The 2002 season would be remembered for one incredible moment that would rival Billy Cannon's punt return as the most amazing play in LSU football history. It would also be remembered as a year of almosts but not quites, rife with frustrations and near misses. The Tigers would have to learn to get by in 2002 without Davey, Reed, and linebacker Trev Faulk, who also revealed in January that he was turning pro. The quarterbacking duties were handed off to Mauck, now a sophomore, and junior Marcus Randall from Baton Rouge's Glen Oaks High. Filling Reed's cleats would be Michael Clayton and Devery Henderson, while Toefield returned from his knee injury in the SEC championship game to share the bulk of carries with Davis. Alhough Faulk was gone, his running mate, Bradie James, was back for what would be an All-American campaign. The front four was growing more and more imposing with Marcus Spears and Marquise Hill at ends, and Chad Lavalais and Kenderick Allen at tackles.

Picked 14th in the preseason AP poll and the choice for the second straight year to win the SEC West, the Tigers would find out immediately what kind of team they had on the road September 1 at No. 16 Virginia Tech. For a moment in the first quarter, everything seemed wonderful as Davis sped downfield with an apparent 81-yard punt-return touchdown. But a flag, a familiar site on LSU returns that season, lay on the turf. Would that touchdown have altered the outcome? Bit by bit the Hokies edged farther in front of the Tigers until they led 24–0 early in the fourth quarter. Toefield saved the Tigers from total embarrassment with a 1-yard run in a 26–8 defeat. "I didn't think we played like we had the eye of the tiger today," Saban said, "with the kind of intensity that you need to be a good football team."

LSU didn't need to overwhelm The Citadel with intensity in its September 7 home opener. Plain talent was more than enough in a 35–10 victory over a Division I-AA opponent that was a January replacement, late by football scheduling standards, when Bowling Green canceled. Miami (Ohio) was next, a team that always made veteran LSU fans nervous because of its memorable 21–12 upset of the Tigers in 1986. No worries this time as LSU rolled 33–7, with Mauck throwing the first three touchdown passes of his LSU career.

LSU fans grumbled about an 11:30 A.M. kickoff for the Tigers' next game against Mississippi State on September 28, the first home game moved up for Jefferson Pilot SEC telecasts in five years. For a while it looked as though the Tigers, who usually rise at 10 A.M. for a 7 P.M. night game, had hit the snooze button as State took a 10–7 second-quarter lead. "We finally said enough of this," Mauck commented later. "We decided to pound it down their throats until they could stop it." LSU rushed 10 times in a row to take a 14–10 lead, eight of the carries by Davis capped by a 5-yard touchdown run. Davis finished with 122 yards on 18 attempts as the Tigers finished off State 31–13.

It had been decades since LSU had played a Division I-A in-state opponent other than Tulane. So one of Skip Bertman's first major acts as athletic director was to sign up Louisiana–Lafayette, Louisiana Tech, and Louisiana–Monroe for a series of games on a rotating basis. The Ragin' Cajuns were the first on deck, and the result on October 5 was the same as the last time they met the Tigers, in 1938: a bleaux-out. Joseph Addai and Davis each rushed for two scores and Mauck threw for three more while the Tigers' defense held ULL to 70 total yards in a 48–0 victory. The only negative: a broken arm that would sideline Toefield for six weeks.

For all its resurgent success, LSU still longed for victory in one place as of 2002: Florida Field. The Gators hadn't lost to LSU in their home swamp since 1986. But these weren't Steve Spurrier's Gators anymore, as the Tigers' 36–7 on October 12 would attest. This time, the "brook trout looks" belonged to the Gators, especially Rex Grossman, who went from five touchdowns in Tiger Stadium in 2001 to four interceptions in 2002, one of them returned 45 yards by Corey Webster for a touchdown. Webster had three interceptions in all, but again victory was tinged by disappointment. This time it was Mauck who went down, suffering a season-ending foot injury running an option play on a drive long after LSU had the win salted away. Surgery would leave Randall as LSU's lone experienced quarterback. His first start was against South Carolina on October 19, which had Tiger Stadium jittery with LSU down 14–6 at halftime. But LSU erupted in the third quarter with a 12-yard touchdown run by Randall, a 13-yard scoring run by 5-foot-6 tailback Shyrone Carey, and a 10-yard interception return by cornerback Demetrius Hookfin that put LSU on its way to a 38–14 victory. "Marcus did an outstanding job," said Saban of his quarterback after he threw for 183 yards and ran for 36 more. "He had poise, confidence, and managed the game well."

Ben's Big Compliment

The Miami (Ohio) RedHawks came to Tiger Stadium on September 14, 2002, led by a talented young quarterback with an impossible-to-pronounce name. He was a sophomore named Ben Roethlisberger, who completed 22 of 34 passes for 195 yards with a touchdown and an interception but was unable to avert the 33–7 loss LSU inflicted on his team. Roethlisberger may have been forgotten by LSU fans until he became the Pittsburgh Steelers' Super Bowl–winning quarterback were it not for this e-mail he sent Nick Saban after returning home.

I hope you get to read this. I wanted to first and foremost congratulate you and the team on the game Saturday. You guys are the best team that I have ever played against, and I think you guys will go a long way this year. Your defense was very confusing and had us on the run all game. But that is not the main reason that I am writing you this e-mail. I really was impressed with your team after the game. They had the most class out of any team that I have ever played against in high school or college, and I commend you for that. Many of the players, including your big-name players, came up to me and congratulated me and told us good luck and have a safe trip home. I just want to commend you and your team for all the class you have. Best of luck and win the SEC.

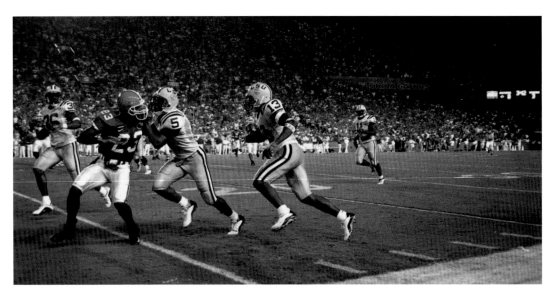

Corey Webster returns a 45-yard interception for a touchdown at Florida, 2002.

Matt Mauck scrambles at Florida. It would be his last game of 2002.

LSU went to Auburn on October 26 riding a six-game winning streak, in possession of a No. 10 national ranking and rolling on a tidal wave of momentum. All of that came to a crashing halt in a 31–7 defeat. Actually, it came to a halt in the first half, when four of the day's five turnovers put LSU in a 17–0 hole. Randall regressed, completing just 9 of 20 passes for 79 yards with four interceptions. "They got the best of us today," Saban said. "It's as simple as that." At least LSU still left atop the SEC West standings at 3–1.

Because of the conference's new 5–1–2 scheduling format, LSU was heading to Kentucky for the second year in a row before the Tigers and Wildcats rotated off each other's schedule until 2006. What happened in that game made LSU's winning pass with 13 seconds left in 2001 seem like luxury instead of desperation.

It was called Dash Right 93 Berlin, a play designed to be used when only desperation would do. The idea was to have the ball come raining down like bombs falling on Berlin in World War II, then hope the prayer was answered with a tipped ball or a lucky bounce. In practice it never, ever worked, but late on the afternoon of November 9, 2002, the Tigers had no other chance at victory. It looked as though LSU had blown it, squandering a 21–7 third-quarter lead that became a 30–27 deficit when Wildcat Taylor Begley kicked a 29-yard field goal with 11 seconds remaining. Blue-clad fans started pouring out of the stands, ringing the field in Commonwealth Stadium, ready to charge. Henderson caught the kickoff, running out of bounds at the 13. Nine seconds left. LSU was pushed back 5 yards for delay of game, adding to what appeared to be the futility of the Tigers' final plays. Someone doused Kentucky coach Guy Morriss with a cooler just after Randall went over the middle to Clayton, who popped up and called time out at his 25. What good would that do? Two seconds remained. In a suite behind the end zone the Tigers were trying to reach, Sandy Bertman, Skip Bertman's wife, turned to Terry Saban and said, "We need a miracle."

One Bluegrass Miracle coming up.

Bluegrass Miracle: Marcus Randall is poised to let it fly . . .

STEVE FRANZ, LSU SPORTS INFORMATION

. . . and Devery Henderson has Kentucky fans in retreat after they storm the field, 2002.

Randall took the shotgun snap, rolled to his right, and let the ball fly from his 18. Henderson, Clayton, and Reggie Robinson lined up to his right, sped downfield, and slowed inside the UK 30 as the ball began its downward arc. At the 24, UK's Morris Lane tipped the ball instead of knocking it down, giving it a forward impetus that carried it through the hands of teammate Earven Flowers. Near the 19, Henderson, who didn't remember he was supposed to be the short receiver on the play, got his right hand on the ball, then brought it in to his chest. Kentucky's Derek Tatum got his fingers on Henderson's left knee for a fleeting second at the 10, but Henderson shook free and scored to shake the college football world. "It was like a dream," he said. "I saw it tipped and tipped again. I reached out and it fell into my hands. I couldn't believe it. All I remember was bobbling the ball and pulling it in, then running like hell." For Randall, thrust into the starting role when Mauck went down, it was simply fate. "This is the biggest play of my life," he said. It took longer for the play to register than for it to unfold. Fireworks boomed overhead, and Kentucky fans charged the field and started to jump on the goalpost at Randall's back. "Did we just lose this game?" one UK fan asked another as they stood on the crossbar. They did. "If you threw the ball 1,000 times you might complete it once," Wildcats quarterback Jared Lorenzen said, "much less for a

Instead of UK fans, Devery Henderson is mobbed by his teammates, 2002.

STEVE FRANZ, LSU SPORTS INFORMATION

touchdown." As the LSU buses pulled away from the stadium, Kentucky fan Chris Holian watched with a bemused look on his face. "Fifty-nine minutes and 58 seconds," he said. "I knew it was too good to be true."

Saban spent the next week trying, unsuccessfully, to get everyone to stop buzzing about the Bluegrass Miracle and getting fitted for tuxedos for the ESPY Awards. "It's time to move on," an irritated Saban said during his Monday news conference. "Just because the most exciting play in college football happened, that doesn't mean there's not a lot of things that need fixing." A 31–0 rout by Alabama on November 16 was a slap of reality. The Crimson Tide didn't need divine intervention or pinball wizardry to run its record to 15–1–1 in Tiger Stadium over the last thirty-one years. Bama led just 6–0 late in the second quarter when it began ramming sprint draws at an LSU defense ranked No. 1 nationally but depleted by the dismissal of senior free safety Damien James after the Auburn game for violating team rules. The Tide drove 96 yards in nine plays to score on Tyler Watts's 2-yard keeper with 12 seconds left, putting Bama well on its way to victory up 14–0 after a two-point conversion. The Tide finished with an even 300 yards rushing on 54 attempts. "I didn't think Alabama was one of those teams that could just manhandle us," Lavalais said. "But they did."

At 7–3 and 4–2 in the SEC, the Tigers needed a win over Ole Miss on November 23 to stay alone in first place in the SEC West. LSU got it, but it was a struggle. The Tigers trailed 10–0 in the second quarter before Randall's

New Year's Day, 2003: Marcus Randall sets sail on a long run against Texas in the SBC Cotton Bowl.

19-yard scoring pass to Henderson with 2.3 seconds left before halftime, a play that ended Henderson's miracle making as he exited the game with a broken arm. Randall found Clayton on a 27-yard scoring pass in the fourth to pull out a 14–13 win, setting up a winner-take-all finale with Arkansas in Little Rock to represent the Western Division in the SEC championship game. "This is it," strong safety Norman LeJeune said. "The title's on the line."

There were a lot of things that could be said about LSU's 21–20 loss to Arkansas on November 29. Blown coverages. Conservative play calling. Maybe, though, the Miracle on Markham Street was simply about the football gods leveling the playing field. LSU led 17–7 midway through the fourth quarter and 20–14 with just 40 seconds left after a 13-play, 53-yard drive that took 5:53 ended in a 29-yard Corbello field goal. Arkansas got the ball back at its 19 with 34 seconds left. Three plays later the Razorbacks were in the end zone. Quarterback Matt Jones hit receiver Richard Smith for a 50-yard gain to the LSU 31 when Webster blew the coverage. After an incompletion, Jones found DeCori Birmingham in the back of the end zone just over the hands of Randall Gay for the winning score with 9 seconds remaining. David Carlton's extra point sent Arkansas (9–3, 5–3 in the SEC) to the SEC championship game and LSU (8–4, 5–3 in the SEC) to the SBC Cotton Bowl to play No. 9 Texas. "All I can think about is agony," said offensive tackle Rodney Reed. "It's very discouraging, but we know how it feels to be on the other end."

The last time the Tigers' season ended in Dallas, they broke No. 2 Arkansas' 22-game winning streak with a 14–7 shocker in the 1966 Cotton Bowl, one of the monumental upsets in school history. This time, the Tigers got up early on January 1 and jumped to a 21–7 second-quarter lead on the favored Longhorns. Unlike the Razorbacks in 1966, Texas didn't blink. Randall did his best, throwing for 193 yards and running for 78, most of it on a 76-yard bolt to set up a second-quarter touchdown by Davis. Texas's Roy Williams more than compensated. He had four catches for 142 yards and a touchdown plus a 39-yard scoring run on his only carry that punctuated a 35–20 Texas victory. "As you can see," James said, "there's no shutting that guy down." LSU would shut it down for the season with an 8–5 record, its worst under Saban, and out of the top 25. As 2003 began, contending for a national title didn't seem impossible, but definitely a long way off.

5

CHAMPIONS OF THE GREAT DIVIDE
2003–2004

In the 1980s, a marketing executive named Roy Hamlin was charged with creating a trophy that southern independent college football teams like Miami and Florida State could play for each year. Hamlin was more ambitious than that, and took the idea all the way to the executive director of the American Football Coaches Association: Charles McClendon.

Waterford was commissioned to craft the crystal football that would crown the trophy, but on the first attempt its Irish artisans produced something resembling a rugby ball. "We've got to fix that, partner," McClendon told Hamlin. It was fixed, and when Penn State beat Miami to win the 1985 national championship in the 1986 Fiesta Bowl, one of the prizes bestowed on the Nittany Lions was the AFCA's new trophy. In time, lifting the crystal football off the big, black-lacquered base would become symbolic of capturing college football's national championship, like donning the green jacket after winning The Masters. That pleased McClendon. There was only one thing that would please him more.

"One of these days," McClendon told his wife, Dorothy Faye, "I hope it goes back to LSU."

LSU's head coach from 1962 through 1979, McClendon was an assistant to Paul Dietzel when the Tigers won their only wire-service national championship in 1958. There were times in the intervening years when another national championship for LSU seemed as far away as the green hills of Ireland. LSU's football fortunes waxed and waned and waxed again as a parade of Southeastern Conference rivals—Alabama, Georgia, Florida, and Tennessee—hoisted national championship trophies and hung national championship banners. Finally, with the arrival of Nick Saban in 2000, LSU fans could talk realistically of reaching the mythical "next level." In fits and starts the Tigers seemed to be getting there after seasons of 8–4, 10–3 (including the 2001 SEC championship), and an 8–5 record in 2002. But LSU had not actually been to the mountaintop. The 2003 Tigers possessed a growing pool of talent, but had anything happened so far under Saban to indicate that LSU belonged among the nation's very best?

There was, among the members of the football team, a deep and confident desire. For quarterback Matt Mauck, the desire started that bittersweet night in Gainesville in 2002 when LSU crushed Florida 36–7 and his season ended with his foot crushed under a Gator tackler. "We were 5–1 and ranked high and I get hurt against Florida," he said. "It was a great win for us. We blew them out of The Swamp. But coming off that game we went 3–4, and that was a little disappointing because we knew we were a lot better team than that. That helped us as far as being hungry for 2003. We wanted to prove how good we were." Doubts remained. Mauck's repaired foot had never been tested in game conditions. The tailback slot was unsettled. And the defense had yet to become the impregnable fortress that Saban's genius was supposed to deliver.

But there was one area in which the 2003 team excelled above any other Saban had at LSU. He was able to spot it easily as the Tigers hurtled toward their season opener. "There were two distinct differences from the 2001 team," he said. "In 2001, Rohan Davey was a great leader, and he impacted everyone who played. When he didn't impact them we weren't very good, but he impacted them most of the time. The consistency of the 2003 team was the difference. There was so much character on that team they didn't need a leader to inspire them to play. Matt Mauck was a great leader. Michael Clayton, Marcus Spears, Marquise Hill in his own way was a great leader. Randall Gay was a leader and he didn't even start. Kyle Williams? He didn't need anyone to get him to play. I don't know if I'll ever have an opportunity to coach a group of football players who have as much character as that team had. I think they thought they could win the championship long before I did." Spears was a believer. "We knew we would do something big before the season started," he said. "We had every element. Every position was covered. There was not one time when we walked on the field in doubt.

"There was always something that season. It just seemed like whenever we needed some-

A New Tradition

As the season approached, LSU athletic director Skip Bertman unveiled a plan to help generate the money needed to pay for the facility improvements Saban had asked for in 1999—and to help pay Saban. The right to purchase season tickets in Tiger Stadium would now depend on "donations" to LSU's Tradition Fund, at a cost of $85 to $400 above the cost of the ticket. This would generate some $7.5 million in revenue annually. The money would be used to retire the debt and build a $15 million football operations complex, grafted onto the indoor practice building at the recently named Charles McClendon Football Practice Facility. The whole plan would go into effect for the 2004 football season. To make it more palatable to season-ticket holders accustomed to paying $50 extra for sidelines seats and $25 in the end zones, Bertman needed the Tigers to make the product on the field worth it. "This whole thing is a belief in Nick Saban," Bertman said in the summer of 2003. "I'm counting on him. Not to just have a winning season but to win nine games—minimum—because he won eight last year. Never before have I rooted for the football coach as much as I'm rooting for him now."

thing to go right, it was there for us. It was just amazing. Everything fell into place."

LSU was expected to be good again, ranked No. 14 in the preseason Associated Press media poll and No. 15 according to the coaches. Some Tigers from the SEC West were expected to contend for a national championship, but they weren't from LSU. Auburn was favored to win the SEC and opened at No. 6 in the polls. The purple-and-gold Tigers were picked to finish second in the SEC West at SEC Media Days.

August 30: LSU 49, Louisiana–Monroe 7

LSU's march to glory would begin with a soggy first step. The Tigers were slated to play Louisiana–Monroe for their first game of the season. Swirling sheets of rain from nearby Tropical Storm Grace swept over Tiger Stadium the night of August 30, accompanied by lightning that forced a 39-minute delay with 11:09 left in the first quarter. It took the Tigers a quarter to get the water out of their gas tank; then they were off to a 49–7 rout. Mauck, the former baseball player, pitched three touchdown strikes in the final 6:37 before halftime, covering 8 yards to wide receiver Devery Henderson, 17 yards to tailback Joseph Addai, and 40 yards on a graceful grab and run by wide receiver Michael Clayton. A 1-yard touchdown run by 5–6 tailback Shyrone

The 2003 season gets off to a soggy start against Louisiana–Monroe.

STEVE FRANZ, LSU SPORTS INFORMATION

All-American defensive tackle Chad Lavalais and the Tigers crush the Arizona Wildcats in week two, 2003.   STEVE FRANZ, LSU SPORTS INFORMATION

Carey and a 31-yard interception return by strong safety Jack Hunt put the Tigers up 35–0. Mauck retired after completing 13 of 28 passes for 153 yards, a number matched by Marcus Randall on 5 of 7 passing that included a 66-yard bomb to Clayton. Freshman Alley Broussard capped the night with a 1-yard touchdown plunge. Despite the margin of victory, the Tigers sounded like perfectionists. "I thought we really came out slow," Mauck said, "and you know we can't do that next week."

September 6: LSU 59, Arizona 13

LSU hadn't played west of Dallas since winning at Southern California in 1984, so a trip to the desert to face Arizona on September 6 was an uncharted challenge. Coming off a 4–8 season but emboldened by a 42–7 win over UTEP, the Wildcats were talking upset. As much as anything, the Tigers were a bit of a mystery team. But after this game, the rest of the nation would take notice of what the Tigers had. An explosive offense and a relentless defense combined for a 59–13 rout that represented Arizona's worst home loss and LSU's most lopsided road win since 1958. The Tigers sizzled from the start, piling up 331 of their 481 total yards in the first half. LSU drove 80 yards for touchdowns three times, converted seven of eight third downs, and held the ball for 20 of 30 minutes. "They thoroughly whipped us," Arizona coach John Mackovic said. Addai scored on runs of 1 and 8 yards and Mauck got in on a 4-yard keeper early in the second quarter to make it 24–0. He then connected with Clayton on a 48-yard touchdown pass before Randall hit Henderson with a 55-yard strike to go into the locker room up 38–0. A roadrunner-quick 60-yard punt return for a touchdown by sophomore Skyler Green highlighted the second half. The LSU defense didn't give up a score until it was 52–0, and allowed only 182 net yards. "I think we answered some questions tonight about being ranked so high and if we could play on the road," Saban said with uncharacteristic delight. "We came into someone's house and played dominant football."

September 13: LSU 35, Western Illinois 7

Despite the lopsided win, Saban lacked for none of his trademark intensity at Arizona, demanding his team compete to the last second. "We look at him storming the sideline with all that energy and we're thinking, 'He's 51 years old,'" defensive end Marquise Hill said. "We're half his age. We could at least go out there and play hard for him so he doesn't have to do that." Hill and his teammates had to wonder whether their effort in a 35–7 win over Western Illinois on September 13 would qualify. The Tigers had to work for what they got against Division I-AA's No. 1 team, leading just 13–7 in the third quarter after the Leathernecks scored on a 3-yard touchdown pass from Russ Michna to Terrance Hall. But LSU responded with 22 unanswered points on Mauck

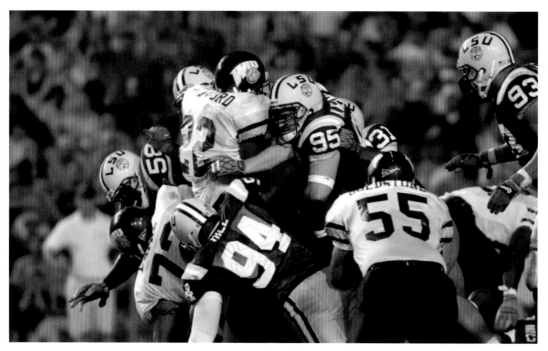

Marquise Hill (94), Kyle Williams (95), and others swarm a Western Illinois ball carrier, 2003.

STEVE FRANZ, LSU SPORTS INFORMATION

touchdown passes of 8 and 40 yards to Green and 16 yards to Henderson. Mauck had a career night, completing 23 of 32 passes for 305 yards with four touchdowns, one going to Clayton in the first half among his 11 catches for 162 yards. Saban seemed satisfied. "I told our players we won't play anybody all year that will want to beat us any worse than these guys," he said. "They took it to us."

September 20: LSU 17, Georgia 10

All the intensity the Tigers and their coach could muster was not enough to subdue Georgia when the Bulldogs visited LSU on September 20. To do that, LSU would need some ad-libbing and a little luck in the kicking department. The No. 11 Tigers and No. 7 Bulldogs traded body blows before the biggest crowd ever in Tiger Stadium (92,251), a national TV audience on CBS, and the added glare of ESPN's College GameDay crew. Georgia drew first blood on Billy Bennett's 33-yard field goal in the first quarter. The Bulldogs would mount several scoring threats over the next three quarters, but they all came to nothing as Bennett misfired from 43, 42, and 36 yards. With 3:10 left before halftime, the Tigers took a 7–3 lead when Carey slipped through the heart of the Georgia defense, and went up 10–3 on a 47-yard Ryan Gaudet field goal in the third. The score stayed that way until the dramatic final 4½ minutes. From his 7, Georgia quarterback David Greene flipped a screen pass

Skyler Green eyes a game-winning touchdown pass from Matt Mauck against Georgia, 2003. STEVE FRANZ, LSU SPORTS INFORMATION

in the left flat for Tyson Browning, who got a block and rumbled 93 yards up the Georgia sideline to tie the game 10–10 with 4:25 remaining. Called to task, the Tigers answered—if in slightly unorthodox fashion. Henderson returned the ensuing kickoff from his 1 to the LSU 49. Five plays later, the Tigers faced third-and-4 at the Georgia 34. Skyler Green was supposed to set a screen for Clayton, the intended receiver, but instead he ran a figure-7 post route toward the end zone. "I saw him out of the corner of my eye," said Mauck, who lofted the pass just before Georgia linebacker Odell Thurman drilled him in the gut. Green caught up with the ball in the end zone, giving LSU a 17–10 lead with 1:22 remaining. Georgia had one last shot, but cornerback Corey Webster picked off David Greene at the 22 to end the threat. "I don't think our team really knew how good it was going into that game," Saban said. "That game gave us the confidence and kind of verified that we had a good football team."

September 27: LSU 41, Mississippi State 6

LSU's critics said the Tigers were lucky to escape Georgia, that the Bulldogs were still the better team. There was little question on the night of September 27 that LSU was better than the Mississippi State Bulldogs. Once again, the Tigers simply outclassed State, this time in a 41–6 rout. It was over by

Strong safety Jack Hunt churns downfield on a 34-yard interception return at Mississippi State, 2003. STEVE FRANZ, LSU SPORTS INFORMATION

halftime with Carey scoring on a pair of 1-yard plunges—the second set up by Hunt's interception return to the 1—and capped by a 48-yard interception return by cornerback Travis Daniels off Kevin Fant to make it 24–0 at the break. LSU went up 31–0 after a State fumble set up a 36-yard Mauck touchdown pass to Henderson, who had seven catches for 114 yards. Freshman tailback Justin Vincent made his presence felt as Saban emptied the bench in the second half. He scored on a 3-yard run and led the Tigers with 58 yards rushing on just six carries. Saban seemed relieved at the way his team responded. "I think you always have a lot of worries about the things that happen in college football today," he said, "people winning big games and then going and dying the next week." It was LSU's 11th win in its last 12 tries against State, and the Tigers were 5–0 for the first time since 1973.

October 11: Florida 19, LSU 7

It looked like a reversal of fortune for LSU and Florida when the Gators came calling on October 11. It was the Tigers flying high, undefeated and nationally ranked at No. 6. It was the Gators who were struggling, 3–3 overall and 1–2 in the SEC. But LSU learned that nothing was for certain. The Tigers looked like they were on their way to another victory when Green zipped into the end zone on an 80-yard punt return with 11:51 left in the first quarter. It would be all the points LSU would get, as Gator freshman quarterback Chris Leak played keep-away with a ball-control offense that burned the Tigers' vaunted defense twice over the middle on big scoring plays. The first was on a 22-yard pass to wide-open tailback Ran Carthon to make it 7–7 in the first quarter. A pair of Matt Leach field goals made it 13–7 but allowed LSU to stay within striking distance. That is, if LSU could have found its offense. LSU turned the ball over three times as the offense completely broke down. After losing Addai with a knee injury, the Tigers managed just 56 net yards rushing on 24 attempts. LSU could do nothing to counter another Leak toss over the middle, this time to a wide-open Ciatrick Fason for a 35-yard touchdown with 5:21 left in the third quarter in a 19–7 Florida win. Saban sensed that the Tigers, and even their fans, had assumed victory. "It's too bad that something bad has to happen for people to be willing to learn and actually change how they're thinking in terms of how they need to go about things," he said.

September 18: LSU 33, South Carolina 7

The Tigers would lose a spot in the top 10 if they didn't return from South Carolina with a victory over the 4–2 Gamecocks on October 18. The challenge appeared daunting. LSU went in minus Addai and Carey, both sidelined with knee injuries. The Tigers' ground attack would have to depend on

Skyler Green's 80-yard punt return for a score was a rare LSU highlight on a frustrating day against Florida, 2003. STEVE FRANZ, LSU SPORTS INFORMATION

a pair of game freshmen in Vincent and Broussard. The success they had was as unexpected as Florida's upset was a week earlier, as Vincent and Broussard combined for 185 yards and two touchdowns in a 33–7 victory. LSU simply ran and ran and ran the ball right at the Gamecocks, draining the home team's will and ability to win. The Tigers mounted three lengthy touchdown drives in the first half that chewed up a combined 19:47 of the first 30 minutes of game time. A 5-yard Mauck-to-Henderson pass completed an eight-play, 64-yard drive that took 4:19. A 4-yard Mauck scoring pass to tight end Eric Edwards capped an epic 97-yard, 21-play drive that took 9:37. And Vincent pushed across from the 1 with 55 seconds left before halftime to finish a 14-play, 91-yard march for a 19–0 LSU lead. In the second half, middle line-

A 15-yard fumble return by linebacker Jason LeDoux gives LSU a 26–7 lead late in the third quarter at South Carolina, 2003.   STEVE FRANZ, LSU SPORTS INFORMATION

backer Jason LeDoux picked up a fumble by Gamecocks quarterback Dondrial Pinkins after he was hit by end Kirston Pittman, returning the ball 15 yards for a touchdown. "I'm really proud of the way our team bounced back," Saban said. "We controlled the line of scrimmage on both sides." "We wanted to re-establish our ability to run," center Ben Wilkerson said. The Tigers outrushed South Carolina 263–0.

October 25: LSU 31, Auburn 7

No. 17-ranked Auburn came to Tiger Stadium on October 25 rejuvenated after an 0–2 start dropped the preseason SEC favorite out of the national rankings. Four straight wins, all in conference, actually had LSU with its 3–1 SEC record looking up at 4–0 Auburn and 4–0 Ole Miss in the SEC West standings. The game had all the markings of another LSU-Auburn classic. Instead, LSU made it a classic rout, 31–7. Once again, LSU's No. 1-ranked rushing defense couldn't be breached, not even by Auburn's Cadillac Williams. He gained 61 yards on 20 carries but got stuffed on a fourth-and-1 play by All-American defensive tackle Chad Lavalais, who spent part of his time after graduating from high school working as a prison guard. The rest of Auburn's team lost a collective 11 yards. Mauck made it 21–0 by halftime with two of his three touchdown passes, starting with a 64-yarder to Henderson just two minutes into the game. Clayton then caught a short screen pass and helicoptered into the end zone on an 18-yard scoring play, followed by a 5-yard Brous-

Chad Lavalais rides Auburn quarterback Jason Campbell to the turf, 2003.

sard touchdown run. Gaudet added a field goal and Mauck a 16-yard scoring pass to Henderson in the third before Auburn could even get on the board, exactly the same scoring progression as in Auburn's 31–7 win over LSU the year before. "They were making plays, moving around," Williams said. "It kind of reminded us of last year." LSU's Vincent had no trouble running the ball, picking up 127 yards on just 14 carries. "We have no excuses," Auburn coach Tommy Tuberville said. "They lined up and whipped us on both sides. They were the better team today."

November 1: LSU 49, Louisiana Tech 10

November 1 was a day for scoreboard watching—for how rapidly LSU hung points on Louisiana Tech and how swiftly some of the nation's mightiest teams fell. Three of the six teams ahead of the Tigers tumbled: Virginia Tech blasted No. 2 Miami 31–7, Florida toppled No. 4 Georgia 16–13, and No. 6 Washington State was routed by No. 3 Southern California 43–16. The Tigers would rise to No. 4 in the polls that comprised two-thirds of the Bowl Championship Series formula, but would remain stuck at No. 7 in the overall BCS standings because the computers in the BCS mix were unimpressed with

Matt Mauck and Devery Henderson celebrate one of their two touchdown connections against Louisiana Tech, 2003.　　　　STEVE FRANZ, LSU SPORTS INFORMATION

LSU's nonconference schedule. A lot of humans were impressed with the Tigers after they crushed Tech. "If they're not the best team in the country, I'd be shocked," said Tech coach Jack Bicknell, whose Bulldogs lost to Miami 48–9 in their season opener. "I promise you, I even feel like they were better than Miami, I really do." LSU scored 35 points in the game's first 15:13 on three Mauck touchdown passes and an interception return by Hunt. The Tigers' defense held Tech to 341 total yards, nearly 119 below its season average. "If they don't win the rest of them, I'll be mad at them," Bicknell said.

November 15: LSU 27, Alabama 3

LSU had an open date before traveling to play Alabama on November 15, but the Tigers' national title hopes could have scarcely been more enhanced if they had played. Clemson upset No. 3 Florida State 26–10, while two more teams ahead of LSU in the BCS—Virginia Tech and Miami—tumbled to Pittsburgh 31–28 and Tennessee 10–6, respectively. Now the Tigers went to Tuscaloosa No. 3 in the human polls and No. 4 in the BCS overall, trying not to trip up against a 4–6 Bama team that hardly resembled the one that humbled LSU 31–0 in Tiger Stadium in 2002. Playing in the same Bryant-Denny Stadium where Bama lost stubbornly 20–13 to No. 1 Oklahoma in September, the Tigers again trotted out the D-word: dominant. No big scoring explosions, just a methodical 27–3 LSU victory. Mauck was 24 of 36 for 251 yards, throwing a 23-yard touchdown pass to Clayton in the first quarter and

One of 12 passes Michael Clayton hauled in for 130 yards at Alabama, 2003.

STEVE FRANZ, LSU SPORTS INFORMATION

a 3-yarder to Edwards on a brilliant over-the-shoulder grab in the second to give LSU a 17–0 halftime lead. Vincent rushed for 83 yards, Broussard had 79 and a touchdown, and the Tigers' defense limited Bama to 219 total yards. Afterward, everyone wanted to know how LSU compared to the mighty Sooners. "They're every bit as good," Bama quarterback Brodie Croyle said. "We didn't play well, and I'm sure it had a lot to do with them."

November 22: LSU 17, Ole Miss 14

Beating the Crimson Tide in Alabama for the eighth time since 1982 faded to insignificance compared with the most crucial LSU–Ole Miss game in decades. The Tigers held at No. 3 in the polls and No. 4 in the BCS, but at 9–1 overall and 5–1 in the SEC were still second in the Western Division behind the No. 15-ranked Rebels (8–2, 6–0 in the SEC). LSU had to win in frenzied Vaught-Hemingway Stadium on November 22 to keep not only its national championship dreams alive, but its SEC title hopes as well. An Ole Miss win would automatically send the Rebels to the SEC championship game. Things looked grim for LSU on its first play from scrimmage when Mauck rolled right in his end zone looking for Clayton. Mauck's pass sailed long, right into the hands of Ole Miss's Travis Johnson, who ran in from the 6 for a quick 7–0 lead. LSU settled down and took a 10–7 halftime lead on Chris Jackson's

45-yard field goal in the first quarter and a screen pass to Clayton that he took in from the 9 with 2:42 left before intermission. After a scoreless third Mauck found Henderson wide open behind the Rebels' secondary, a 53-yard pass that gave LSU a 17–7 lead with 14:50 to play. The Tigers' breathing room was a short gasp, as Eli Manning and the Rebels answered immediately with a 10-yard touchdown pass to Brandon Jacobs with 10:51 left. Nearly 11 minutes of taut, defense-dominated drama remained. Ole Miss had a chance to tie with 4:15 left, but Jonathan Nichols (that year's Lou Groza Award winner as the nation's top kicker) was wide right on a 36-yard field goal. It was just his third miss of the season but his second of the game after failing on a 47-yard attempt in the first half. With 1:50 remaining, the Rebels faced fourth-and-10 at their 42. Manning dropped back to pass but tripped over the foot of left guard Doug Buckles, who was being shoved back as he tried to block Lavalais. Manning tumbled to the ground otherwise untouched. He got the ball back for one last desperation heave, but there would be no Magnolia Miracle. LSU won 17–14 and defense was the reason, limiting the Rebels to just 27 yards rushing and 227 yards overall. "Our defense played like gangbusters," Saban said. "We could have melted down, but they showed a lot of character. It wasn't always pretty, but they showed a lot of maturity."

Linebacker Cameron Vaughn helps LSU limit Ole Miss to 27 net yards rushing, 2003.

STEVE FRANZ, LSU SPORTS INFORMATION

November 28: LSU 55, Arkansas 24

A 35–21 loss by BCS No. 2 Ohio State to Michigan allowed LSU's BCS ranking to match its No. 3 poll rankings going into the final weekend of the regular season, behind No. 1 Oklahoma and new No. 2 USC. With so much at stake against 8–3 Arkansas, soon-to-be All-American guard Stephen Peterman reflected on his decision to come to LSU during the lean years at the end of the Gerry DiNardo era. "I could have gone to Florida or some other places where they were winning," he said. "But something hit me when I came on this campus. I said, 'This is where I want to play—in front of these people.'" The 92,213 people in Tiger Stadium on November 28 appreciated Peterman and the Tigers' efforts in a rousing 55–24 win. Arkansas stunned LSU early on a 53-yard pass from Matt Jones to DeCori Birmingham—shades of their winning touchdown connection the previous year in Little Rock. But LSU got rocking later in the quarter, when linebacker Eric Alexander scooped up a Jones fumble, running 25 yards to give the Tigers a 10–7 lead. The Razorbacks tied it 10–10 but couldn't keep pace in a rapid-fire second quarter as the Tigers scored in a 24-point rush. Mauck completed 12 of just 19 passes for 189 yards but was efficient, throwing four touchdown passes. Three were in the second quarter, covering 10 yards to Clayton, 2 yards to Green, and 22 yards to Henderson. Vincent carried 18 times for 112 yards and two second-half scores. "That second-quarter flurry really hurt," Arkansas coach Houston Nutt said. "That's hard to overcome, especially against a team that good."

Marcus Spears chases down Arkansas quarterback Matt Jones, 2003.

Freshman tailback Justin Vincent breaks off a long run against Georgia, 2003.

STEVE FRANZ, LSU SPORTS INFORMATION

The SEC Championship Game: LSU 34, Georgia 13

The SEC championship game on December 6 was almost a distraction to LSU fans consumed with BCS talk. Some experts said a rematch with No. 5 Georgia might even hurt the Tigers with the BCS computer polls. First, LSU had to win the game. "Our focus needs to be on Georgia," Saban said, remembering the Tigers' dramatic 17–10 victory in September. "Nothing else." As often the case, the sequel didn't live up to the original, as LSU staked its claim to the national championship game with an emphatic 34–13 victory. Vincent, who didn't get a carry in the first Georgia game, earned MVP honors with 18 carries for 201 yards and two touchdowns, including an explosive 87-yard touchdown run around right end late in the first quarter. Jackson's extra-point try hit the crossbar, but it would be one of LSU's few miscues. The Tigers were soon up 8–0 when Georgia punter Gordon Ely-Kelso dropped the snap and was tackled for a safety by Broussard. A 43-yard pass over the middle from Mauck to Clayton and a 35-yard field goal by Gaudet gave LSU a 17–0 lead before Georgia made it 17–3 at the half. In the third quarter, LSU's defense stopped sacking Greene long enough to score a touchdown when middle line-backer Lionel Turner ran back an interception 18 yards for a 24–6 lead. Vincent added his second touchdown on a 3-yard run in the fourth, and Gaudet's 22-yard field goal after a 62-yard Vincent run to the 18 completed the scoring—and began the speculation.

While LSU was dismantling Georgia, No. 1 Oklahoma was getting crushed by No. 13 Kansas State 35–7 in the Big 12 championship game, a completely bewildering upset that threw fresh fuel on the already smoldering BCS controversy. Despite the loss, and the fact that it dropped to No. 3 in the AP and coaches' polls, 12–1 Oklahoma was still assured of being the BCS No. 1 and in the Sugar Bowl because it went into the Kansas State game with such a big lead in the BCS computer rankings. That drew the battle lines between 12–1 LSU and 11–1 USC (the Trojans beat Oregon State 52–28 that day) for the other spot. "I think our team deserves the opportunity to play for a national championship," Saban said. "But if we wouldn't have had that loss [to Florida] we wouldn't be in this place." Late into the night the last few results of the season were awaited like election returns, games that would turn the final BCS rankings a fraction either way. In the end, what pushed LSU past USC was Boise State's seemingly isolated 45–28 win over Hawaii. What made it a win for LSU as well was that USC beat Hawaii 61–32 in September, tamping down the Trojans' strength of schedule just enough to allow LSU to slip by. In the final BCS rankings, LSU had a total of 5.99 to USC's 6.15, a difference of 0.16, lower score as in golf being better. Hawaii's loss to Boise State added an extra 0.20 to USC's total. The Tigers' schedule ranked 29th toughest, while USC's was 37th.

Now No. 2 in the BCS, the Tigers were headed down the road to play Oklahoma in the Sugar Bowl while BCS No. 3 USC was staying home to play Michigan in the Rose Bowl. Still No. 1 in the AP poll, the Trojans would stay there with a 28–14 win over Michigan and actually gain votes. "Given everything that has happened this year, split polls are the right outcome," wrote *Atlanta Journal-Constitution* sportswriter and AP voter Tony Barnhart. He would switch his No. 1 vote from LSU to USC.

Nokia Sugar Bowl (BCS Championship): LSU 21, Oklahoma 14

The Tigers couldn't worry about that. They had enough to handle with Oklahoma. The Sooners obviously weren't the best college football team ever as some gushed during the regular season, but on their way to New Orleans they won by some frightful scores. The Sooners clubbed Texas 65–13, routed a No. 14-ranked Oklahoma State team coached by Les Miles 52–9, and the capper, destroyed Texas A&M 77–0, the most lopsided score in Big 12 history. When the individual postseason awards came out, the Sooners cleaned up.

Quarterback Jason White won the Heisman Trophy and the Davey O'Brien Award, while linebacker Teddy Lehman won the Bednarik and Butkus awards. Defensive tackle Tommie Harris won the Lombardi, and cornerback Derrick Strait took home the Thorpe and Nagurski awards. Saban's advice to his players was simple and direct. "Focus on dominating the guy you've got to play against every play," he said, "and assume that guy's going to be the best you've ever played against." What he didn't want was talk of winning the game. That to Saban was focusing on the result, not the process of winning, and would get his Tigers beat. "The players were pretty good about that," he said. "That's how we practiced and that's how we played. We were practicing to beat the team we were playing, not to win the national championship."

Before a Superdome-record crowd of 79,342, the game started brilliantly for the Tigers, then segued into nervousness. On the first play from scrimmage, Vincent broke up the middle on a 64-yard run before being caught from behind at the Oklahoma 16. LSU failed to score as Mauck fumbled on first-and-goal at the 1. The Sooners turned the ball right back over, Webster returning a White interception 18 yards to the OU 32. Three plays later, Green scored on a 24-yard end-around

Sugar Bowl Starters			
For the Nokia Sugar Bowl against Oklahoma on January 4, 2004, the LSU Fighting Tigers lined up this way:			
	Ht.	Wt.	Class
WR Devery Henderson	6–0	189	Sr.
LT Andrew Whitworth	6–7	325	Soph.
LG Nate Livings	6–5	313	Soph.
C Ben Wilkerson	6–4	296	Jr.
RG Stephen Peterman	6–4	321	Sr.
RT Rodney Reed	6–4	287	Sr.
TE Eric Edwards	6–5	244	Sr.
WR Michael Clayton	6–4	200	Jr.
HB David Jones	6–4	259	Soph.
TB Justin Vincent	5–10	208	Fr.
QB Matt Mauck	6–2	213	Jr.
DE Marcus Spears	6–4	297	Jr.
DT Kyle Williams	6–3	288	Soph.
DT Chad Lavalais	6–3	292	Sr.
DE Marquise Hill	6–7	295	Jr.
LB Eric Alexander	6–3	223	Sr.
LB Lionel Turner	6–2	257	Jr.
LB Cameron Vaughn	6–4	220	Soph.
CB Corey Webster	6–0	201	Jr.
SS Jack Hunt	6–1	197	Sr.
FS LaRon Landry	6–2	180	Fr.
CB Travis Daniels	6–1	187	Jr.
PK Ryan Gaudet	5–6	155	Fr.
P Donnie Jones	6–3	217	Jr.

down the LSU sideline for a 7–0 lead with 11:38 left in the first quarter. The Tigers were in control early, but their mistakes would keep the Sooners in the game. OU's Brandon Shelby broke through to block a Donnie Jones punt that Russell Dennison returned to the LSU 2. Three plays later, running back Kejuan Jones smashed over from the 1 at left guard to tie it 7–7 with 7:31 left in the second quarter. Just as when Georgia tied the game in Baton Rouge, the Tigers immediately responded. Keyed by a 15-yard pass from Mauck to David Jones on third-and-7 to the OU 30, Vincent blasted off left guard and cut to the pylon to score on an 18-yard run with 4:21 remaining, giving LSU a 14–7 halftime lead.

The game's biggest play came early in the third quarter. White, who completed just 13 of 37 passes for 102 yards with two interceptions, didn't see

Skyler Green's 24-yard end-around gives LSU an early 7–0 lead against Oklahoma in the 2004 Sugar Bowl.   STEVE FRANZ, LSU SPORTS INFORMATION

Marcus Spears dances into the end zone after a 20-yard interception return to give LSU a 21–7 lead in the Sugar Bowl.   STEVE FRANZ, LSU SPORTS INFORMATION

The clincher: Lionel Turner sacks Heisman Trophy winner Jason White to seal the win.

STEVE FRANZ, LSU SPORTS INFORMATION

Spears dropping back from his defensive end spot into coverage. He picked off White at the 20 and rumbled into the end zone for a 21–7 LSU lead just 47 seconds into the second half. "It was a zone blitz and the defensive end drops into the flats," Spears explained. "Usually quarterbacks never see that, and Jason White hadn't seen that all year. I knew from watching film that their tendency on third down was to throw a slant rout to Mark Clayton. We called the play and I ended up being in the right position at the right time." Again, though, the Sooners weren't done. Brodney Pool intercepted a badly thrown Mauck pass in coverage and returned it 49 yards to the LSU 31. Another 1-yard run by Kejuan Jones nine plays later made it 21–14 with 11:01 remaining. As LSU's offense bogged down, Oklahoma went three-and-out on its next possession, then turned the ball over on downs. The Sooners had one last chance to score, starting from their 49 with 2:09 left. But after three back-to-back incompletions, Turner zoomed untouched on a safety blitz to sack White at his 40 with 1:51 left. With OU out of time-outs, LSU needed just four more snaps and a Donnie Jones punt that rolled out of bounds as time expired to start the celebration. Vincent was named the MVP for his 16-carry, 117-yard effort, his second straight in a huge game. "It's kind of a fantasy land I'm living in right now," he said. Oklahoma's season ended with a two-game night-

Chad Lavalais (93), Michael Clayton (14), and others celebrate as Nick Saban holds the crystal football aloft after winning the Bowl Championship Series in the Nokia Sugar Bowl, 2004.   STEVE FRANZ, LSU SPORTS INFORMATION

mare. "They are a great defense," White said. "They out-executed us, and we didn't execute through most of the night. You've got to give them credit." LSU limited Oklahoma's explosive offense to 154 total yards, at the time the fewest ever allowed in a BCS game. From New Orleans to Baton Rouge and across much of Louisiana, the party began. "You can imagine walking through the New Orleans streets afterward and people knew who you were," Spears said. "It was unbelievable." For LSU fans who suffered through eight of 11 losing seasons in the 1980s and '90s it would take a while to sink in, but it was true. The LSU Tigers were BCS national champions.

Some observers, especially those who wanted to see a college football playoff, took shots at LSU's title. The system could be debated, but there was no debating that it was the system agreed upon by USC and the rest of college football going into the 2003 season. Nor was there debating the fact that LSU deserved to be in the Sugar Bowl, the only one of the three between USC and OU to be ranked No. 2 in the AP and coaches' polls and BCS rankings entering the bowl season. And when it was done, six of the seven BCS computers had LSU ranked No. 1 over USC.

In the final analysis, nothing will ever be settled from the controversy-scarred season of 2003. USC has its national championship trophy, and LSU has its—the one crowned by the crystal ball.

Farewell, for Now

Afterward, there was much to savor. There was a parade through downtown Baton Rouge shared with Southern University's team, that year's black-college national champion. There were a trio of national coach-of-the-year honors for Saban—the Eddie Robinson, Bear Bryant, and Associated Press awards. Lavalais, Peterman, Green, and Webster were named to a patchwork quilt of All-American teams, while Clayton, Spears, and Wilkerson were first-team All-SEC selections. And for Saban, there was a new seven-year contract that guaranteed he would be the highest-paid coach in college football, starting at $2.3 million per year and climbing to $3 million per year if he stayed through to the end. As always with Saban, though, there were reports he was going to leave for the NFL. On January 10, Saban took the unprecedented step of calling a news conference to say he was staying after shunning an offer from the Chicago Bears reportedly worth $3.5 million per year. But not until after an eight-hour meeting the night before between Saban and his friend, Bears general manager Jerry Angelo. Saying the Chicago job "was a very good situation," Saban said he was making a commitment to stay at LSU because he was happy there. "I have a great job," he said, "a great job." LSU fans were relieved, but how many seasons were there in Saban's "commitment"?

Committed high school football players were still more than willing to flock to Baton Rouge. After pulling in a No. 1-ranked class in 2003 that included Vincent, Broussard, Will Arnold, Dwayne Bowe, and two highly regarded quarterbacks named JaMarcus Russell and Matt Flynn, the 2004 class was ranked No. 2 nationally with names like Glenn Dorsey, Early Doucet, Ali Highsmith, and Tyson Jackson. A nation of college football observers believed in Saban and the Tigers, too. Despite losing 10 starters—including seniors Lavalais, Henderson, Peterman, and Rodney Reed; and juniors Mauck, Clayton, and Hill, who were turning pro early—the Tigers opened at No. 3 in the coaches' poll and No. 4 in the AP. Those rankings interchanged with Georgia, essentially the co-favorite in the SEC.

Mauck's departure after throwing for 2,825 yards and a school-record 28 touchdowns left the quarterback job back in Marcus Randall's hands. Almost a forgotten man except for occasional mop-up duty in 2003, Randall played in just eight games and attempted only 40 passes. But he could rely on a stacked backfield that included Justin Vincent (who rushed for 1,001 yards as a freshman), Alley Broussard, a now-healthy Joseph Addai, and senior Shyrone Carey. Skyler Green and sophomore Dwayne Bowe manned the receiver spots with sophomore Craig "Buster" Davis coming up fast. Marcus Spears returned at defensive end for what would be an All-American senior season, the anchor of a still-imposing line that included junior tackle Kyle Williams, sophomore end Melvin Oliver, and talented junior-college transfer Claude Wroten, who quickly claimed a starting spot. Lionel Turner was back at middle linebacker, while All-American cornerback Corey Webster and future All-American free safety LaRon Landry roamed the secondary.

Saban insisted the Tigers were not defending their BCS national championship because it was not something that could be lost. Instead, he wanted his team to focus on trying to climb the mountain again. It was fitting, then, that the Tigers opened on September 4 against a team that had to come over the Rockies to get to Baton Rouge, Oregon State, in an ESPN-brokered made-for-TV deal. After surviving to win 22–21 in overtime, LSU appeared to have a long climb. The night was as strange as the score. A 47-minute weather delay featured a male streaker slip-sliding away what otherwise would have been a tedious wait for kickoff. Getting kicks off was a major problem for Oregon State's Alexis Serna, who bounced two extra-point tries off the right upright in regulation. For the Beavers it was the difference between a stunning upset and a painful defeat. LSU trailed 9–0 at halftime and 15–7 late before Russell came off the bench to throw a 38-yard touchdown pass to Bowe with 1:05 left, the first of many connections the two would have over the next three seasons. Russell then ran a keeper for two points to force overtime. In the extra period, Randall returned and scored on a 5-yard run while Chris Jackson added the all-important extra point. Oregon State answered the touchdown, but Serna's extra-point try was spectacularly wide right to bring an end to it. "They outplayed us and beat us all over the field," Williams said. "We snuck one out."

Nothing sneaky about the next game. LSU's talent was there for all to see in a 53–3 pasting of Arkansas State on September 11. Vincent rushed for 102 yards and two touchdowns, Randall and Russell combined for 210 yards passing three TDs, and the Indians managed just 201 yards. But what did it mean with a trip to Auburn the next week?

It looked like this LSU-Auburn clash would be called the Hurricane Game after it was nearly postponed when Hurricane Ivan smashed ashore near Orange Beach, Alabama. But the game was played—and became remembered at LSU as the Penalty Game. No. 4 LSU struck first on a 9-yard touchdown pass from Randall to Bowe, but Ryan Gaudet's extra-point try was no good. No. 14 Auburn made it 6–3 on a 29-yard John Vaughn field goal before Jackson's 42-yarder in the second put LSU up 9–3. With less than seven minutes left, Auburn mounted what looked like a do-or-die drive, culminating with

Ronnie Prude (8) goes up high to try to block John Vaughn's kick, 2004. Where he came down would be the problem.

a 16-yard Jason Campbell to Courtney Taylor touchdown pass with 1:14 remaining. Auburn had made 190 straight extra points going back to 1999, but Vaughn yanked the kick wide left. Overtime seemed likely—except for a flag. Attempting to block the kick, LSU's Ronnie Prude leaped up high and came down on top of Auburn deep snapper Pete Compton, invoking a new rule called 9-1-2-q. The rule essentially stated that no defensive player could jump and land on an opponent while trying to block a kick. It gave Auburn a second chance, and this time Vaughn drilled it to give his team a dramatic 10–9 victory. "It's a tough way to lose a game," said Saban, a member of the NCAA football rules committee. "I'm not criticizing the officials. It's just a tough—kind of a cheap—way, cheap penalty, to end up losing the game on."

Another year, another rout of Mississippi State. The Tigers took out their frustrations on the Bulldogs on September 25, sprinting to a 34–0 halftime lead in a 51–0 blowout despite the 11:30 A.M. kickoff for Lincoln Financial Sports. Broussard rushed for LSU's first three touchdowns, then was joined in the end zone by Spears, whose 35-yard interception return brought back happy memories of his crucial score in the Sugar Bowl.

On the road again to take on the SEC's other Bulldogs, it was No. 13 LSU that felt No. 3 Georgia's frustration. A lot of people said that Georgia was the better team when it lost at LSU a year earlier. On October 2, the Bulldogs proved they were better this time with a sound 45–16 thrashing, the most points allowed by a Saban-coached LSU team. "That was a curveball to me," Saban said. Georgia quarterback David Greene threw fastballs, picking the Tigers' proud defense apart with surgical precision. He threw five touchdown passes, including two each to Reggie Brown and Fred Gibson, as Georgia built a 24–0 lead midway through the second quarter. "It's a good feeling," Greene said. "We wanted this one bad."

Its season on the verge of slipping away, LSU next headed to Florida on October 9 to meet the No. 12 Gators. This time it was the Tigers' turn to exact some revenge for their only loss of 2003, though that hardly looked possible early. Russell made a disastrous first start, throwing two rapid-fire interceptions that led to touchdown mini-drives of 5 and 3 yards and a 14–0 first-quarter Florida lead. Enter Randall, who threaded a needle with a 15-yard touchdown toss to Doucet just 12 seconds before halftime to pull the Tigers within 21–14. Jackson made a 47-yard field goal in the third quarter, setting up an impressive 50-yard, six-play drive for the win. With 27 seconds left, Addai crashed into the end zone on a 10-yard pass from Randall as the Tigers came back from the grave to register a 24–21 victory. "I can't tell you how proud I am of this team," Saban said. "I don't want to be harsh, but humiliated is what we all felt just one week ago."

After a month of hostile road trips to Auburn, Athens, and Gainesville, the Tigers got an open-date breather before returning home against Troy University on October 23. LSU looked as though it might fall victim to an October surprise when the Trojans took a 20–17 lead with 3:59 left on a 24-yard Greg Whibbs field goal. Xavier Carter returned the kickoff near midfield, from where Randall took the Tigers 54 yards in four plays to win 24–20 on a 30-yard pass to tight end David Jones. Randall was 24 of 37 passing for 328 yards, but his last throw was the biggest.

JaMarcus Russell started a week later against Vanderbilt, but as he and Randall alternated, they performed essentially the same task: handing the ball off. LSU ran on 44 of its 55 offensive plays to grind out a 24–7 victory. Randall and Russell were just 6 of 11 combined passing for 102 yards, but the Tigers picked up 273 yards on the ground led by 80 from Broussard. Now 6–2 and ranked 15th, the Tigers ran right into the teeth of the nation's No. 1 defense and came away with some stellar defense of their own in a 26–10 win over Alabama on November 13 before a crowd of 91,861. LSU managed just 283 total yards, but the Crimson Tide eked out only 196. His team trailing 10–6 at halftime, linebacker Cameron Vaughn scooped up a Spencer Pennington fumble after he was sacked by Spears and returned it 8 yards for a touchdown and a 13–6 lead in the third quarter. Another Bama threat was snuffed out by a Webster interception that the Tide bitterly claimed was created by pass interference. No flag, no penalty, no chance for Alabama to win again at Baton Rouge as the Tigers prevailed.

A crowd of 91,413 bid farewell to one of LSU's most successful classes ever in a 27–24 win over Ole Miss on November 20. Alley Broussard made sure

Two-time All-American Corey Webster: 16 career interceptions.

STEVE FRANZ, LSU SPORTS INFORMATION

they would go out winners. He carried 26 times for a school-record 250 yards and three scores, eclipsing Kevin Faulk's 246 yards rushing against Houston in 1996. Broussard and the Tigers still found themselves trailing 24–17 going into the fourth quarter before Broussard scored the game winner on a 7-yard run with 10:51 left.

After a string of squeakers, the Tigers wrapped up the regular season with a convincing 43–14 victory on November 26 at Arkansas. Randall never looked better or more efficient, throwing for two touchdowns and rushing for two in an easy win. The Tigers rolled up 468 yards total offense while their defense held lanky Matt Jones to just 12 of 29 passing for 152 yards with two interceptions and minus 10 yards rushing.

Ranked No. 11 and armed with a six-game winning streak, the 9–2 Tigers were appealing to the Capital One Bowl in Orlando, which paired LSU in a first-ever meeting with the Big Ten co-champion Iowa Hawkeyes (9–2). Meanwhile, Spears, Webster, and Wilkerson spent the down time collecting All-American awards. Wilkerson, whose season had ended with a late-game knee injury against Vanderbilt, earned a share of the Rimington Trophy as the nation's top center.

The story of December wasn't that the Tigers would spend their holidays in Florida. The question was whether their coach would be coming back with them. The Miami Dolphins were in the market for a coach again, and team officials, including former LSU graduate and team president Eddie Jones, flew to Baton Rouge and met with Saban on December 14. "I'm not driving the wheel here," Saban said. "They're continuing their search and I'm continuing my job and that's it. Nothing else." Before the week ended, a Florida paper was reporting that Saban would get an offer from the Dolphins. Charles Weems, chairman of the LSU Board of Supervisors athletic committee, said the school had to be prepared for the worst—that Saban would leave.

The Dolphins made an offer on December 22, but Saban didn't budge at first. "I didn't want to leave," Saban said. "I actually turned the job down December 23 at 11 o'clock at night. I called [Dolphins' owner] Wayne Huizenga and said, 'Wayne, I don't think I can do this. I'll sleep on it, but I've got too many relationships here. It's too much of an emotional decision for me to leave here with my kids, the players on the team, the program, the fans.'"

At eight o'clock on Christmas Eve morning there was a knock at the Sabans' door. It was Huizenga and his wife, come to put on the full-court press. Although he wouldn't announce his decision until Christmas Day once his team arrived in Orlando for the Capital One Bowl, Saban basically made his mind up right then. "He [Huizenga] kind of talked us into doing it," Saban said. "I don't mean that in a bad way. I love college football. I loved LSU. But I always had it in the back of my mind that maybe the last job I'd take would

Nick Saban talks to reporters in Orlando after announcing he is leaving LSU to coach the Miami Dolphins, 2004.   STEVE FRANZ, LSU SPORTS INFORMATION

be in the pros for that last challenge. I guess Wayne convinced me that was the best opportunity I would ever get." It was a lucrative deal worth close to $5 million per year, plus virtually total control of the Dolphins' player personnel decisions. It was a combination Athletic Director Skip Bertman said LSU couldn't match. "We changed his mind several times," he said, "but quite honestly this is a once-in-a-lifetime opportunity."

As LSU's search for its next coach cranked up, Saban would coach the Tigers one more time in the Capital One Bowl on New Year's Day, 2005. His imminent departure clearly appeared to have an impact on his team. Despite a dazzling 74-yard scoring run by Broussard in the second quarter, LSU trailed 24–12 in the fourth before Russell directed a comeback. He threw a pair of touchdown passes to Green, the second a 3-yard toss with 46 seconds left to give the Tigers a 25–24 lead after a two-point pass failed. Iowa took over at its 29, and in two plays moved to its 44 for one last play. Prude missed his assignment, leaving Warren Holloway uncovered. He found a seam to score on a 56-yard touchdown pass from Drew Tate as time expired. For Holloway, an Iowa senior, it was his first career touchdown catch, the perfect ending to a college career. For Saban and the LSU seniors, the 30–25 loss was perfectly awful. "The disappointing thing is the last 14 seconds, 20 seconds tarnishes what a lot of good football players have been able to accomplish in their career here," Saban said. "I feel badly myself that there's not something that I could do to help the players play better in this game." As good as Saban was in five years at LSU—a national championship, two SEC titles, five bowls, and an overall record of 48–16—he couldn't do enough in the end to help his team overcome the distractions he helped create. It was up to someone else now to help the Tigers through the good times and the bad times that were just ahead.

Nick Saban bids farewell to LSU fans after the Tigers lose to Iowa in the 2005 Capital One Bowl.
STEVE FRANZ, LSU SPORTS INFORMATION

6

MILES AND MILES TO GO

2005–2006

It was an emotional farewell in Orlando on New Year's Day 2005 as the LSU Tigers lost in the Capital One Bowl in their last game under Nick Saban. It was an emotional day in Stillwater, Oklahoma, as well, as Kathy and Les Miles and their four children were going house to house, telling the Oklahoma State assistants of Les's decision to go to LSU.

LSU's 30–25 last-play loss to Iowa wasn't the only big postseason letdown. It was preceded on December 29, when Miles's Oklahoma State team was routed by Ohio State 33–7 in the Alamo Bowl in San Antonio. LSU athletic director Skip Bertman had flown to San Antonio on December 26 to interview Miles, who was just completing his fourth season in Stillwater. Miles was definitely interested, but as with the Tigers and Saban's imminent departure, the reports and rumors surrounding Miles apparently weighed on the Cowboys and hampered their efforts against the Buckeyes. "I've got to be honest," Miles said. "I was distracted. I did nothing differently. I worked harder to prepare. I realized that it was a distraction for my team, especially by game day. It was everywhere that I was in contention for the job." By game's end, Les and Kathy figured LSU's interest in Miles had cooled. "In the world of football you're usually about as good as your last game," Kathy Miles said. "When you take a beating like we did from Ohio State, we were both thinking, 'Nah, LSU probably won't call again.'"

Since this was the first LSU football coaching search Team Miles was involved in, they probably didn't realize how bizarre those searches could be. First, there was a strange non-interview in Daytona Beach on New Year's Eve with Jacksonville Jaguars coach Jack Del Rio, who refused to meet with LSU officials face-to-face for fear of what it would do to his status with the NFL team. Del Rio went back to Jacksonville and LSU officials went back to Orlando, both sight unseen. Then there was the evening Skip Bertman's wife, Sandy, answered a call to their Orlando hotel room—a call from former president George H. W. Bush. "She gave me the phone and I said, 'Mr. President,'" Bertman recalled. "He said, 'I normally don't get involved, but I'd like to recommend somebody.'" So, on a former president's request, Bertman met with former Texas A&M coach R. C. Slocum. "He's a man's man, a gentleman," Bertman said of Slocum. "But we wanted a sitting head coach."

An interview with Bobby Williams, Saban's wide receivers coach and one-time successor at Michigan State, was basically a courtesy. Bertman tested the waters with former Miami Hurricanes and Cleveland Browns coach Butch Davis, Iowa coach Kirk Ferentz, USC's Pete Carroll, and Oklahoma's Bob Stoops before settling on two main candidates: Miles and Louisville coach Bobby Petrino. Petrino failed to impress the interview committee when they met December 26, leaving Miles as the primary candidate. "You have to be comfortable with the coach. I felt real comfortable with him," Bertman said of Miles, "and so did the others on the [selection committee]. He was upbeat, enthusiastic. And he knew a lot about LSU." Miles had just signed a contract extension with Oklahoma State that would take him through 2011 and pay an average of $1.5 million per year plus a handsome annuity. "Do you know what I'm giving up here, Coach?" Miles asked Bertman. Bertman replied, "Coach, I won some baseball national championships, but my legacy here will be with Les Miles, good or bad. I'm in this thing with you. You've got to trust me, and I've got to trust you."

On January 2, Kathy and Les Miles and his agent, George Bass, flew to Baton Rouge to work out details of his contract that would initially pay Miles $1.25 million per year plus $200,000 per year paid into a deferred account. But it was much more than money that led Miles to LSU. "The grand scope of the success this place can have," Miles said at a January 3 news conference, "the ability to recruit for and compete for national championships very quickly, my competitive spirit would not let me say no." Miles's first competitor would be the specter of Saban's success, a ghost the new coach didn't shy away from. "The goal—and Coach Saban set it up for us—is to run the finest football program in the country so our guys will have an experience second to none." Miles would have to fight Saban to keep some of his former assistants. Four of them—defensive coordinator Will Muschamp, running backs and special teams coach Derek Dooley, defensive line coach Travis Jones, and Williams—followed Saban to Miami. Saban offered offensive coordinator Jimbo Fisher a noncoordinator position, so Fisher remained at LSU. The only other coaches staying were offensive-line coach Stacy Searels and strength and conditioning coach Tommy Moffitt. Miles lured Karl Dunbar, an LSU player from 1986 through 1989 and an assistant for him at Oklahoma State, from the Chicago Bears to coach defensive line. Coming from Oklahoma State would be tight ends and recruiting coordinator Josh Henson, defensive backs coach Doug Mallory, wide receivers coach Todd Monken, and running backs coach Larry Porter. Bo Pelini left a co–defensive coordinator position at Oklahoma to run the defense for Miles, while Bradley Dale Peveto came

Miles of smiles: Les Miles meets the media at LSU for the first time, 2005.

from Middle Tennessee State to coach linebackers and special teams. Mack Butler, also from Oklahoma State, joined Sam Nader as administrative assistant.

Leslie Edwin Miles was born on November 10, 1953, in Elyria, Ohio, a quintessential working-class midwestern town about twenty-five miles southwest of Cleveland. Sports, particularly football, were a constant companion, and Les's father, a big, hulking ex-Navy man named Hope Miles, was his biggest supporter and toughest critic. The father, a lover of John Wayne movies, called the son "Duke." And the son thought the world of him. "I don't think anyone on our teams called him Duke," said Les's schoolmate Steve Sunagel. "That was between him and his father." Hope could be demanding of Duke, though. Once, before Elyria High School's sophomore team faced rival Sandusky, Hope tried to inspire his son with the promise of a new coat if he played well. After two holding penalties, Les was back on the sideline when he heard his father grumble, "It's going to be a cold winter, Duke."

Many in Elyria expected to see Les head to Ohio State to play for legendary coach Woody Hayes. But he gravitated toward another Ohio native turned Michigan man, Hayes protégé Bo Schembechler. Miles lettered for Bo in 1974 and '75 despite his small size for an offensive lineman (6–1, 230). "He was an undersized offensive guard," Schembechler said. "But I would describe him as a feisty player. He would do anything to get you blocked." When he finished playing, Miles took a job as a trucking agent making $32,000 per year, pretty good money in 1976. But the work left him unfulfilled, and he decided to ask Schembechler to take him back. Miles tried to contact his former coach 33 times before Bo finally took his call. "He would tell me, 'Oh, Miles, you sure you want to do this?'" Les recalled. "To get him convinced probably took me six months." Miles started as a graduate assistant in July 1977 making $8,200 a year—and couldn't have been happier.

A full-time assistant by 1980, Miles left Michigan in 1982 to follow former Michigan defensive coordinator Bill McCartney to Colorado, where he would coach alongside a former Notre Dame offensive guard and future LSU head coach, Gerry DiNardo. Miles returned to Michigan in 1987 as its offensive line coach. That year he met and fell in love with Kathy LaBarge, a Michigan women's basketball assistant, whom he married on June 5, 1993.

In 1995, Miles left for the first of two stints at Oklahoma State, this time as the Cowboys' offensive coordinator. Three seasons as the Dallas Cowboys' tight ends coach from 1998 through 2000 (where he coached former LSU All-American David LaFleur) put NFL experience on his résumé before Oklahoma State brought Miles back as its head coach in 2001. The Cowboys went only 4–7 that season, but one of those wins was a colossal 16–13 upset of No. 4-ranked Oklahoma in Norman. After the season, someone from Oklahoma groused, "Some people are happy with four wins." Miles, still the feisty offensive lineman, shot back, "We are not happy with four wins. But we enjoyed that victory more than they enjoyed any of theirs." Shortly after the season, Miles was plagued with intense headaches that were the result of a cyst on his brain caused by a buildup of fluid. An operation on Christmas Eve 2001 in Cleveland to relieve the pressure solved the problem, and soon Miles was back on the road recruiting. He led Oklahoma State to an 8–5 season in 2002 (including another upset of Oklahoma) and a 9–4 record in 2003 before going 7–5 in 2004.

As soon as Miles arrived at LSU, fans began questioning whether he had the intensity to match the volcano inside Saban. Friends said not to worry. "He has a fire inside him that probably won't be shown publicly," Sunagel said. "Don't let that laissez-faire kind of appearance fool you. He'll beat you on the field." In February, Miles beat Texas and Mack Brown for a national letter-of-intent signature from East St. John High quarterback Ryan Perrilloux. Perrilloux had committed to the Longhorns months before Saban left for Miami, a commitment some said Saban would have never gotten. Like DiNardo with Kevin Faulk ten years earlier, Miles made visiting the Gatorade national player of the year an early top priority, and eventually made Perrilloux the shining star of a truncated 13-man class that also included linebacker Darry Beckwith, wide receiver Brandon LaFell, and a receiver/track sprinter from Zachary named Trindon Holliday.

Miles's first recruits joined a veteran, talented team. There was prototypical sophomore quarterback JaMarcus Russell (6–5, 248), who beat out classmate Matt Flynn for the job, and a backfield stacked with Joseph Addai, Alley Broussard (he would be lost for the season with an August knee injury), Justin Vincent, and Shyrone Carey. Junior Buster Davis beat out senior Skyler Green for one starting wide receiver spot, while Dwayne Bowe was at the other. Senior Andrew Whitworth, who would never miss a practice in his LSU career, much less a game, was at left tackle. The defensive front was anchored by a pair of senior All-Americans, Kyle Williams and Claude Wroten, while safeties LaRon Landry and Jessie Daniels patrolled the secondary. Little surprise, then, that LSU opened the season at No. 5 and was picked to win the SEC West. The football program moved into its new football operations facility in mid-August, mere weeks before LSU was supposed to open the season on September 3 against North Texas.

The evening of August 28, Tiger running back Jacob Hester and defensive end Chase Pittman, former teammates at Evangel, made an eerie drive south from Shreveport down I-49 bound for Baton Rouge. "Traffic was backed up from Shreveport to Baton Rouge bumper to bumper," he recalled. "I just remember me trying to get [to LSU] and everyone else trying to get out. It was like a deserted road." Early on the morning of August 29, Hurricane Katrina's eye came ashore below New Orleans near the village of Buras and followed a straight-arrow track northward toward the Louisiana-Mississippi border. Soon New Orleans was almost completely flooded and much of southeast Louisiana was rendered a shambles, forcing LSU's campus to be converted into a primary care site for hurricane victims being brought out of the shattered city. The North Texas opener was postponed, LSU's first weather-related postponement since the 1964 Florida game was moved from October

Shelter from the Storm

After working for hours helping Hurricane Katrina victims being brought to the Pete Maravich Assembly Center and nearby Carl Maddox Field House, Bill Martin returned to the LSU Sports Information office across the street, where he worked as a student assistant. Early on the morning of August 31, he sent out an emotionally charged e-mail that its readers would forward again and again around the world. Here is what he wrote:

Little did I know what I would be doing following Hurricane Katrina's aftermath but as I type right now, there won't be a more gratifying or more surreal experience [than what] I went through tonight. We went up to the office today and held a press conference regarding the postponement of the [LSU–Arizona State] game and it was the right decision. As the PMAC and Field House are being used as shelters we decided as an office to do everything we could to help the situation.

At first, we were just supposed to make copies of this disaster relief form for all of the people. The copiers will never print a document more important than that. It's weird. Nearly 12 hours ago we were running off copies of game notes for a football game that is now meaningless. We printed the copies and carried them over to the Field House at 6:30 p.m. I wouldn't leave the area for another 8 hours.

On the way back to the PMAC in a car, it looked like the scene in the movie "Outbreak." FEMA officials. U.S. Marshals, National Guard, and of course the survivors. Black Hawks were carrying in victims who were stranded on roofs. Buses rolled in from N.O. with other survivors. As Michael [Bonnette, LSU Sports Information director] and I rode back to the PMAC, a lady fell out of her wheelchair and we scrambled to help her up.

We met Coach Miles and Coach Moffitt in the PMAC to see all the survivors and it was the view of a hospital. Stretchers rolled in constantly and for the first time in my life I saw someone die right in front of me. A man rolled in from New Orleans and was badly injured on his head. 5 minutes later he was dead. And that was the scene all night.

What did we do, we started hauling in supplies. And thousands of boxes of supplies. The CDC [Centers for Disease Control] from Atlanta arrived directing us what to do. One of the U.S. Marshals was on hand so the supplies could not become loot. I asked him what his primary job was. He serves on the committee of counter terrorism, but once he saw of the disaster, he donated his forces to come help. He said the death toll could be nearing 10,000. It was sickening to hear that.

After unloading supplies, I started putting together baby cribs and then IV poles. Several of our football players and [basketball players] Big Baby [Glen Davis] and Tasmin Mitchell helped us. At the same time, families and people strolled in. Mothers were giving birth in the locker rooms. The auxiliary gym "Dungeon" was being used as a morgue. I couldn't take myself down there to see it.

I worked from 8 p.m. until 2:45 a.m. Before I left three more buses rolled in and they were almost out of room. People were standing outside, the lowest of the low from N.O. The smells, the sights were hard to take. A man lying down on a cot asked me to come see him. He said, "I just need someone to talk to, to tell my story because I have nobody and nothing left." He turned out to be a retired military veteran. His story was what everybody was saying. He thought he survived the worst, woke up this morning and the levees broke. Within minutes water rushed into his house. He climbed to the attic, smashed his way through the roof and sat there for hours. He was completely sunburned and exhausted. Nearly 12 hours later a chopper rescued him and here he was.

We finished the night hauling boxes of body bags and more were on the way. As we left, a man was rolled in on a stretcher and scarily enough he [had] suffered gunshots. The paramedic said he was shot several times because a looter or a convict needed his boat and he wouldn't give it to him. Another man with him said it was "an uncivilized society no better than Iraq down there right now." A few minutes later he was unconscious and later pronounced dead. I then left as they were rolling a three-year-old kid in on a stretcher. I couldn't take it anymore.

That was the scene at the PMAC and it gives me a new perspective on things. For those of you who I haven't been able to get in touch with because of phone service, I pray you are safe. Send me an email to let me know. God Bless.

Bill Martin
LSU Sports Information

Matt Flynn distributes LSU T-shirts to Hurricane Katrina evacuees at Baton Rouge's River Center, 2005. Bill Martin stands at right.   STEVE FRANZ, LSU SPORTS INFORMATION

to December because of Hurricane Hilda. The September 10 game with Arizona State was originally to be played as scheduled, but soon was hastily shifted to the Sun Devils' home field in Tempe. There would be grumbling among some LSU football fans, but new LSU chancellor Sean O'Keefe held firm. Evacuees were being treated in LSU's Carl Maddox Field House and Pete Maravich Assembly Center, whose basement-level auxiliary gym was converted into a morgue. Helicopters ferried in victims for days, using the Bernie Moore Track Stadium as a landing pad. "We are not going to conduct any activities that could deter from our mission of assisting in the recovery," O'Keefe said. Miles, his first season now plagued by uncertainty, agreed. "It's a football game," Miles said. "It's not necessarily ranked in the scale of what the state's experiencing."

Soon the September 10 Arizona State game was widely seen as a necessary—if far away—distraction from Katrina's death and destruction. "I think we have to go out and just play football and come back with a win," said Green, a native of the New Orleans suburb of Westwego and among the 60 percent of LSU players who came from Katrina-affected areas. A crowd of 63,210 turned out at Sun Devil Stadium, LSU's temporary "home" field, where game organizers raised over $1 million for hurricane relief. For the Tigers and their storm-tossed fans, relief wouldn't come until the game ended. It was, to say the least, a wild one. In one strange move, LSU punter Chris Jackson cocked his arm to pass to Ronnie Prude for a 12-yard gain on fourth-and-3 from the Tigers' 10. Jackson wasn't supposed to do it, and the Tigers weren't supposed to have so much trouble reining in Arizona State quarterback Sam Keller. He riddled the Tigers all night, completing 35 of 56 passes for 461 yards and four touchdowns, helping the Sun Devils take a 17–7 lead going into the fourth quarter.

That's when the game really began. Wroten blocked Jesse Ainsworth's 47-yard field-goal attempt, which Mario Stevenson picked out of midair for a 55-yard touchdown return. Then Hester nailed ASU punter Chris MacDonald on a rollout punt, forcing a fumble that Craig Steltz returned 29 yards for a score. The lead would change hands three more times before LSU faced fourth-and-10 at the ASU 39 with just over a minute left. Russell rolled right, sensed pressure, spun to his left, and flung a pass into the corner of the end zone for wide receiver Early Doucet. Doucet had dropped three passes earlier that night but hung onto this one for the winning score in a 35–31 thriller with just 1:13 remaining. "It was designed to get a first down," Russell said, "but they came after me and I just improvised."

Improvisation seemed to be the word for the entire season. LSU was supposed to host Tennessee on September 24, but early that morning Hurricane Rita stormed ashore on the Texas-Louisiana border south of Lake Charles. The game was pushed back two days, setting up a *Monday Night Football* en-

Fats Finds a Home

It was one of the few bright spots in the gloom and despair following Hurricane Katrina: New Orleans music legend Fats Domino was alive, and he was living in JaMarcus Russell's apartment.

For days after Katrina struck, most of the world didn't know whether Domino, who still lived in the storm-ravaged Ninth Ward neighborhood where he grew up, survived or not. It turned out he was rescued from the balcony of his home, was transported first to the Superdome then on to the Pete Maravich Assembly Center like so many other evacuees, and was processed there under his given name: Antonie Domino. Russell, who was dating Domino's granddaughter, came across the rock and roll hall-of-famer while volunteering at the PMAC. Soon, Fats and about twenty family members were heading out to Russell's off-campus apartment on Highland Road. Shortly before Domino left, LSU Sports Information director Michael Bonnette got a phone call from Russell. "Fats Domino's here," Russell said. "What did you say?" Bonnette asked incredulously. "Yeah, Fats Domino has been staying with me for two days. We're trying to keep it under wraps, but we wanted to let people know he was safe and here." Bonnette and LSU photographer Steve Franz rushed over and got this photograph of Domino and Russell before the music icon departed. "Tell the people of New Orleans that I'm safe," Domino told Bonnette. "I wish I was able to still be there with them, but I hope to see them soon." With that, Domino and three carloads of relatives were off to parts unknown.

Ain't that a shame.

Fats Domino and JaMarcus Russell say good-bye as Domino leaves after a two-day stay in Russell's apartment following Hurricane Katrina.

STEVE FRANZ, LSU SPORTS INFORMATION

Desert fox: Early Doucet hauls in a 39-yard, fourth-down pass to beat Arizona State, 2005.

STEVE FRANZ, LSU SPORTS INFORMATION

counter on ESPN2 between No. 4 LSU and No. 10 Tennessee. LSU built a 21–0 lead on a 10-yard run by Addai, a 1-yard keeper by Russell, and a 3-yard interception return by Kenny Hollis when Tennessee quarterback Erik Ainge flung the ball out of his end zone under pressure. Ainge was so ineffective (7 of 19 for 54 yards) and the Volunteers so far behind, Tennessee coach Phillip Fulmer figured he had nothing to lose sending former LSU quarterback Rick Clausen out for the second half. Clausen, who left LSU after the 2002 season, picked the Tigers apart with short, accurate passes, forcing overtime with a 24–24 tie. In the extra frame LSU had to settle for a 31-yard Colt David field goal. Tennessee drove inexorably for a 1-yard touchdown run by Gerald Riggs for a 30–27 victory.

There were more anxious moments five days later at Mississippi State. The Bulldogs grabbed a quick 7–0 lead on a 66-yard pass from Omarr Conner to wide-open Joey Sanders—but that was all. State gained 80 yards on its first drive but just 149 the rest of the way as LSU rolled again 37–7. Xavier Carter put LSU up for good 10–7 on a 36-yard run late in the first quarter, followed by a pair of Russell-to-Bowe touchdown passes in the second and third quarters, covering 14 and 44 yards. "We couldn't get them on the ground," State coach Sylvester Croom lamented.

Another road trip, this one to Vanderbilt on October 8, lay ahead before the Tigers came home for two tough games with Florida and Auburn. The 4–1 Commodores promised to be no traditional pushover, led by quarterback Jay Cutler, soon to be a first-round draft pick in 2006 by the Denver Broncos. But LSU's rapidly improving defense harassed Cutler throughout, sacking him five times and allowing him to complete a feeble 11 of 32 passes for 113 yards with two interceptions in a 34–6 Tiger romp. "They determined what we did," Vandy wide receiver Erik Davis said. "My hat goes off to them."

The Florida Gators were 5–1 and ranked No. 11 coming into Tiger Stadium on October 15, while 3–1 LSU was No. 10. After LSU completed its 21–17 victory, first-year Florida coach Urban Meyer was moved to tears, and Miles sounded like he wanted to tear into his team over the Tigers' five turnovers and 11 penalties. "I'm coming after somebody," he snarled. Meyer was weepy over seeing quarterback Chris Leak, who beat LSU's BCS champions as a freshman in 2003, battered and bruised by a defense that sacked him five times and held him to 11 of 30 passing for 107 yards. Florida came in leading the SEC with 258.2 yards passing per game. "Obviously," Meyer said, "our throw game was nonexistent." Addai had 156 yards rushing on a career-high 32 carries, including a 3-yard game-winning touchdown run with 12:35 left.

By 2005, Auburn had grown into LSU's most intense rivalry, defined by a string of taught, critically important games. The winner had gone on to the SEC championship game four of the previous five years, and a combination of crazy earthquakes, interceptions, burning buildings, and smoking cigars gave the series its color. "You know they don't like us," Williams said. "Their fans don't like us, our fans don't like them. It's always a passionate game." For the second year in a row, this one came down to Auburn kicker John Vaughn's foot, but this time Ronnie Prude didn't fall on Auburn snapper Pete Compton to give Vaughn a shot at redemption. On October 22 before a crowd of 92,664, the largest to that point in Tiger Stadium thanks to the new west upper deck, LSU struck first on a 66-yard punt return by Green with 5:20 left in the first quarter. A Vaughn field goal and a 74-yard bolt by Kenny Irons put Auburn up 10–7 in the third quarter. LSU bounced back to go up 14–10 on an 18-yard Russell-to-Bowe strike before Auburn's Anthony Mix grabbed what looked like the winning score on a 5-yard, fourth-and-goal pass from Brandon Cox with 4:52 left in regulation. LSU forced overtime with a 44-yard field goal by Jackson with 1:40 left, then settled for a 30-yard Jackson three-pointer in overtime. An Auburn touchdown could have ended it but the LSU defense stiffened, bringing Vaughn out for a 39-yard field-goal try. The kick looked good at first, but clanged high off the left upright to make LSU a 20–17 winner. "It was a good snap, good hold," Vaughn said. "I've got to come up bigger than that."

Because of Katrina, LSU's only midseason open date, Ocotber 29, was now filled by the North Texas game postponed from September 3. The Tigers paid North Texas a $500,000 guarantee and $50,000 each to Louisiana–Lafayette and Louisiana–Monroe to juggle their games with the Mean Green to accommodate the switch. It proved to be money well spent, as the Tigers took a break from the SEC wars to manhandle the visitors 56–3. A week later, LSU eased past Division I-AA foe Appalachian State 24-0, needing a 9-yard Russell-to–Keith Zinger touchdown pass and a 34-yard field goal by Jackson in the fourth quarter to pad an uneasy 14–0 lead. The Mountaineers went on to prove why they were such a tough out, winning the next three I-AA championships and posting an epic upset of Michigan to open the 2007 season.

The two nonconference wins set up the biggest game of the year: a battle royal in Tuscaloosa on November 12 between No. 4 Alabama (9–0, 6–0 in the SEC) and No. 5 LSU (7–1, 4–1 in the SEC). Victory would lock up the SEC West for the Crimson Tide, or put LSU in charge with two games to go. A defensive struggle seemed likely—Alabama led the nation allowing just 8.2 points per game, while LSU was sixth at 13.9. The Tide appeared to have all the points it would need in the first half, taking a 10–0 lead on a 28-yard Jamie Christensen field goal and an 8-yard touchdown pass from Brodie Croyle to DJ Hall. It could have been worse: Alabama held a 196–31 advantage in total yards and a 12–2 edge in first downs. "Halftime was hectic," Bowe said. "Coach [Miles] came out there, screamed at us, told us we needed to be calm, collected and don't worry about anything else but the game." To make sure his players weren't confused by the contradictory message, he told them one more thing: "Play LSU ball." The Tigers took the second-half kickoff and marched 80 yards for a 1-yard run by Vincent on fourth-and-goal. LSU's defense pinned Bama deep, forced a punt, and allowed the Tigers to tie the game 10–10 with a 42-yard field goal by Jackson. Neither team scored again until overtime, when Bama opened on offense first but could only manage a 35-yard field goal by Christensen. In the huddle on third-and-6 from the 11, Bowe pleaded with Russell to look his way, though he had dropped key passes in the fourth quarter against Auburn and again Saturday. "Just keep coming back to me," Bowe said. "I'm hot." Russell did just that, firing a heat-seeking missile over the middle that found Bowe for the winning points. "We felt going into overtime that we would win because of the kind of football team we are," said Miles, the first LSU coach ever to beat Florida, Auburn, and Alabama in the same season.

Now 8–1 overall and 5–1 in the SEC, the Tigers needed two more wins to go to Atlanta to play for the SEC title. The first was easy to come by—the

Dwayne Bowe cradles the game-winning pass from JaMarcus Russell in overtime at Alabama, 2005. KENT GIDLEY, ALABAMA SPORTS INFORMATION

Tigers overwhelmed Ole Miss 40–7 in Oxford on November 19, holding the Rebels to seven net yards rushing and 175 yards overall. The second would take considerably more work. At 4–6 overall and 2–5 in the SEC, Arkansas had already given up its postseason hopes. Now the Razorbacks were out to wreck LSU's plans. They almost succeeded in the regular-season finale on November 25. The Tigers appeared well on their way to a win, going up 19–3 with 10:40 left in the third quarter on a 4-yard touchdown run by Vincent. But in a span of less than nine minutes the Razorbacks cut the deficit to 19–17 on a 29-yard pass from Casey Dick to Cedric Washington and a 1-yard run by Darren McFadden. LSU had to repel three Arkansas drives over the final 10 minutes, the last threat snuffed out when Landry intercepted Dick near the goal line with 57 seconds left. The difference ended up being a second-quarter safety when Doucet fell on Arkansas punter Jacob Skinner in the end zone after a faulty snap.

How narrow was the margin of success for the 2005 Tigers? LSU was 10–1, ranked No. 3, and headed to the SEC championship game to face No.

With the rebuilt west upper deck, Tiger Stadium seated 92,400 by 2005.

13 Georgia at the end of a season in which six of its games were decided by four points or less, three of them in overtime. "I think just playing football by itself takes years off your life," said center Rudy Niswanger, who won the Draddy Trophy that season as college football's top student-athlete. "I don't know how many more of these my ticker can handle." Niswanger's ticker was in luck: the Tigers were about to make two straight trips to the Georgia Dome, and neither game would qualify as heart-pounding—just poundings.

Going into Championship Saturday on December 3, LSU still held out slim hopes that either unbeaten No. 1 Southern California or unbeaten No. 2 Texas would slip up and allow the Tigers to play for the national title in the Rose Bowl. Neither happened, as USC crushed UCLA 66–19 and Texas annihilated Colorado 70–3 in the Big 12 championship game. Just as well, because LSU was thoroughly dominated by Georgia, 34–14. The Bulldogs blitzed to a quick 14–0 lead on a pair of long touchdown passes from D.J. Shockley to Sean Bailey, taking advantage of an LSU secondary depleted by injuries. Craig Steltz had to start at strong safety for Jessie Daniels, while Jonathan

Zenon played an expanded role to help cornerback Chevis Jackson. Russell scored on a 1-yard keeper in the second, but the Tigers still trailed 21–7 at intermission. Any hopes of a second-half rally were snuffed out when Russell went down with a separated left (non-throwing) shoulder that would keep him out of the bowl game. Georgia finished with just a 250–230 edge in total offense but seemed to capitalize on every mistake, including a 15-yard interception return for a touchdown off of Flynn by Tim Jennings. "They did everything well on both sides of the ball," Green said, "and we struggled to do anything well."

The loss sent LSU tumbling down through the SEC's bowl hierarchy, as the three bowls below the Sugar picked teams the Tigers beat during the regular season. The Capital One Bowl took 9–2 Auburn because LSU had been there the year before. The Cotton Bowl picked 9–2 Alabama, its first time there in twenty-four years, despite a personal trip by Miles and Bertman to Dallas in the days before the SEC championship game that drew criticism from LSU fans because of its "what if we lose?" overtones. The Outback Bowl picked 8–3 Florida because Gators fans were expected to make the short drive to Tampa and buy plenty of tickets. Still ranked No. 10 nationally, the Tigers were in danger of dropping to the Independence or Music City Bowl before the Chick-fil-A Peach Bowl stepped in and invited LSU to play No. 9 Miami (9–2) on December 30. "The [SEC] championship game loser should not fall to where they are not playing a top-ranked team," Peach Bowl president Gary Stokan said.

Peach Bowl officials were not completely disappointed—this was the first matchup of top-10 teams in the bowl's 38-year history. The question was whether the Tigers could live up to their part. Russell was definitely out and didn't even make the trip for disciplinary reasons. Making his first start would be Flynn, taking on a speedy Miami defense that allowed more than 17 points only once all season. With Doucet also out with an ankle injury, the Tigers looked the part of a serious underdog. Instead, a season that started with hurricanes ended with the complete domination of the Hurricanes, as LSU crushed Miami 40–3. Flynn earned MVP honors, completing 13 of 22 passes for 196 yards and two touchdowns, including a brilliant 51-yard bomb to Davis that helped LSU build a 20–3 halftime lead. When Flynn—a much better runner than Russell—wasn't throwing, he was weaving through disheartened Miami defenders for 39 yards on five carries. The revitalized LSU running game piled up 272 yards led by Addai, soon to be a first-round draft pick of the Indianapolis Colts. Finally recovered from an ankle injury he suffered against Florida, a fresh and physical Addai had 130 yards on 24 carries, including a 6-yard touchdown run in the third. The Tigers outgained the 'Canes 468–153 in LSU's biggest-ever margin of victory in a bowl game and Miami's worst bowl defeat. "They met their part of the bargain," Miami coach Larry Coker said of LSU. Marring the outcome was a fight that started when Bowe, a Miami native, was ribbing a Miami player after the game. Two of the Hurricanes were left unconscious in the brawl. Despite the melee, the coaches ranked 11–2 LSU No. 5 in their final poll, while the Associated Press voters had the Tigers at No. 6.

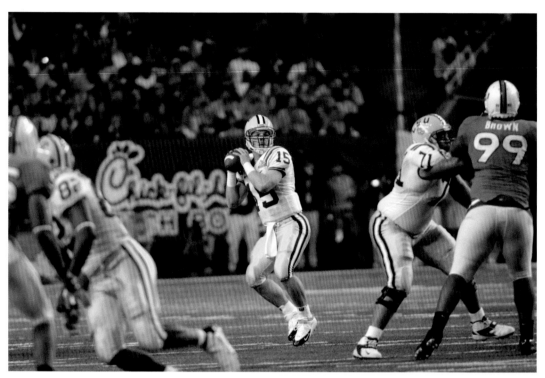

Chick-fil-A Peach Bowl MVP Matt Flynn drops back to pass against Miami, 2005.

STEVE FRANZ, LSU SPORTS INFORMATION

Sweet Enough

The months between the Peach Bowl and LSU's September 2 opener with Louisiana–Lafayette were, to say the least, eventful. First, Miles had to begin to fill the holes left by the departure of the most successful senior class in LSU history—51 wins over five years, a BCS national championship, and two SEC titles. He needed a strong recruiting class and got it, a top-10 haul highlighted by Al Woods of Elton, Louisiana, the nation's No. 1 defensive tackle; wide receiver and baseball center fielder Jared Mitchell; running backs Charles Scott and Richard Murphy; and speedster Trindon Holliday, counting against the 2006 class because he wasn't academically qualified in 2005. Two days after the signing period began, Lafayette running back Keiland Williams, who spent the 2005 season at Hargrave Military Academy in Virginia, chose LSU over Southern California to complete the class. Over the next two months Baton Rouge was enveloped in basketball fever as the LSU men's and women's basketball teams marched through the madness to their respective Final Fours. It was a thrilling ride, but soon LSU fans were consumed again by talk of the upcoming season, talk that almost always seemed to begin and end with questions about who would be the Tigers' starting quarterback: junior JaMarcus Russell, classmate Matt Flynn, or redshirt freshman Ryan Perrilloux. Whoever was behind center, he would have to deal with two new significant clock rules. To speed up play, the clock would now start when the ball was kicked on kickoffs instead of when the receiving team touched it, and the clock would start on the referee's ready-for-play signal, not when the ball was snapped. It was estimated a dozen or more plays per game would be sacrificed.

The questions even followed Miles home, when he returned from his USO trip to Iraq and Kuwait to find his wife asleep. "So tell me," Kathy supposedly asked him, "Who you going to play at quarterback?" Miles delighted in telling the joke as he toured the South in the weeks leading up to the season.

The question had only one answer. Flynn had experience. Perrilloux had promise. But Russell had sheer talent and perhaps the strongest arm in football, college or pro. How strong? At SEC Football Media Days, senior wide receiver Dwayne Bowe had reporters scribbling furiously when he described putting Russell's arm to the test. "He threw it about 75 yards," Bowe said. On one knee. Standing or with a running start, "he could probably throw it the length of the field," Bowe said.

The legend grew in the season opener

> ### In the Danger Zone
>
> What would happen, Les Miles asked the USO staffer accompanying him, if they went outside the perimeter of the U.S. military base in Iraq they were visiting? "In 10 minutes we'd be shot and killed," the USO worker replied. Danger was an ever-present companion, but in June 2006 Miles went anyway, taking part in a USO-sponsored tour to visit bases in Iraq and Kuwait. "I got more from my trip than I could possibly have given," Miles said. "I'm very grateful that I was allowed to go over and represent a very common thought here, which is thanks."
>
> It took two years for Miles to get permission to visit American troops in the war zone. When it came, Les needed a final okay from wife Kathy and their four children, Kathryn, Manny, Ben, and 2-year-old Macy Grace, who asked, "Daddy, are you going to take me to Di-rack with you?" A few days later, Les was flying over Baghdad in a Blackhawk helicopter. When he told the C-130 pilot flying him out of Iraq about the helicopter ride, Miles recalled, "he said, 'You flew in a helicopter out of Baghdad? That would scare me to death.' I said, 'You know what? Me, too.'" Miles said he came back not questioning whether what he was doing was important, but with a renewed desire to do it well. "It brings a desire to be excellent," he said. "With the price that's being paid for our civil liberties and our freedoms, we should fully enjoy what we have."

as Russell threw sparingly but effectively, completing 13 of 17 passes for 253 yards and three touchdowns in an easy 45–3 victory for No. 8-ranked LSU over Louisiana–Lafayette. Flynn and Perrilloux played, too, and cornerback Zenon punctuated a trademark stifling night for the LSU defense (the Tigers outgained the Ragin' Cajuns 469–176) with a 20-yard interception return in the first quarter. LSU's depth was clearly evident. The Tigers possessed not only three quality quarterbacks but also three NFL-caliber receivers, the "Three Amigos" Bowe, fellow senior Buster Davis, and junior Early Doucet. The tailback spot was five deep with senior Justin Vincent trying to recapture the glory of his 2003 freshman season, but sharing the load with a repaired Alley Broussard, Jacob Hester, and freshmen Scott and Williams. Another year, another pair of All-Americans on LSU's defense, this time senior free safety LaRon Landry, a four-year starter, and defensive tackle Glenn Dorsey, who didn't even break into the starting lineup the year before.

Except that the game was in Tiger Stadium instead of Tucson, a week-two encounter on September 9 had the familiar feel of the game LSU played at Arizona in 2003. Back then, the Tigers manhandled the Wildcats 59–13 in a game that was supposed to provide a sterner test. This game was billed the same way and again LSU dominated, winning 45–3 for the second week in a row. The Tigers brutalized the Wildcats, with Tyson Jackson knocking Arizona quarterback Willie Tuitama loopy with a helmet-to-helmet hit on the game's first play. Jackson drew a roughing-the-passer penalty, but a message was sent. "It was real important that the defense come out and let them know they were in Tiger Stadium and nothing was going to be easy," Dorsey said unapologetically. "We stepped up in class to the heavyweight division," Arizona coach Mike Stoops said. "We didn't handle it very well."

Everything that happened in the first two games resembled an NFL team's preseason schedule. LSU at Auburn on September 16 was for real. On a Showdown Saturday featuring, among others, No. 11 Michigan at No. 2 Notre Dame, No. 7 Florida at No. 13 Tennessee, and No. 15 Oklahoma at No. 18 Oregon, No. 6 LSU at No. 3 Auburn represented the biggest game in America. By day's end, the game represented the height of frustration for LSU as it came up on the short end of a 7–3 score. A series of calls, four in particular, went against LSU, drawing bitter complaints from Baton Rouge that echoed the rest of the season:

- In the first quarter, Russell lobbed a pass in the right flat to Hester on fourth-and-1 at the Auburn 33. Hester was ruled to have made a catch, but the replay official said Hester never had possession.
- Just before halftime, Russell threw for Brandon LaFell in the end zone. Auburn cornerback David Irons appeared to hold LaFell as the ball arrived, but there was no flag. LSU settled for a 42-yard Colt David field goal and a 3–0 halftime lead.
- Early in the fourth quarter, strong safety Jessie Daniels intercepted a Brandon Cox pass but cornerback Daniel Francis was called for pass interference, negating the turnover.
- The big one. Trailing Auburn 7–3 with 2:43 remaining, Russell threw incomplete for Doucet at the 3. Zach Gilbert was initially flagged for pass

interference, a 15-yard penalty that would have given LSU a first down at the Auburn 16. But the call was waved off because safety Eric Brock tipped the ball as it came in. LSU got it back, but Davis was tackled by Brock at the 4 as time expired.

Good play or bad call? Auburn's Zach Gilbert collides with Early Doucet in the closing minutes against Auburn, 2006.   STEVE FRANZ, LSU SPORTS INFORMATION

"If somebody would have told me that we would have won the turnover battle [1–0] and we'd have outgained our opponent [311–182], you'd have thought we'd have won," Miles said. "It wasn't meant to be." After getting home and reviewing the tape of what he thought were questionable calls—LSU took issue with a dozen in all—Miles wasn't so magnanimous. "Hopefully my view of the officials in this conference gets better," Miles said. New SEC coordinator of football officials Rogers Redding stood by his crew. "The score of the game is not going to change," Skip Bertman said.

Fortunately for LSU, the Tigers didn't have another blockbuster game immediately on the horizon, just a new look at its oldest rival. The game on September 23 was the first of a home-and-home series between LSU and Tulane to run through 2015. LSU would pay Tulane $600,000 for each of the first four games of the series in Tiger Stadium, and $650,000 for the last one in 2015. For games at the Superdome, LSU would keep the revenue from the sale of 40,000 tickets. The Tigers opened the series with a rush, Doucet scoring on a 12-yard pass from Russell and a 17-yard run in the first quarter. They hooked up on a 4-yard touchdown pass in the second quarter as LSU built a 28–0 halftime lead en route to a 49–7 victory. LSU returned to SEC play a week later as it hosted Mississippi State, but again the challenge was minimal, the Tigers routing the Bulldogs 48–17. Russell was pinpoint accurate, completing 18 of 20 passes for 330 yards and a touchdown to each of the Three Amigos. "This game made a statement," Davis said. "Stack the box all you want to stop the run, but you better respect our passing game. We're going to hurt you downfield if you focus too much on our run."

That's if the Tigers weren't too busy hurting themselves. Next, No. 9-ranked LSU (4–1, 1–1 in the SEC) traveled to face No. 5 Florida (5–0, 3–0 in the SEC) on October 7, the first time the Tigers and Gators had played each other when both ranked in the top 10. When it was over, only Florida belonged after a 23–10 victory. Again, a crucial call didn't go the Tigers' way—Hester appeared to score by rolling over a Florida defender at the goal line but was ruled down at the 1. On the next play, Russell fumbled the snap, one of LSU's five turnovers. Once again, the Tigers were victimized by a freshman Florida quarterback—this one named Tim Tebow. He helped the Gators score 16 straight points without LSU running an offensive play, throwing a 1-yard jump pass touchdown to Tate Casey just before halftime and a 35-yard play-action pass to Louis Murphy in the third. The touchdowns bookended Doucet's fumble of the opening second-half kickoff that led to a Florida safety. "The turnovers took a lot of air out of us," kicker Chris Jackson said.

Now 4–2 and ranked No. 16, the Tigers took out their frustrations on October 14 on visiting Kentucky. Reprising their efforts against Louisiana–Lafayette and Arizona, LSU returned home and blasted the Wildcats 49–0. Once again the Tigers started strong, racing to a 28–0 halftime lead on a pair of touchdown runs by Hester and a pair of Russell-to-Bowe touchdown passes. LSU had nine ball carriers who ran for 268 yards and seven receivers who caught for 278. "We had the balance that we're looking for," Miles said, "both run and pass. We didn't have a turnover. We played like we were supposed to."

The Tigers stepped out of conference to take on Fresno State on October 21 in another made-for-TV matchup, this one on ESPN2. The Bulldogs were typically one of the most rugged of the "mid-majors," taking on BCS powers like LSU with an "anytime, anywhere" mentality. This wasn't a vintage Fresno State team, however, limping into Tiger Stadium with a 1–5 record. The Bulldogs limped out at 1–6 after a 38–6 defeat. LSU was off and running after a 38-yard run by Holliday and a 77-yard punt return by Davis for a 14–0 LSU lead before the first quarter ended.

Saddled with an 0–2 road record, the Tigers ventured on November 4 to a place where their success was rarer than snow in south Louisiana: Knoxville, Tennessee. In thirteen trips there, LSU was 1–11–1, its only victory coming in 1988. Now facing a No. 8-ranked Tennessee team revving up dreams of another championship run, LSU saw a rocky path to victory ahead. But LSU did win, 28–24, in a game that exemplified everything great and frustrating about JaMarcus Russell's boundless talent. Russell nearly cost LSU the game with three interceptions, two of them badly conceived attempts to thread passes through Tennessee defenders, the third a high lob returned for a touchdown early in the third quarter. But Russell was also the reason LSU won. It was Russell who calmly waited, waited, waited in the pocket until Doucet popped open on a 4-yard touchdown pass with 9 seconds remaining. "I'd say for myself," Russell offered casually, "I kind of proved myself today." He ended up completing 24 of 36 passes for 247 yards and was LSU's leading rusher with seven carries for 71 yards on a series of unscripted scrambles. "He's an amazing guy to play with," center Brett Helms said. "He's one of the best athletes I've ever seen. He makes mistakes, but so what? He knows how to keep his head on."

The Tigers had won five of their last six games against Alabama, and had finally rediscovered the ability to beat the Crimson Tide in Tiger Stadium.

Early Doucet cradles the winning pass from JaMarcus Russell at Tennessee, 2006.

STEVE FRANZ, LSU SPORTS INFORMATION

Bama wasn't the unbeaten juggernaut LSU took down in Tuscaloosa the year before, but at 6–4 it was still good enough to give the Tigers a test. LSU did just enough to hold back the Tide in a 28–14 win on November 11. The Tigers bolted to a 14–0 first-quarter lead on a 38-yard run by Keiland Williams and a 30-yard Russell-to-Doucet pass, but Bama wouldn't fold. Twice John Parker Wilson—who threw for 291 of Bama's 369 yards to repeatedly confound the nation's No. 1 defense—brought the Tide within a touchdown. But LSU's defense stiffened in the second half, the only scoring of the final two quarters on a 17-yard middle screen from Russell to Hester with 7:14 left in the third quarter. It was the second game of a regular season–ending three-game losing streak for Alabama, a losing streak that would cost former Bama quarterback Mike Shula his job and open the door for a man LSU fans figured never to see again in the college game—Nick Saban.

The Tigers were now 13–0 under Miles against unranked opponents, usually taking them out of it early. But unranked Ole Miss took the fight to an unsuspecting LSU team on November 18, leading 20–7 in the third quarter to make the crowd of 92,449 fans squirm in their seats. The Tigers pulled within 20–14 with 8:46 left on a 4-yard Russell-to-Doucet pass, but as the final moments ticked away, LSU faced a desperate fourth-and-goal at the 5. In need, where did Russell look? Right at Bowe, zipping a touchdown pass to him with 14 seconds left. The scoring strike was the 22nd between the two, eclipsing Tommy Hodson and Wendell Davis as the most prolific touchdown passing duo in LSU history. It appeared to give LSU victory, but John Jerry blocked David's extra-point try to force overtime. In the extra period, Daniel Francis stripped the ball from Ole Miss quarterback Brent Schaeffer, allowing LSU to escape with a 23–20 win with a 26-yard field goal by David.

Although his team faced a short week preparing for the now-typical Friday-after-Thanksgiving season finale with Arkansas, Miles flew to Ann Arbor, Michigan, on Monday morning to pay his respects to his mentor: Bo Schembechler. The legendary Michigan coach died November 17, the day before unbeaten No. 2 Michigan faced unbeaten No. 1 Ohio State. "We all are subject to personal needs and wants," Miles said candidly. "I needed to get back there and pay tribute to someone very influential in my life." Miles had to know he was opening himself to criticism if the Tigers didn't win. Again, the road looked treacherous. No. 5-ranked Arkansas (10–1, 7–0 in the SEC), the fourth top-10 team LSU had faced in as many road games, had already clinched a trip to the SEC championship game. LSU was playing for pride—and possibly a different prize.

In mid-November, Pasadena Tournament of Roses chairman Paul Holman visited Baton Rouge to extend an invitation to the Rose Parade to a local high school marching band. During his visit, Holman and Miles met at a gathering at the home of Shaw Group CEO Jim Bernhard, where Miles expressed LSU's desire to play in the Rose Bowl. Holman said the Rose would enjoy having LSU, but that it would take an unlikely series of events to bring LSU to California for the game. Just in case, though, LSU began taking orders from season-ticket holders for any bowl it was possible for the Tigers to play in—including the Rose.

LSU was heading somewhere special down the holiday road, thanks in part to Trindon Holliday. Moments after Arkansas running back Darren Mc-Fadden, runner-up for the 2006 Heisman Trophy, sprinted up the middle on an 80-yard touchdown run to cut the Tigers' lead to 24–19, Holliday zoomed 92 yards up the LSU sideline with the ensuing kickoff for a 31–19 advantage with 10:14 remaining. Felix Jones came back and scored on a 5-yard run to make it 31–26 with 4:53 left. But when Arkansas got the ball back one last time, it didn't put McFadden behind quarterback in the Wild Hog formation that had vexed LSU all day. Casey Dick threw four straight incompletions and LSU ran out the final 1:31 to finish 10–2 and lay claim to the unofficial title of best in the West. "It was our championship game," Doucet said. "I think we showed who is the real SEC West champion."

If you had told LSU fans when the Tigers were 4–2 that they would go to the Allstate Sugar Bowl and play Notre Dame, they would have been grateful

Trindon Holliday revs up on his 92-yard kickoff return at Arkansas, 2006.

and giddy. But in the week after the Arkansas game it became more and more apparent that LSU, which rose to No. 5 in the second-to-last BCS poll, was seriously on the Rose Bowl's radar. One reason: a bowl full of ticket orders. Tiger fans, sensing a potential once-in-a-lifetime trip to Pasadena, put in orders for 42,600 tickets before LSU cut sales off the day before the SEC championship game between Florida and Arkansas on December 2. It appeared that if Southern California would beat UCLA in their regular-season finale that day, the No. 2-ranked Trojans would go to the inaugural BCS national championship game in Glendale, Arizona, to play No. 1 Ohio State, opening a slot for a highly ranked team in the Rose likely opposite Miles's alma mater, Michigan. Then, the unlikely series of events crowned LSU's Rose Bowl hopes with thorns. First, UCLA upset USC 13–9, sending the Trojans to the Rose Bowl. LSU could still have gone to play USC if Michigan stayed in the BCS top two, but Florida's 38–28 win over Arkansas in the SEC championship game did just enough to push the Gators past the Wolverines into the national title game. That sent Michigan to the Rose Bowl and shut the door on No. 4 LSU, which was quickly snapped up by the Sugar Bowl to play No. 11 Notre Dame. "You want to celebrate a great season with a quality opponent, and Notre Dame, any way you cut it, is a quality opponent," Miles said. Still, the whole experience was bittersweet for LSU.

JaMarcus Russell throws for 332 yards and two touchdowns against Notre Dame in the All-state Sugar Bowl, 2007. STEVE FRANZ, LSU SPORTS INFORMATION

Sugar Bowl MVP JaMarcus Russell.

STEVE FRANZ, LSU SPORTS INFORMATION

Among its many facets, the 73rd Allstate Sugar Bowl on January 3 looked like an audition for the No. 1 overall pick in the 2007 NFL draft between Notre Dame quarterback Brady Quinn and LSU's JaMarcus Russell, who was all but certain to forgo his senior season. Russell won the matchup and the game, earning MVP honors as he led LSU to an easy 41–14 victory. Quinn tied the game 14–14 in the second with a 10-yard touchdown pass to favorite receiver Jeff Samardzija, but was under attack the rest of the way by LSU's defense. Quinn completed just 15 of 35 passes for 148 yards with two interceptions. Russell completed 21 of 34 passes for 332 yards and two touchdowns—one last touchdown toss going to Bowe for 11 yards in the first quarter. Russell's signature play came late in the third quarter when he was drilled in the midsection by Irish defensive tackle Trevor Laws and still hit LaFell with a perfect 58-yard strike for a touchdown. "Just average," Davis said when asked to rate Russell's performance, "but an average game by JaMarcus Russell is better than your usual quarterback."

With another 11–2 finish, the Tigers wound up No. 3 in the final polls, behind only national champ Florida and Ohio State. It marked LSU's first back-to-back top-five finishes since 1958–59 and first-ever back-to-back seasons of 10 wins or more.

Ranked fifth in the final 2005 coaches' poll. Third to end the 2006 campaign. As 2007 began, the LSU Tigers and Tiger fans everywhere knew what continuing that stair-step progression would mean and where it could lead them: back to the top of the college football world, and back to the Superdome for the BCS national championship game.

Few doubted the Tigers could make it. Few could have imagined that their path to glory would be perhaps the most dramatic chapter in LSU football history.

7

FOREVER LSU

2007

LSU football is a cradle-to-grave love affair. Weddings are planned to coincide with weekends when LSU is on the road. Births, when possible, are scheduled so they don't conflict with home games. Coffins are lined with purple-and-gold items in hopes that you can really take it with you—and to guard against the possibility that heaven doesn't get ESPN. Every year, LSU officials are asked for permission to sprinkle a loved one's ashes over Tiger Stadium's eternally green grass.

The passion for LSU football never really goes away. But as the 2006 season ended with the Tigers' emphatic 41–14 victory over Notre Dame in the Allstate Sugar Bowl, the victory seemed to be only the jumping-off point to a year of unprecedented anticipation of another championship season in Tigertown. A season that would bring victories, and one dramatic moment after another.

The drama started in the hours before the Fighting Tigers dispatched the Fighting Irish in the Superdome on January 3. Earlier that day, the news broke that former LSU coach Nick Saban was returning to college football after two up-and-down NFL seasons with the Miami Dolphins. And not to just any college program, but to Alabama, LSU's SEC Western Division rival. On the streets of New Orleans that day, anger with Saban, LSU's one-time savior, was evident as his return to the SEC threatened to steal some of the Tigers' Sugar Bowl thunder. "He could have at least stayed out of the SEC," said one fan. Even before the Sugar Bowl kicked off, fans were figuring out that November 3, the date LSU was to visit Alabama in 2007, would be not only circled in red but dripping crimson. "I look forward to seeing [Saban] in Tuscaloosa next year so we can beat him," LSU chancellor Sean O'Keefe said with a laugh.

LSU fans weren't laughing on January 10, though what happened that day seemed inevitable. JaMarcus Russell had secretly decided during the 2006 season that he was going to forgo his senior year—even though Coach Les Miles spelled out for Russell the possibility that returning in 2007 would mean a serious shot at both the national championship and the Heisman Trophy. "I'm telling momma," Russell said, "in the next couple of days or couple of months she can quit her job."

April's NFL draft brought unprecedented demand for LSU football talent. After months of speculation, Russell was indeed taken with the No. 1 overall pick by the Oakland Raiders, the first former Tiger selected first in the draft since Billy Cannon in 1960. Three other Tigers were also No. 1 picks, the most in the program's history. Free safety LaRon Landry went sixth to the Washington Redskins. Wide receiver Dwayne Bowe went 23rd to the Kansas Chiefs, while wideout Craig "Buster" Davis was taken 30th by the San Diego Chargers.

If not for a nagging shin injury, defensive tackle Glenn Dorsey could have been LSU's fifth first-rounder. But Dorsey thought the injury would hurt his draft stock. He also thought of the fans who loved him and the Tigers, and how much he loved them right back. "You see one-year-old girls at the games in cheerleader outfits," Dorsey said. "She doesn't know what's going on, but she's out there cheering us. That's what I think of when I'm tired in a game. Here's a 90-year-old guy out there at the game. He can't do much, but he's pulling for LSU. I love playing in that kind of environment. I love being around LSU."

Roscoe I

Mike V, LSU's Bengal tiger mascot, succumbed to renal failure in May 2007, prompting a nationwide search for his successor. In August, Mike VI arrived, a two-year-old Bengal-Siberian mix who grew up with the name "Roscoe" at a nonprofit sanctuary called Great Cats of Indiana. Mike VI would make his debut at the LSU-Florida game on October 6, and was expected to grow about twice the size of his predecessor—or to about 700 pounds.

Mike VI makes his first trek around Tiger Stadium before the LSU-Florida game, 2007.

STEVE FRANZ, LSU SPORTS INFORMATION

Dorsey wasn't the only experienced player the Tigers were counting on to help make LSU a contender in 2007. The Tigers returned 23 seniors—minus often-injured tailback Alley Broussard, who transferred to Division II Missouri Southern State in August. Overall, LSU returned 15 starters—and one quarterback who had paid his dues to get his chance. Matt Flynn was a redshirt freshman with Russell in 2003, watching from the sidelines as Matt Mauck quarterbacked LSU to the BCS national championship over Oklahoma. He watched in 2004 as Russell and Marcus Randall shared time behind center. Except for his brilliant pinch-hitting MVP role in the 2005 Peach Bowl when Russell was injured, Flynn had watched as Russell started through 2005 and 2006. Now with Russell gone to the NFL, the team was

Glenn Dorsey: He came back to win a championship. STEVE FRANZ, LSU SPORTS INFORMATION

finally his, and the fifth-year senior from Tyler, Texas, was eager to make the most of it. "It's been a long road," Flynn said. "I didn't really come here expecting not to play, but I've got my chance now and I can't ask for a better opportunity.

"This has a chance to be one of the best teams we've ever had at LSU."

Many observers figured highly touted sophomore Ryan Perrilloux might brush past Flynn to the starting job. But Flynn was steady, while Perrilloux flirted with off-the-field troubles all year long: a federal counterfeiting probe, an attempt to use his older brother's driver's license to board a Baton Rouge casino riverboat, and his part in a brawl at an off-campus bar. That last incident earned Perrilloux a second suspension and resulted in the dismissal of linebackers Derrick Odom and Jeremy Benton.

In some ways, the 2007 season would be a referendum on Les Miles's tenure as LSU's coach. Consecutive 11–2 records and top-five finishes—the best back-to-back seasons in Tiger history—were not enough to satisfy a faction of fans for whom the losing seasons of the late 1980s and 1990s were a fading memory. Miles, it was true, had yet to lead a glittering roster of talent to a championship. The pressure to deliver would be on, as preseason magazines and polls almost unanimously picked LSU to win the SEC and ranked the Tigers in the top two behind USC.

Miles didn't shun great expectations. Unlike Saban before him, he seemed to embrace them. In

Matt Flynn: Finally, a chance to lead.
STEVE FRANZ, LSU SPORTS INFORMATION

fact, he upped the ante on his own. Miles was criticized coast to coast for some supposedly off-the-record statements he made in June about the level of difficulty competing in the SEC as opposed to the Pac-10, where USC played. Miles's brash talk and the fact that Saban was now leading an enemy program made many LSU fans love their coach more than ever. From jokes about his high-riding hat, the Tiger faithful now coined a new phrase: "Fear the hat."

If LSU were to capture another national championship, two Tigers who helped bring home the 2003 title wouldn't be around to celebrate. Defensive end Marquise Hill, then a member of the New England Patriots, died Memorial Day weekend in a watercraft accident on Lake Pontchartrain. In July, linebacker Dave Peterson was killed in a motorcycle accident in Baton Rouge. Hill was just twenty-four, Peterson twenty-six.

In Focus

LSU's first two national championship teams went into their respective seasons unburdened by the crushing pressure of great expectations. The 1958 Tigers were ranked 35th in the preseason, not even cracking the top 10 until October. LSU's 2003 team started out No. 14 and wasn't even picked to win the SEC West. Somehow for the 2007 Tigers, there was no fear of the daunt-

Les Miles embraced LSU's great expectations.   STEVE FRANZ, LSU SPORTS INFORMATION

ing pressure facing them. This was a group of players and coaches—indeed, an entire program—used to winning and winning big. The previous seven seasons had been the greatest period of prosperity in LSU football history. The expectation that the Tigers would put the exclamation point on that success with a run at another national title bounced off their collective psyche, just like every obstacle that would be thrown in their way over the course of the season. "We don't need to play to anybody else's expectations but ours," Miles said. "Our expectations are all that we have to meet. If we play well, if we do that and have great focus, we'll do fine."

Craig Steltz returns one of his three interceptions against Mississippi State.

August 30: LSU 45, Mississippi State 0

If anything made Miles cranky, it was the fact that the no. 2 Tigers were opening with an SEC road game. An ESPN-brokered deal moved the Mississippi State game from the third Saturday of the season to Thursday, August 30, the first day of the 2007 season. Despite the Tigers' long run of success against the Bulldogs—LSU had won 14 of the last 15 against Mississippi State—an opposing SEC stadium is always a dicey place to debut a new offense. This would be the Tigers' first game under new offensive coordinator Gary Crowton—Jimbo Fisher had left to call plays at Florida State—as well as offensive line coach Greg Studrawa and wide receivers coach D. J. McCarthy. Not surprisingly, the Tigers started off cautiously, taking a 17–0 halftime lead on a 27-yard Colt David field goal and a pair of 1-yard touchdown runs by backup tailback Keiland Williams. The Tigers extended their lead to 24–0 to start the third quarter with their only sustained drive, a six-play, 73-yard march culminating with an 11-yard touchdown lob from Flynn to senior wide receiver Early Doucet. After that, the Tigers were content to let the Bulldogs dig their own hole. Senior strong safety Craig Steltz tied a school record with three of LSU's six interceptions off State quarterback Michael Henig, two of them setting up touchdowns. Miles knew his Tigers would have to improve with No. 9 Virginia Tech coming to Tiger Stadium. "Certainly we're going to have to get better," Miles said. "We understand that."

LSU fans had to come to an understanding of their own: a season of speculation about their coach and his alma mater. Appalachian State's historic 34–32 upset victory at No. 5 Michigan on September 1 set an improbable, roller-coaster season into motion—and ignited talk that Miles would replace Michigan coach Lloyd Carr.

September 8: LSU 48, Virginia Tech 7

First, LSU paid tribute to the Hokies, a team playing its first game away from its Blacksburg campus since the horrifying massacre of 32 Virginia Tech students and faculty members in April. The Golden Band from Tigerland performed Virginia Tech's alma mater before playing LSU's own and the national anthem. It was believed to be the first time LSU's band performed the other school's song before a football game.

Pregame activities were where the sentimentality ended. Before a Tiger Stadium–record crowd of 92,739, the Tigers crushed the Hokies 48–7, certainly LSU's most impressive performance of the season and arguably its best ever against a quality opponent. A 3-yard run by senior running back Jacob Hester capped a 10-play, 87-yard drive to start the game against what was the nation's No. 1-ranked defense in 2006. Flynn added a 7-yard keeper for a 14–0 lead before David tacked on a 30-yard field goal with 14:55 left in the second quarter. Then the Tigers got tricky, unholstering the "Pistol" formation, a shortened version of the shotgun where the quarterback lines up ahead of the tailback. On this play, Flynn rolled right and made a slightly awkward pitch to Williams, who was trailing too closely. Didn't hurt the play, though. Williams hurdled fullback Shawn Jordan at his 40 and set sail on a 67-yard touchdown run for a 24–0 halftime lead. Williams tacked on a 32-yard touchdown run in the fourth quarter, finishing with 126 yards rushing on just seven carries. The Tigers outgained the Hokies 598–149 and controlled the ball for 34½ minutes.

Keiland Williams hurdles teammate Shawn Jordan en route to the end zone on his 67-yard touchdown run against Virginia Tech. STEVE FRANZ, LSU SPORTS INFORMATION

"I'm not sure if this isn't the No. 1 football team in the country," Virginia Tech coach Frank Beamer said. As it turned out, Virginia Tech would finish No. 1 in the computer polls in the final BCS rankings and could have been in the BCS championship game if not for a decision made in 2004. That year, Virginia Tech backed out of a game at LSU in favor of playing in a preseason classic against USC. Had the Hokies gone to LSU three years earlier, then scheduled a beatable team at home instead of traveling to Baton Rouge in 2007, Virginia Tech might have played for the BCS title—not LSU. Instead, the Hokies ranked as one of LSU's signature wins.

September 15: LSU 44, Middle Tennessee 0

The Tigers gained a little on No. 1 USC in the polls after slamming Virginia Tech, but lost a lot to the training room. Flynn suffered the dreaded high ankle sprain on a keeper against Virginia Tech. Near the end of a Friday's workout before the Middle Tennessee game, wide receiver Early Doucet went down with a severe groin pull and would miss all but one play in the next five games. Against Middle Tennessee the LSU defense was again a star— the Tigers outgained the Blue Raiders 505–90, the fewest yards LSU allowed since 2002—but Perrilloux was the big story. He completed 20 of 25 passes

Ryan Perrilloux is pressed into starting for Matt Flynn against Middle Tennessee and throws for 298 yards and three touchdowns.   STEVE FRANZ, LSU SPORTS INFORMATION

for 298 yards with three touchdowns and an interception. David added three field goals—one of them clanging off the left upright and through from 35 yards—while redshirt freshman Richard Murphy completed the scoring with his first career touchdown on an 8-yard run. Perrilloux, who had been off limits to the media until now, toed the party line. "Without my teammates I wouldn't be at this point," he said. "They stuck with me, stayed behind me, and knew I was going to one day be able to lead this team."

September 22: LSU 28, South Carolina 16

LSU's next game with No. 12-ranked South Carolina was shrouded in anxiety. First, the weather called for slippery conditions, always an equalizer in football. Second, kickoff was moved up to 2:30 P.M. for the first of a record seven LSU games broadcast nationally on CBS in 2007, sunlight often having the same effect on the Tigers as it has on Dracula. Third, Steve Spurrier was coming to town. True, he didn't have the talent at South Carolina that he once commanded at Florida, but no one since Bear Bryant had been so dominant over the purple and gold. As the Gators' Heisman-winning quarterback (1964–66) and Florida's coach (1990–2001), Spurrier was a combined

14–1. What's more, Spurrier took pleasure in bating the opposition. Asked about LSU being the preseason favorite during SEC Media Days in August, Spurrier said: "They led in all the categories last year—offensively, defensively—yet they didn't win the conference. They didn't win much really, except their bowl game." The unspoken worry buzzing through Tiger Stadium was that Spurrier would conjure some magical plays and topple the Tigers once again.

Red Alert Roxie: Colt David heads for the end zone against South Carolina.

Instead, it was Miles and the Tigers who would pull trick-play perfection. Leading 14–7, LSU's drive stalled at the South Carolina 15 with little over a minute left before halftime, sending the kicking unit onto the field. Unknown to the Gamecocks, Flynn, the holder on David's place kicks, went out with instructions from special teams coordinator Bradley Dale Peveto to call "Red Alert Roxie" if South Carolina was in the right formation. It was. With the Gamecocks bunched in tight, Flynn barked out "Roxie!" He took the snap from Jacob O'Hair, faked a placement and flipped a no-look pass over his right shoulder to David, who took off running immediately to the right. Flynn hit David in stride, and the former Dallas-area soccer player sped untouched into the end zone while Miles laughed and Spurrier grimaced. "They got me, you're right," Spurrier admitted. "It worked perfect. Obviously when they work, it's a good call." Hearing the call didn't make David as nervous as what came after. "The nerves hit me worse after I scored the touchdown because I didn't want to miss that kick," he said. "I can't wait to watch it." Asked in December to review a season of great plays and pick their favorite, readers of *The Advocate* in Baton Rouge chose "Red Alert Roxie."

September 29: LSU 34, Tulane 9

LSU fans hoped the Tigers' first regular-season visit to the Superdome since 1994 to take on Tulane would be but a dress rehearsal for a return engagement three months later to play for the BCS national title. "That's obviously where we want to end up," Flynn said. "But we know that we're not going to get there by thinking about it." For a half against the 1–2 Green Wave, 4–0 and still No. 2 LSU made it look like playing in the national championship game would be just a dream. Either still asleep when the game kicked off at 11 A.M. or distracted by their never-before-seen uniform combination—white helmets, purple jerseys, and white pants designed to help spur souvenir sales that would go toward Hurricane Katrina relief efforts—the Tigers showed a rare lack of effort against an outclassed opponent. LSU gave up a safety when right guard Lyle Hitt was flagged for holding in the end zone, trying to keep Tulane's surprising pressure off a relatively immobile Matt Flynn. Moments later, Tulane's Andre Anderson zipped five yards around left end through a suddenly porous LSU defense to give the Green Wave a surprising 9–7 lead with 1:40 left before halftime. The Tigers regained the lead with a 36-yard Colt David field goal with three seconds left before intermission, but as they left the field Tulane players taunted that the Tigers were overrated.

Defensive end Rahim Alem sacks Tulane quarterback Anthony Scelfo.

In the second half the Tigers found their focus and took control as expected, with David adding another field goal, Hester scoring standing up from the 1, and Charles Scott breaking through on touchdown runs of 35 and 3 yards. Meanwhile, LSU's defense finally stiffened, allowing just 15 total yards in the fourth quarter. Tulane running back Matt Forte, who would finish as the nation's second-leading rusher with 2,127 yards, managed just 74 yards on 16 carries, his second-lowest total of the season. As the day unfolded, LSU's early struggles looked less and less significant. Seven of the nation's top 13 teams—No. 3 Oklahoma, No. 4 Florida, No. 5 West Virginia, No. 7 Texas, No. 10 Rutgers, No. 11 Oregon, and No. 13 Clemson—would lose that Saturday. And USC would lose its Associated Press No. 1 ranking to LSU after a shaky 27–24 win at Washington, a three-touchdown underdog. Despite 15 penalties for 91 yards and troubles pass blocking and pass catching, LSU was No. 1 in the AP poll for the first time since 1959.

October 6: LSU 28, Florida 24

In a season rife with anticipation and excitement, the Florida game stood out. Not only was ESPN's GameDay program returning to campus for the second time in a month, but CBS finally agreed to use its once-a-year prime-time slot on the contest. That made Florida the first night game in Tiger Stadium televised by an over-the-air network since the 1981 season opener against Alabama on ABC. There was also Florida itself, the reigning national champion. The Gators were coming off a 20–17 loss to Auburn that dropped them to No. 9 in the polls, taking a bit of luster off what could have been a No. 1 vs. No. 3 matchup. But still, the 4–1 Gators were led by quarterback Tim Tebow, the year's eventual Heisman Trophy winner. A record crowd of 92,910 wedged into Tiger Stadium on October 6, with another estimated 70,000 to 80,000 drawn to the campus for the party. Cars were parked as far away as City Park to the north of the campus and all the way down Burbank Drive to West Lee Drive to the south. The game would deliver excitement worthy of the setting.

Florida jumped on top early as Tebow proved to be as elusive as advertised. He rolled left from the two on what looked like another keeper early in the second quarter, only to dump a short touchdown toss to tailback Kestahn Moore for a 10–0 lead at the 13:45 mark. Clearly the Tigers would have to make the extra effort to beat the Gators. Miles elected to go for it five times on fourth down and called for Flynn to run on a fake field goal, LSU converting every time. Florida led 17–7 at halftime before Keiland Williams pulled LSU within 17–14 with a 4-yard TD run in the third, bringing a huge cheer from the LSU faithful. An even bigger cheer followed seconds later, when public-address announcer Dan Borné told the crowd that USC, still No. 1 in

A record crowd of 92,910 jams Tiger Stadium for the Florida game, with another 70,000–80,000 estimated to be on campus.   STEVE FRANZ, LSU SPORTS INFORMATION

the coaches' poll, had fallen to 41-point underdog Stanford at home 24–23 in one of the biggest upsets ever. The crowd knew the Tigers could have the top of the polls all to themselves finally, if only they could avoid the upset, too.

Tebow quickly silenced the crowd, putting Florida up 24–14 with a 37-yard touchdown pass to wide-open receiver Cornelius Ingram with 5:16 remaining in the third. Defensive end Kirston Pittman, a starter after sitting out the previous two seasons with injuries, intercepted a deflected Tebow pass at the Florida 27 that led to fourth-and-goal for LSU at the 4. This time, Flynn escaped the pass rush and found Demetrius Byrd for the touchdown with 10:15 remaining. Florida 24, LSU 21. The Tigers then got a crucial defensive stop, taking over at their 40 with 9:10 remaining. Flynn scrambled for 15 yards on third-and-16 before Hester pounded away for 2 yards to keep the drive going. Hester developed his powerful legs as a boy growing up in Shreveport in a

Glenn Dorsey closes in on Florida quarterback Tim Tebow.

drill he and his brothers would call "running the hill." They would tie a rope around their waists with an old tire at the other end and scramble up the side of an interstate embankment near their home. Those legs served him well again, as he converted another fourth down and scored on third-and-goal from the 2 with 1:09 remaining, finishing with 106 yards on 23 carries. "Things weren't going our way until the fourth quarter," Hester said. "We said that if we keep moving the ball and playing our game, everything will work out for us." It still took Chad Jones batting down a Hail Mary pass from Tebow in the end zone to secure the victory, but at last LSU was everybody's No. 1. "I enjoy the character of this football team," Miles said. "Down the road, that is what will sustain this team—character."

October 13: Kentucky 43, LSU 37 (3 OT)

The Tigers' character would be sternly tested a week later as LSU visited Kentucky's Commonwealth Stadium for the first time since the legendary Bluegrass Miracle victory in 2002. Sandwiched between home showdowns with Florida and Auburn, the trip to Kentucky looked like a trap game from the outset. Indeed, the No. 17-ranked Wildcats, led by a Heisman contender in quarterback Andre Woodson, had a lot more fight than the team LSU crushed

49–0 in Tiger Stadium a year earlier. LSU seemed to be in command again, extending a 17–14 halftime lead to 27–14 on a 4-yard Flynn-to–Richard Dickson touchdown pass and a 30-yard field goal by David. But David's 3-pointer came after a catchable pass went off the hands of tight end Keith Zinger in the back of the end zone. Kentucky stormed back to force overtime with 13 unanswered points, capped by a 27-yard Lones Seiber field goal with 4:21 left in regulation. The teams traded touchdowns in the first overtime, field goals in the second. In the third extra period, Kentucky's Steve Johnson faked LSU cornerback Jonathan Zenon off his feet to free himself up for a 7-yard touchdown catch and a 43–37 lead. LSU still had hope, especially when the Wildcats came up empty on the mandatory try for two points. The Tigers took over at their 25 and after three straight Hester runs faced fourth-and-1 at the 16. Hester had to come off with a thigh injury, leaving the ball in Charles Scott's hands. This time, the fourth-down heroics belonged to the other team as Kentucky linebacker Braxton Kelley broke through to nail Scott short of the first-down marker with a solo tackle. Kentucky fans stormed the field just as in 2002, this time with no Bluegrass Miracle to make them sound retreat. LSU's Bluegrass bummer was as much on the Tigers as it was because of Kentucky.

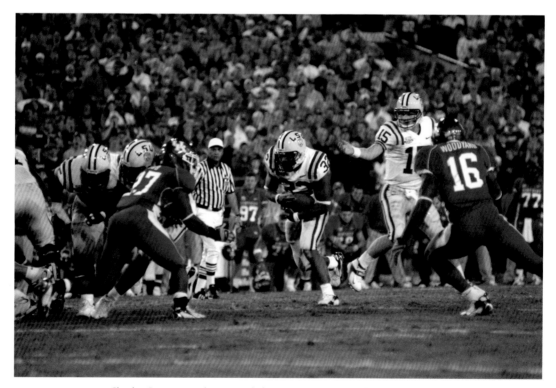

Charles Scott scored two touchdowns against Kentucky but couldn't pick up the two yards LSU needed to stay alive. STEVE FRANZ, LSU SPORTS INFORMATION

The Wildcats played well—Woodson was 21 of 38 for 250 yards. But the Tigers couldn't sack him, the first time in 26 games they could say that about an opposing quarterback. LSU also committed 12 penalties for a season-high 103 yards, several of them momentum killers. "We've got a team that's sick," Miles said. "Maybe I need to be a better coach. I thought this football team fought, and I don't think we were good. There's a lot of things we can correct.

"It cost us tonight. It cost us victory."

October 20: LSU 30, Auburn 24

As painful as the Kentucky loss was, it didn't hurt LSU much in the national rankings. Second-ranked California became No. 1 for only a couple of hours before falling to Oregon State 31–28, one of four teams in the AP top 25 to lose to unranked opponents on October 13. When the polls came out the next day, LSU was No. 5 in the AP, coaches', and Harris Interactive polls (the last two each comprising one-third of the BCS formula) and No. 4 in the season's first BCS standings. "One loss isn't going to kill you," said ESPN BCS analyst Brad Edwards, "so the key is the pecking order among one-loss teams. Right now, LSU's in the best spot." The Tigers wouldn't be there much longer if they couldn't beat No. 18 Auburn. The home team had won every game in this series since 2000, the last three meetings decided by a total of eight points. With the winner of this game representing the SEC West five times since 2000, the contest took on added significance. "This Auburn-LSU thing," Les Miles said. "I want you to know something: It's not normal." Some would be saying that about Miles by game's end.

Just like Florida two weeks earlier, Auburn was able to plow through LSU's defense for a 17–7 halftime lead. Again, LSU didn't seem fazed, thanks to Early Doucet. He played one snap as a decoy late in the Kentucky game, but this time he was Flynn's top target. Flynn completed 22 of 34 passes for a career-high 319 yards and a career-best matching three touchdowns, seven passes going to Doucet for a game-high 93 yards. Slowly LSU forged a 23–17 lead with three Colt David field goals of 29, 26, and 33 yards sandwiched around a 5-yard pass from Flynn to Hester with the tailback lunging into the end zone for the score right at the pylon. LSU's defense held up despite a chop block by Auburn right guard Chaz Ramsey on Glenn Dorsey midway through the third quarter, bending the All-American backward and forcing him from the game. Auburn finally broke through to take a 24–23 lead with 3:21 remaining on a 3-yard pass from Brandon Cox to Rod Smith, giving the ball back to LSU at its 42 with 3:13 remaining. A field goal would have sufficed, but LSU would have none of it. LSU went for it after Demetrius Byrd signaled up to offensive coordinator Gary Crowton in the press box that the fly route, a play called "144 Go," was open. "I said, 'OK, Gary,'" Miles recalled. "Seven points was right there for us and I didn't mind us taking that chance."

With seconds ticking down, Flynn sauntered up to the line slowly, dropped back with Hester and fullback Shawn Jordan picking up the blitz, and arched a toss in the left corner of the end zone toward Byrd, who took the pass away from Auburn cornerback Jerraud Powers with 4 seconds showing on the clock. Byrd hit the turf with 3 seconds remaining, and the clock ran down to one second as the official waited to see if Byrd had possession. "I wasn't aware [of the time] until I got up," Byrd said. "I saw there was one second left and I was like, 'Damn!'" Critics across the country would wrongly take Miles to task for going for it with one second left, not realizing or refusing to acknowledge that Byrd caught the ball with four ticks left. Still, the man people were starting to call "the Mad Hatter" knew his team had cut it close. "I did not expect that play would take [us] to one second," Miles said. "I didn't have it quite timed out that far."

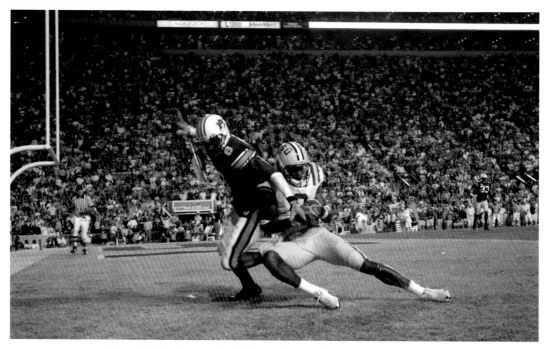

Demetrius Byrd wrests the ball away from Auburn's Jerraud Powers in the end zone for the game-winning touchdown. STEVE FRANZ, LSU SPORTS INFORMATION

November 3: LSU 41, Alabama 34

During the summer, the LSU athletic ticket office was swamped with a record 33,000 requests for the 7,500 tickets LSU was allotted for the game at Alabama (the previous record was 14,000 requests for the 2006 game at Tennessee). Brokers wanted hundreds of dollars for prime tickets in 92,138-seat Bryant-Denny Stadium—and why not? Even though LSU and Alabama play every year, the "Saban Bowl," as the first showdown between predecessor and successor came to be billed, would only happen once. Les Miles tried to keep the focus on the game, rather than who would be coaching it. "Our staff and our team, our guys," Miles said, "they play for LSU." Saban, who had recruited 18 of the Tigers' 24 starters in that game, gave No. 3 LSU its respect but reminded everyone who paid his $4 million annual salary. "I'm on this side of the fence now," Saban said. "It's not difficult for me. I'm not affected by external things. It's not about me." Some LSU players begged to differ. "He said leaving [LSU for the Dolphins] was probably one of the biggest mistakes he ever made," senior offensive tackle Carnell Stewart said. "But at the same time, you don't come back to Alabama."

There was no escaping the deep feelings and volatile emotions of the matchup. Saban rebuilt LSU's football fortunes and drove them to heights not seen since the days of Dietzel and the Chinese Bandits. Miles had come into the house that Saban built, literally—Miles now occupied the office in an LSU football operations building that Saban asked be built but had never seen—and enjoyed the fruits of his predecessor's labor. There was one last crucial factor: Both 7–1 LSU and 6–2 Alabama were 4–1 in the SEC. The winner would have the inside track to the SEC title game; the loser would almost certainly be out.

The game followed a familiar script for LSU: trick plays (Doucet threw a 35-yard pass to Flynn, who for a moment looked like he was injured), penalties (14 for 130 yards), seven video- reviewed plays (five of which went LSU's way), and the now-patented dramatic comeback from a double-digit deficit. The Tigers were seemingly in command 17–3 in the second quarter when defensive end Tyson Jackson was flagged for roughing the passer. Bama quarterback John Parker Wilson launched a 67-yard bomb to wideout DJ Hall on the next play, helping Bama storm back to take a 20–17 halftime lead and a 27–17 edge in the third quarter on a 14-yard Wilson-to–Keith Brown touchdown pass. LSU tied it with a 61-yard heave from Flynn to Byrd and a career-long 49-yard David field goal, but Bama regained the lead 34–27 with 7:33 remaining on a 61-yard punt return by Javier Arenas. Back came the Tigers, who made it 34–34 on a 32-yard Flynn-to-Doucet pass with 2:49 left, but now they needed a stop. On third-and-12 from the Alabama 29, freshman Chad Jones (a Les Miles recruit who decided to play football for LSU instead of baseball in the Houston Astros system) flashed in on a safety blitz and spun Wilson to the ground. The ball came free and bounded toward the end zone before LSU's Curtis Taylor fell on it at the 3. It seemed inevitable that Hester would score, leaping over second-and-goal from the 1 with 1:26 remaining for the winning points.

Alabama quarterback John Parker Wilson loses the ball as Chad Jones pulls him to the turf.

Afterward, Saban congratulated Miles midfield, then bristled at more coach-vs.-coach talk in the interview room. "They didn't want to win the game for me," Saban said. "We never talked about that, and I don't want to talk about it, either." That wasn't the sentiment in the LSU locker room,

Les Miles with the Alabama score visible behind him. This was a game he had to win.

where Hester handed Miles the game ball. "He's been through so much," Hester said. "I think tonight he really proved that he's a great coach—one of the best in the country." To date, Miles and Saban are the only two LSU coaches to beat Alabama three times.

Jacob Hester gives Les Miles the Alabama game ball.   STEVE FRANZ, LSU SPORTS INFORMATION

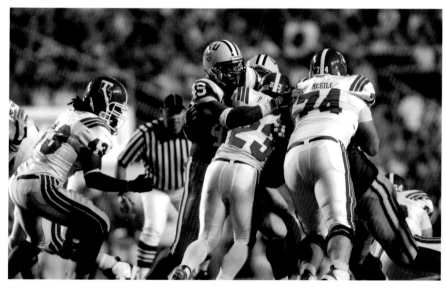

Kirston Pittman wraps up Louisiana Tech running back Patrick Johnson.

STEVE FRANZ, LSU SPORTS INFORMATION

November 10: LSU 58, Louisiana Tech 10

LSU's win at Alabama, coupled with a 27–17 loss by BCS No. 2 Boston College to Florida State a few hours later, vaulted the Tigers back into the No. 2 spot in the new BCS standings. It was an important shift, meaning LSU would likely be in the BCS championship game if it could "hold serve" against Louisiana Tech, Arkansas, and in the SEC championship game. The first step would be no problem for the Tigers, who throttled the visitors from Ruston. Flynn, coming off a 353-yard effort against Alabama, ran for a touchdown and threw for three, including a 71-yarder to Terrance Toliver and a 37-yarder to Brandon LaFell. Jacob Hester rushed for 115 yards on 11 carries, including an 87-yard burst up the middle for a score in the third quarter. "I'd like to sit here and sugarcoat it," said first-year Tech coach Derek Dooley, an assistant on LSU's 2003 BCS championship team. "Across the board, they've got a lot better players than we've got." When the rout, LSU's most lopsided win of the season, was over, there was a little lagniappe waiting: No. 1 Ohio State lost to Illinois 28–21, meaning the Tigers would be back atop the polls on Sunday.

The fastest man in college football: Trindon Holliday on his 98-yard kickoff return at Ole Miss. STEVE FRANZ, LSU SPORTS INFORMATION

November 17: LSU 41, Ole Miss 24

To play for the national championship, it seemed No. 1 LSU would have to win out. To play for the SEC title, all the Tigers (9–1 overall, 5–1 in the SEC) needed to do was win one of their last two against Ole Miss or Arkansas. Once again, Ole Miss proved to be a tougher test than LSU wanted. The problems were equal parts LSU's doing and the Rebels'. The Tigers committed nine penalties, allowed their second punt return for a touchdown in three games, and gave up 466 total yards to the nation's No. 97-ranked offense. But there were certainly highlights for LSU. Trindon Holliday answered Marshay Green's punt return touchdown with a 98-yard return for a touchdown on the ensuing kickoff. And the Tigers were able to use a balanced rushing attack to pile up four touchdowns and 228 net yards on the ground. Afterward, Miles said he wasn't worried about scoring style points to impress the pollsters enough to keep LSU at No. 1. "Style points—honestly—don't carry a lot of weight with me," Miles said.

November 23: Arkansas 50, LSU 48 (3 OT)

Six days after the Ole Miss win the Tigers could have used style points or, rather, some way to keep Arkansas from scoring so many, as for the second straight week the LSU defense was simply overwhelmed. This time the culprit was Arkansas—more particularly, two-time Heisman runner-up Darren McFadden. Operating either at tailback or at quarterback in Arkansas' "Wild Hog" formation, McFadden spent the day carving up the LSU defense. He had 32 carries for 206 yards, including touchdown runs of 16, 73, and 9, and threw for a score, helping Arkansas pile up a stunning 385 yards rushing. Arkansas led only 7–6 at the half, belying the fireworks to come. Three times in the second half LSU would rally to tie the score, the final time on a 2-yard pass from Flynn to Byrd with 57 seconds left. A moment earlier, Flynn's two-yard touchdown run was nullified by an Arkansas time-out called just before the snap.

In overtime, LSU simply couldn't keep the Razorbacks out of the end zone. The Tigers had a chance to end things in the first overtime after Flynn scored on a 12-yard keeper. Arkansas faced fourth-and-10 at the 22, but quarterback Casey Dick found fullback Peyton Hillis open along the Razorbacks' sideline for a 12-yard gain. Three plays later, Dick hit Hillis with a 10-yard touchdown pass to tie the score 35–35. Both teams traded touchdowns in the second OT; then Hillis plowed in from the 3 in the third. That and a two-point run by Felix Jones gave Arkansas a 50–42 lead. LSU came back with a 9-yard Flynn-to-LaFell touchdown pass, but by rule was required to try a two-point conversion. Flynn, who was in and out of the locker room with a separated

Matt Flynn separates his shoulder on this play but stays in the game against Arkansas.

shoulder suffered on a two-point run in the third quarter, had pressure and tried to thread a pass to Byrd in the back of the end zone. But Arkansas cornerback Matterral Richardson stepped in front of it to make the interception and knock LSU out of the No. 1 spot once again.

Arkansas players danced across the Tiger Stadium field in delight, certain that they had slain the giant. LSU's players trooped off to their locker room in stunned silence, not stopping to sing the alma mater with the student section as they had for 19 straight home wins before, certain they had blown their chance at the national title. "We understand what this cost us," Miles said quietly, "what this means." Actually, he had no idea, as the college football season was saving its wildest, most unpredictable Saturday for last.

The SEC Championship Game: LSU 21, Tennessee 14

When the polls were released on November 25, LSU fell only to No. 5 in the AP and Harris rankings but tumbled all the way to No. 7 in the all-important BCS standings. BCS experts like ESPN's Brad Edwards said it was still possible for LSU to play in the national championship game, but the theory seemed outlandish:

1. New No. 1 Missouri (11–1) had to lose to No. 9 Oklahoma in the Big 12 Championship Game.
2. No. 2 West Virginia (10–1) had to lose at home to 4–7 Pittsburgh.

3. LSU had to beat Tennessee impressively enough to vault idle No. 4 Georgia (10–2), No. 5 Kansas (11–1), and No. 6 Virginia Tech (10–2 before beating Boston College in the Atlantic Coast Conference championship game).

Then there were the distractions. Defensive coordinator Bo Pelini met with Nebraska officials on November 25 and a week later would be named the Cornhuskers' head coach, though he was allowed to return to LSU to coach against Ohio State, his alma mater. And reports linking Miles to the soon-to-be-vacant coaching position at his alma mater Michigan only intensified, with LSU officials confirming on Wednesday that Michigan athletic director Bill Martin had been granted permission to speak to Miles after the SEC championship game. By the morning of December 1, ESPN's Kirk Herbstreit reported that Miles was on the verge of becoming Michigan's next coach, leading to an angry denial by Miles just hours before the SEC title game kicked off. As Martin waited and Herbstreit reported, neither apparently knew that Miles had agreed in principle to a new contract the night before the game. There were injuries, too. Glenn Dorsey would be able to play only about half the game because of a tailbone bruise limiting his mobility. Flynn couldn't play because of his separated shoulder, meaning that all of LSU's championship hopes would ride on Ryan Perrilloux.

Tennessee was decked out in solid orange, as was most of the Georgia Dome crowd of 73,832 the night of December 1. Like LSU, the 9–3 Volunteers had overcome big hurdles to win the SEC East, surviving 59–20 and 41–17 blowouts at the hand of Florida and Alabama, respectively, and a 52–50 four-overtime thriller at Kentucky on November 24. Now they were trying to do to LSU what the Tigers did to them in 2001: extinguish LSU's once-bright title hopes and send the Tigers tumbling, likely to the AT&T Cotton Bowl. The Vols opened with an 11-yard touchdown pass from Erik Ainge to tight end Chris Brown before a pair of 30-yard David field goals put LSU down 7–6 at halftime for the second straight week. LSU's offense operated conservatively under Perrilloux, with Jacob Hester getting most of the work. He had 23 carries for 120 yards, giving him 1,017 for

"Have a great day"

He never took a seat. He took no questions. It lasted only 45 seconds. But his statement concerning an ESPN report that he was going to Michigan at a hastily called news conference hours before the SEC championship game was perhaps Les Miles's defining moment in the eyes of many Tiger fans. Here is the complete text of what he said:

"There was some misinformation on ESPN, and I think it's imperative that I straighten it out. I am the head coach at LSU. I will be the head coach at LSU. I have no interest in talking to anybody else. I've got a championship game to play, and I am excited about the opportunity of my damn strong football team to play in it. That's really all I'd like to say. It was unfortunate that I had to address my team with this information this morning. With that being done, I think we'd be ready to play. There will be no questions for me. I represent me in this issue. Please ask me after. I'm busy.

"Thank you very much. Have a great day."

the season. Finally, Perrilloux unleashed a couple of long ones, throwing a 48-yard bomb to Brandon LaFell that set up a 27-yard touchdown pass to Demetrius Byrd at 11:52 of the third quarter for a 13–6 lead. A 6-yard pass from Ainge to Josh Briscoe made it 14–13 Vols going into the fourth. The Vols got the ball back after a Patrick Fisher punt and faced third-and-5 from their 14 with about 10 minutes to go when cornerback Jonathan Zenon made a play for the ages.

Jonathan Zenon (19) gets mugged by teammates Chevis Jackson and Chad Jones after returning an interception for the game-winning touchdown against Tennessee.

STEVE FRANZ, LSU SPORTS INFORMATION

Ainge had been picking on defensive back Danny McCray much of the night but now turned his attention to Zenon, who was locked up in man-to-man coverage on the right side with Tennessee's Quintin Hancock. "Our coaches gave us great preparation," Zenon said. "I'd seen those types of routes maybe four or five times throughout the week. Basically when I saw that formation, I knew exactly what they were going to run." Zenon saw the ball coming and jumped the route, picking off Ainge at the 18 and running straight into the end zone with 9:54 remaining. LSU would have to fend off two more Tennessee threats—the Vols came up empty on fourth down at the LSU 21 with 6:22 left and linebacker Darry Beckwith picked off Ainge at the LSU 7 with 2:42 remaining—but victory, and the Tigers' 10th SEC championship, was theirs. Perrilloux, who at times seemed a liability during the season with his off-the-field troubles, completed 20 of 30 passes for 243 yards and ran for a two-point conversion after Zenon's interception. "I just did whatever Coach [Miles] asked me to do," said Perrilloux, keeping his comments close to the vest. Like Matt Mauck in the 2001 SEC title game against Tennessee, Perrilloux came off the bench in a desperate situation and came away with MVP honors. "I'm happy he got a chance to show what he can do," Byrd said, "and he picked the biggest stage to show the world."

Ryan Perrilloux accepts his MVP trophy after the SEC championship game.

STEVE FRANZ, LSU SPORTS INFORMATION

Afterward, the Miles-Michigan saga took center stage again. Miles spoke wistfully of what had transpired, a man torn between the love of a program he led to a championship and a program where he always dreamed of being. "I'm for them," Miles said of Michigan, "and if there's any way I can help them, I'd love to help them. But I'm not going there. It saddens me at times. I can't be at two places. I've got a great place. I'm at home." Watching her husband speak at the postgame news conference, Kathy Miles was moved to tears. "I'm proud of Les," she said. "He put the team in front of his professional dream."

"We're goin' to the 'ship!"

The night was still young, and there was still plenty of time for dreams to be dashed—or fulfilled. As the Tigers headed back to Baton Rouge, it appeared LSU was destined for a January 1 date in the Allstate Sugar Bowl, probably against unbeaten Hawaii. But the 2007 regular season would be unpredictable to the last. In Morgantown, West Virginia lost quarterback Pat White, who LSU once tried to sign as a defensive back, and with him its offensive punch and its title hopes. Pittsburgh won the one hundredth edition of the game known as the Backyard Brawl 13–9, making the Mountaineers the seventh No. 2-ranked team to fall in 2007 and putting No. 3 Ohio State in the BCS championship game. Now LSU needed Oklahoma to beat No. 1 Missouri in San Antonio, which it did 38–17, opening the door for a new No. 2. "I think it's LSU and Ohio State," ESPN's Brad Edwards predicted. Jerry Palm of www.collegebcs.com likewise thought LSU was Ohio State's likely opponent.

There were other candidates, but every other team's case had a weakness LSU's did not. Georgia and Kansas didn't even play in their respective conference championship games, though as in 2003 with Oklahoma it still wasn't a requirement that a team be a conference champ to play in the BCS title game. Virginia Tech won the ACC, but had the specter of that 41-point September loss to LSU. Some said USC was again the best team going, but the Trojans couldn't shake the ghost of that loss to 41-point underdog Stanford. On the plane ride home, LSU's pilot relayed news of West Virginia's and Missouri's demise to the Tigers' increasingly giddy travel party. Late the next afternoon, LSU's players gathered at the football operations center to watch the BCS bowl pairings on TV. As soon as they saw the LSU logo flash on the screen in the BCS championship game, they erupted. "We're goin' to the 'ship!" they chanted. "We're goin' to the 'ship!" The phrase came from the 2001 movie *Hardball*, about an inner-city youth baseball team that overcame hardships to play for a title. The 2007 LSU Tigers could relate. "We've faced a lot of adversity," Craig Steltz said, "and we just kept on fighting."

Before LSU could wrap up the season against Ohio State, awards season came first. Seven LSU players made one or both of the AP and coaches' All-SEC teams: Glenn Dorsey (the SEC defensive player of the year), linebacker Ali Highsmith, cornerback Chevis Jackson, strong safety Craig Steltz, offensive guard Herman Johnson, kicker Colt David, and punter Patrick Fisher. Dorsey and Steltz were consensus All-Americans. Dorsey captured four of the five individual awards he was nominated for: the Outland, Lombardi, and Lott trophies and the Nagurski Award. When it was all done, Dorsey eclipsed even Billy Cannon as the most decorated player in LSU football history.

Any last concerns there may have been about Miles and Michigan were swept away on December 6, when the coach signed a contract extension through 2012 with an option for a two-year extension on LSU's part. Some cynics said Miles only used the Michigan job to leverage LSU for more money, but his new deal simply put into place the incentives that existed in the previous contract. After winning the SEC championship, LSU would have to make Miles one of the conference's three highest-paid coaches at around $2.8 million. If LSU won the BCS championship, the school would have to make Miles one of the three highest-paid coaches in the entire country at about $3.7 million per year.

Standing between Miles and a big financial windfall was an Ohio State team determined to make amends for what happened a year earlier. The Buckeyes went into the inaugural BCS championship game against Florida in January 2007 with a 12–0 record and the Heisman Trophy winner in quarterback Troy Smith, but were embarrassed by the Gators in a 41–14 rout. The 2007 Buckeyes were supposed to be in rebuilding mode, starting at No. 11, but played with an anger and determination that helped them capture their thirty-second Big Ten title. Linebacker James Laurinaitis, whose father was once a professional wrestler, claimed the Butkus Award and consensus All-American honors, making the postseason awards circuit with Dorsey. The Buckeyes also had Chris "Beanie" Wells at tailback, who had 1,463 yards rushing and 14 touchdowns going in,

The BCS Championship Game Starters

For the Allstate BCS national championship game against Ohio State on January 7, 2008, the LSU Fighting Tigers lined up this way:

		Ht.	Wt.	Class
WR	Demetrius Byrd	6–2	195	Jr.
WR	Brandon LaFell	6–3	205	Soph.
LT	Ciron Black	6–5	320	Soph.
LG	Herman Johnson	6–7	356	Jr.
C	Brett Helms	6–2	270	Jr.
RG	Lyle Hitt	6–2	299	Soph.
RT	Carnell Stewart	6–5	320	Sr.
TE	Keith Zinger	6–4	250	Sr.
WR	Early Doucet	6–0	207	Sr.
TB	Jacob Hester	6–0	228	Sr.
QB	Matt Flynn	6–3	227	Sr.
DE	Tyson Jackson	6–5	291	Jr.
DT	Glenn Dorsey	6–2	303	Sr.
DT	Ricky Jean-Francois	6–3	285	Soph.
DE	Kirston Pittman	6–4	252	Sr.
LB	Luke Sanders	6–5	242	Sr.
LB	Darry Beckwith	6–1	230	Jr.
LB	Ali Highsmith	6–1	223	Sr.
CB	Jonathan Zenon	6–0	180	Sr.
SS	Craig Steltz	6–2	209	Sr.
FS	Curtis Taylor	6–3	204	Jr.
CB	Chevis Jackson	6–0	184	Sr.
PK	Colt David	5–9	173	Jr.
P	Patrick Fisher	6–5	253	Sr.

and a leading receiver in Brian Robiskie, son of LSU's first 1,000-yard rusher, Terry Robiskie.

The Allstate BCS National Championship Game: LSU 38, Ohio State 24

The Buckeyes had waited 51 days since beating Michigan to end the regular season on November 17, the Tigers 37 days since beating Tennessee for the SEC title. Asked how his team felt the day before the big game, Miles replied, "Pent up, trapped, held hostage." Soon they would finally have a chance to expend their energy as would the Buckeyes, both teams in a race to see who would be the first to claim two championships in the BCS era.

Ohio State fired out of the blocks first, just as it did against Florida a year before. Wells blasted through right tackle to score on a 65-yard run just 1:26 into the game, stunning the LSU fans who made up about two-thirds of the Superdome–record crowd of 79,651. After LSU went backward on its first drive, Ohio State tacked on a field goal at the 9:12 mark for a 10–0 lead. It was just the kind of start the Buckeyes needed. It seemed to be, in a perverse way, just what the Tigers wanted, too. They had come back from double-digit deficits against Florida, Auburn, and Alabama; why should the national championship game be any different? LSU pulled within 10–3 on a 32-yard Colt David field goal, then dominated the second quarter. This time it was the opponent that lost its poise, with Ohio State committing two 15-yard penalties as the Tigers moved from their 16 to the Buckeyes' 13. On first down, LSU went into trick-play mode, bunching four wide receivers to the right to draw in the Ohio State defensive backs. Tight end Richard Dickson then fired straight off the left side of the line uncovered, Flynn finding him to tie the score 10–10 at the 13-minute mark.

What happened next completely turned the momentum in LSU's direction. Ohio State drove from its 24 to the LSU 21, where Ryan Pretorius came on for a 38-yard field-goal try. LSU's Ricky Jean-Francois, who saw his first action against Tennessee after a season-long academic suspension, shoved Buckeyes guard Ben Person backward and reached out with his right hand to smother the kick, which LSU recovered at the 34. Ten plays later, Flynn rolled left and lobbed a pinpoint pass to Brandon LaFell in the back of the end zone for a 10-yard touchdown pass and a 17–10 lead LSU would not relinquish. After Chevis Jackson returned a Todd Boeckman interception 34 yards to the Ohio State 24, Hester smashed over from the 1 to give LSU a 24–10 halftime lead. The Tigers' 21 unanswered second-quarter points were more than the Buckeyes' No. 1-ranked defense gave up in any game except the loss to Illinois.

Ohio State needed a stop to start the second half and seemed to get it, but

Tight end Richard Dickson crosses the goal line for LSU's first touchdown in the BCS national championship game.

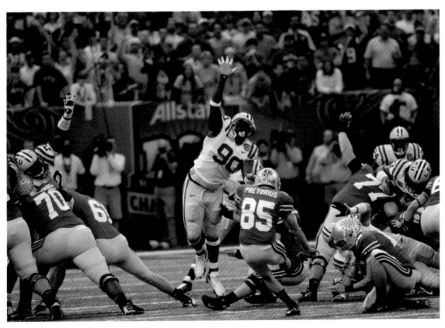

Ricky Jean-Francois reaches up to block Ryan Pretorius's field-goal attempt, shifting the momentum to LSU.

Ohio State's Austin Spitler roughed LSU punter Patrick Fisher, giving the Tigers the ball at the Buckeyes' 45. Four plays later after yet another personal foul penalty on Ohio State, LSU was in the end zone again, Early Doucet breaking three tackles to score on a 4-yard pass from Flynn with 9:04 left in the third quarter. LSU's 31 straight points took the life out of the Buckeyes and the drama out of the game. Ohio State would score twice more but LSU never relinquished control, its defense sacking Boeckman five times and forcing him into three turnovers. Flynn, the offensive MVP after throwing for 174 yards on 19 of 27 passing, tacked on his career-high fourth touchdown pass by hitting Dickson on a 5-yard scoring toss with 1:50 remaining to cap LSU's 38–24 victory. Jean-Francois took defensive MVP honors, though the award could easily have gone to Harry Coleman. He replaced Steltz after the All-American suffered an early shoulder injury and had two tackles, recovered a Chad Jones fumble on a punt return in the first quarter and Boeckman's fumble after he was hammered by Highsmith in the fourth.

When the final polls came out, there was no sharing this time. Aside from an AP voter here and there, LSU was the undisputed No. 1, despite being the first two-loss national champion since Minnesota in 1960. "It was divine intervention," Miles said, reflecting on the season, "a two-loss team winning."

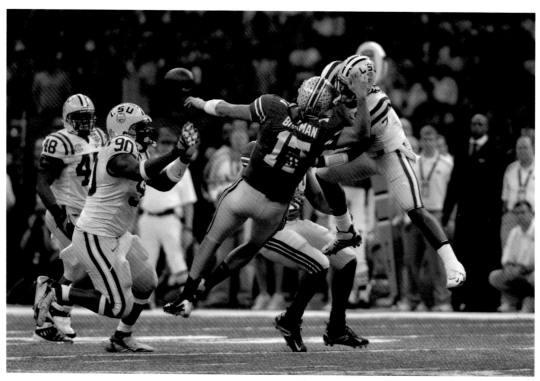

Linebacker Ali Highsmith collars Ohio State quarterback Todd Boeckman in the fourth quarter, forcing a fumble.   STEVE FRANZ, LSU SPORTS INFORMATION

Les Miles lifts the crystal football in triumph.

STEVE FRANZ, LSU SPORTS INFORMATION

"People said we didn't belong," Kirston Pittman remarked. "We belong. Look who's holding up the crystal trophy." The first man to do it was Miles, who at long last had emerged from Nick Saban's shadow.

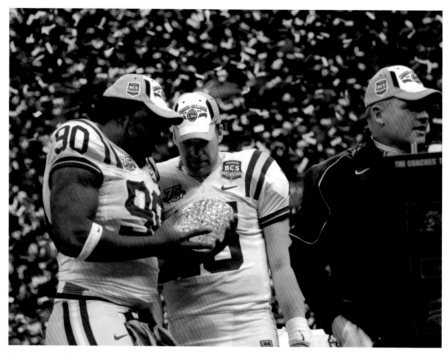

Championship game MVPs Ricky Jean-Francois and Matt Flynn examine their prize.

STEVE FRANZ, LSU SPORTS INFORMATION

When LSU won the BCS title four years earlier, Saban found it difficult to enjoy himself, fretting about sports agents hanging out in the team hotel lobby and the expectations for next year. For Miles, it was a completely different experience. After sharing a celebratory glass of champagne with his wife Kathy, Miles left the Superdome and went across Poydras Street to the ESPN GameDay set. "There's the man with the crystal ball," said ESPN analyst and fellow Michigan alum Desmond Howard. The two embraced before fellow analyst Lee Corso got to tell Miles how wrong he was in picking the Buckeyes to win the game. As Miles headed back to the Superdome one last time, he looked up at the giant arena and considered again what his team had just accomplished. "How about that one!" Miles yelled. "Wahoo!"

Back in the LSU locker room again, senior associate athletic director Herb Vincent approached Miles and asked him if he was willing to make an appearance on Bourbon Street with a replica of the crystal football. "Yeah," Miles said. "Let's go. Let's have some fun tonight." Miles, Kathy, and an LSU entourage piled into two police vans and made the slow trek toward the

Miles holds a replica of the crystal football on a Bourbon Street balcony after the game.

ALEX RESTREPO, LSU SPORTS INFORMATION

French Quarter through the excited throngs, who became more excited still when they realized their championship coach was riding in the lead vehicle. Mounted police cleared a path for the Miles party to the entrance of the Royal Sonesta Hotel, where on a second-floor balcony draped with an LSU banner, Les and Kathy Miles stood and displayed the replica crystal ball for the fans below to see. "This is for you!" Miles yelled, the LSU fight song blaring in the background. LSU Sports Information director Michael Bonnette said he would never forget the joyous scene that night at the corner of Bourbon and Bienville. "People from both ends of Bourbon Street started to converge on that corner," Bonnette recalled. "It was an amazing sight—a sea of purple and gold. He just wanted to share that moment with the fans." After about ten minutes, Les and Kathy Miles headed wearily back to the team hotel on Canal Street. Their rest was short lived, though, as a phone call on their room's private line woke them a few hours later. "Is this Les Miles?" a woman on the phone asked. Miles confirmed it was him. "Please hold," she said, "for the President of the United States." A moment later, President Bush was congratulating Miles and his Tigers on "overcoming the hurdles" it took for them to win the national championship, and inviting the team to the White House that April.

First, Miles was off to the American Football Coaches Association convention in Anaheim, California. There was a photo shoot with all the NCAA champion football coaches, including Appalachian State's Jerry Moore. His

Mountaineers lost to Miles's Tigers in 2005 before embarking on the first of three straight Division I-AA and Football Championship Subdivision titles—and before pulling off their stunning upset at Michigan to open the 2007 season that got so many people talking about Miles replacing Lloyd Carr in the first place. Miles spoke at the convention's banquet, talking about his days as an "average lineman" at Michigan, and how honored he was to be able to coach the "finest sport in the land."

End Game

January 19, 2008, was a cold and blustery day in Baton Rouge, but not so cold that it kept 25,000 fans from turning out to Tiger Stadium one last time to welcome home their conquering heroes. LSU's championship celebration featured all the trophies the Tigers had captured throughout the year, and the hoisting of a new national championship flag to fly over Tiger Stadium in the seasons to come. "That flag is going to fly over Tiger Stadium forever," Miles said, looking toward the flagpole above the north end zone. "It's wonderful to be a part of that." More wonderful, perhaps, to be the coach of a team that dealt with enormous expectations, difficult setbacks, and parlayed its good fortune to emerge on top of the college football world. "Some of the half-times, they were mad at each other," Miles said. "You knew they wanted to play well, and someone was going to turn it around, someone was going to make a play, it was going to work. Yes, there's some talent on this team, but they may be the most competitive group of men I've been around."

Winning doesn't come easily. Or cheaply. Just three days after beating Ohio State, LSU announced $5-per-ticket price increases and hikes in Tradition Fund fees that would within three years double what season-ticket holders have to pay for the right to purchase their tickets. No matter the cost, fans will come and fill Tiger Stadium and make it a fearsome place to play football. Because the love affair between LSU fans and their Tigers is eternal.

And priceless.

APPENDIX
LSU Record Book, 1893–2008

LSU Football by the Numbers

Academic All-SEC selections—312
First-team All-SEC selections—198
All-American honors—64
Bowl games—39
NFL first-round draft picks—31
Academic All-Americans—25

Bowl victories—20
SEC championships—10
College Football Hall of Famers—11
SEC West titles—7
National championships—3 (AP, UPI, or coaches')
Pro Football Hall of Famers—3

LSU All-Americans

(first-team only)

1935–36	Gaynell "Gus" Tinsley, end
	Marvin "Moose" Stewart, center
1939	Ken Kavanaugh, end
1951	George Tarasovic, center
1954	Sid Fournet, tackle
1957	Jimmy Taylor, fullback
1958–59	Billy Cannon, halfback
1958	Max Fugler, center
1961	Roy "Moonie" Winston, guard
1962	Fred Miller, tackle
	Jerry Stovall, halfback
1963	Billy Truax, end
1964	Remi Prudhomme, tackle
1965	Doug Moreau, split end
	George Rice, tackle
1967	John Garlington, end
1969	George Bevan, linebacker
1969–71	Tommy Casanova, cornerback
1970	Mike Anderson, linebacker
1971	Ronnie Estay, defensive tackle
1972	Bert Jones, quarterback
1972–73	Warren Capone, linebacker
1973	Tyler LaFauci, offensive guard
1974	Mike Williams, cornerback
1977–78	Charles Alexander, tailback
1978	Robert Dugas, offensive tackle

1982	James Britt, cornerback
	Albert Richardson, linebacker
1983	Eric Martin, wide receiver
1984	Lance Smith, offensive tackle
1985	Michael Brooks, linebacker
1986–87	Wendell Davis, wide receiver
1987	Joseph "Nacho" Albergamo, center
1988	Greg Jackson, safety
1996	Kevin Faulk, all-purpose
	David LaFleur, tight end
1997	Alan Faneca, offensive guard
	Chad Kessler, punter
1998	Todd McClure, center
	Anthony "Booger" McFarland, nose guard
2001	Josh Reed, wide receiver
2002	Bradie James, linebacker
2003	Stephen Peterman, offensive guard
	Chad Lavalais, defensive tackle
2003, 2005	Skyler Green, return specialist
2003–04	Corey Webster, cornerback
2004	Marcus Spears, defensive end
	Ben Wilkerson, center
2005	Kyle Williams, defensive tackle
	Claude Wroten, defensive tackle
2006	LaRon Landry, free safety
2006–07	Glenn Dorsey, defensive tackle
2007	Craig Steltz, strong safety

LSU Academic All-Americans

1959	Mickey Mangham, end	1980	Benjy Thibodeaux, defensive tackle
1960	Charles "Bo" Strange, center	1982	James Britt, cornerback
1961	Billy Booth, tackle	1982	Alan Risher, quarterback
1971	Jay Michaelson, kicker	1984	Juan Betanzos, kicker
1971	Tommy Butaud, defensive tackle	1986–87	Joseph "Nacho" Albergamo, center
1972	Charles Williamson, tight end	1993–94	Mike Blanchard, center
1973	Tyler LaFauci, offensive guard	1997	Chad Kessler, punter
1973	Joe Winkler, defensive back	2001–03	Rodney Reed, offensive tackle
1974	Brad Davis, running back	2003	Matt Mauck, quarterback
1977	Robert Dugas, offensive tackle	2004–05	Rudy Niswanger, offensive line

National Football Foundation Scholar Athletes

1978	Robert Dugas, offensive tackle	2002	Bradie James, linebacker
1987	Joseph "Nacho" Albergamo, center	2003	Rodney Reed, offensive tackle
1990	Sol Graves, quarterback	2005	Rudy Niswanger, center
1997	Chad Kessler, punter		

LSU Record Book

INDIVIDUAL RECORDS

Rushing

GAME

Rushing Yards

	Player	Yards	Att.	Opponent
1.	Alley Broussard	250	26	Ole Miss, 11/20/2004
2.	Kevin Faulk	246	21	Houston, 9/7/1996
3.	Charles Alexander	237	31	Oregon, 10/22/1977
4.	Cecil Collins	232	27	Auburn, 9/20/1997
5.	Charles Alexander	231	43	Wyoming, 11/26/1977
6.	Terry Robiskie	214	30	Rice, 9/28/1976
7.	Harvey Williams	213	28	Kentucky, 10/20/1990
8.	Kevin Faulk	212	28	Kentucky, 11/1/1997
9.	Justin Vincent	201	18	Georgia, 12/6/2003
	Kevin Faulk	201	30	Alabama, 11/7/1998

Attempts

	Player	Att.	Yards	Opponent
1.	Charles Alexander	43	231	Wyoming, 11/26/1977
2.	Charles Alexander	41	199	Tulane, 11/19/1977
3.	Charles Alexander	40	156	Florida, 10/1/1977
4.	Kevin Faulk	36	138	Arkansas, 11/29/1996
	Dalton Hilliard	36	183	Florida State, 11/20/1982
6.	Rondell Mealey	34	233	Notre Dame, 12/28/1997
7.	Joseph Addai	32	156	Florida, 10/15/2005
	Kevin Faulk	32	177	Miss. State, 10/26/1996
	Charles Alexander	32	144	Indiana, 9/16/1978
	Art Cantrelle	32	95	Auburn, 10/24/1970

Yards per Rush

(min. 10 att.) 19.6   Harvey Williams vs. Rice, 9/19/1987 (196 in 10 att.)

(min. 15 att.) 11.7   Kevin Faulk vs. Houston, 9/7/1996 (246 in 21 att.)

(min. 30 att.) 7.6   Charles Alexander vs. Oregon, 10/22/1977 (237 in 31 att.)

(min. 40 att.) 5.4   Charles Alexander vs. Wyoming, 11/26/1977 (231 in 43 att.)

Touchdowns

	Player	TDs	Opponent		Player	TDs	Opponent
1.	Kevin Faulk	5	Kentucky, 11/1/1997		Dalton Hilliard	4	Kentucky, 10/20/1984
2.	LaBrandon Toefield	4	Utah State, 9/8/2001		Charles Alexander	4	Oregon, 10/22/1977
	Rondell Mealey	4	New Mexico State, 9/28/1996	7.	several players	3	Last: Alley Broussard vs. Ole Miss, 11/20/2004
	Harvey Williams	4	Miami (Ohio), 9/15/1990				

Longest Rush for a Touchdown

	Player	Yards	Opponent		Player	Yards	Opponent
1.	Sal Nicolo	94	Rice, 10/4/1952	7.	Jeff Burkett	86	Georgia Navy, 11/24/1942
	Jesse Fatheree	94	Georgia, 11/16/1935	8.	Kevin Faulk	81	Idaho, 9/26/1998
3.	Cotton Milner	90	Auburn, 11/14/1936		Ripper Rowan	81	Alabama, 9/30/1944
4.	Adrian Dodson	88	Tulane, 11/30/1940	10.	Kevin Faulk	80	Houston, 9/7/1996
5.	Jacob Hester	87	Louisiana Tech, 11/10/2007				
	Justin Vincent	87	Georgia, 12/6/2003				

SEASON

Rushing Yards

	Player	Yards	Att.	TDs
1.	Charles Alexander (1977)	1,686	311	17
2.	Kevin Faulk (1996)	1,282	248	13
3.	Kevin Faulk (1998)	1,279	229	12
4.	Dalton Hilliard (1984)	1,268	254	13
5.	Charles Alexander (1978)	1,172	281	14
6.	Kevin Faulk (1997)	1,144	205	15
7.	Dalton Hilliard (1985)	1,134	258	14
8.	Terry Robiskie (1976)	1,117	224	12
9.	Jacob Hester (2007)	1,103	225	12
10.	Justin Vincent (2003)	1,001	154	10
	Harvey Williams (1988)	1,001	154	11

Attempts

	Player	Att.	Yards
1.	Charles Alexander (1977)	311	1,686
2.	Charles Alexander (1978)	281	1,172
3.	Dalton Hilliard (1985)	258	1,134
4.	Dalton Hilliard (1984)	254	1,268
5.	Kevin Faulk (1996)	248	1,282
6.	Art Cantrelle (1970)	247	892
7.	LaBrandon Toefield (2001)	230	992
8.	Kevin Faulk (1998)	229	1,279
9.	Jacob Hester (2007)	224	1,103
10.	Terry Robiskie (1976)	224	1,117

Yards per Rush (min. 200 att.)

1. 5.585   Kevin Faulk, 1998 (1,279 in 229 att.)
2. 5.580   Kevin Faulk, 1997 (1,144 in 205 att.)
3. 5.4   Charles Alexander, 1977 (1,686 in 311 att.)

Rushes per Game

1. 28.3   Charles Alexander, 1977 (311 in 11 games)
2. 25.5   Charles Alexander, 1978 (281 in 11 games)
3. 23.1   Dalton Hilliard, 1985 (258 in 11 games)

Rushing Yards per Game

1. 153.3   Charles Alexander, 1977 (1,686 in 11 games)
2. 116.5   Kevin Faulk, 1996 (1,282 in 11 games)
3. 116.3   Kevin Faulk, 1998 (1,279 in 11 games)
4. 115.3   Dalton Hilliard, 1984 (1,268 in 11 games)

Touchdowns

	Player	TDs
1.	LaBrandon Toefield (2001)	19
2.	Charles Alexander (1977)	17
3.	Kevin Faulk (1997)	15
4.	Dalton Hilliard (1985)	14
	Charles Alexander (1978)	14
6.	Kevin Faulk (1996)	13
	Dalton Hilliard (1984)	13
	Steve Van Buren (1943)	13
9.	Jacob Hester (2007)	12
	Kevin Faulk (1998)	12
	Terry Robiskie (1976)	12
	Jimmy Taylor (1957)	12

100-Yard Games

	Player	Games		Player	Games		Player	Games
1.	Kevin Faulk (1996)	7	7.	Joseph Addai (2005)	5		LaBrandon Toefield (2001)	4
	Charles Alexander (1977)	7		Justin Vincent (2003)	5		Kevin Faulk (1995)	4
	Steve Van Buren (1943)	7		Kevin Faulk (1998)	5		Jermaine Sharp (1994)	4
4.	Kevin Faulk (1997)	6		Dalton Hilliard (1985)	5		Harvey Williams (1990)	4
	Dalton Hilliard (1984)	6		Dalton Hilliard (1982)	5		Dalton Hilliard (1983)	4
	Charles Alexander (1978)	6	12.	Jacob Hester (2007)	4		Terry Robiskie (1976)	4

Rushing Yards

	Player	Yards	Att.	TDs
1.	Kevin Faulk (1995–98)	4,557	856	46
2.	Dalton Hilliard (1982–85)	4,050	882	44
3.	Charles Alexander (1975–78)	4,035	855	42
4.	Harvey Williams (1986–90)	2,860	588	27
5.	Joseph Addai (2001–05)	2,577	490	18
6.	Terry Robiskie (1973–76)	2,517	578	29
7.	LaBrandon Toefield (2000–02)	2,291	511	26
8.	Rondell Mealey (1996–99)	2,238	453	29
9.	Garry James (1982–85)	2,217	491	27
10.	Brad Davis (1972–74)	2,165	456	15

Attempts

	Player	Att.	Yards
1.	Dalton Hilliard (1982–85)	882	4,050
2.	Kevin Faulk (1995–98)	856	4,557
3.	Charles Alexander (1975–78)	855	4,035
4.	Harvey Williams (1986–90)	588	2,904
5.	Terry Robiskie (1973–76)	578	2,517
6.	LaBrandon Toefield (2000–02)	511	2,291
7.	Garry James (1982–85)	491	2,217
8.	Joseph Addai (2001–05)	490	2,577
9.	Brad Davis (1972–74)	456	2,165
10.	Domanick Davis (1999–2002)	455	2,056

Yards per Rush (min. 400 att.)

1. 5.32 Kevin Faulk, 1995–98 (4,557 in 856 att.)
2. 5.26 Joseph Addai, 2001–05 (2,577 in 490 att.)
3. 4.94 Rondell Mealey, 1996–99 (2,238 in 453 att.)
4. 4.86 Harvey Williams, 1986–90 (2,860 in 588 att.)
5. 4.72 Charles Alexander, 1975–78 (4,035 in 855 att.)

Rushing Yards per Game

1. 111.2 Kevin Faulk, 1995–98 (4,557 in 41 games)
2. 92.0 Dalton Hilliard, 1982–85 (4,050 in 44 games)
3. 91.7 Charles Alexander, 1975–78 (4,035 in 44 games)
4. 73.9 LaBrandon Toefield, 2000–01 (2,291 in 31 games)
5. 72.6 Harvey Williams, 1986–90 (2,904 in 40 games)

Rushes per Game

1. 20.9 Kevin Faulk, 1995–98 (856 in 41 games)
2. 20.0 Dalton Hilliard, 1982–85 (882 in 44 games)
3. 19.4 Charles Alexander, 1975–78 (855 in 44 games)
4. 16.54 Art Cantrelle, 1969–71 (397 in 24 games)
5. 16.48 LaBrandon Toefield, 2000–02 (511 in 31 games)

Touchdowns

	Player	TDs
1.	Kevin Faulk (1995–98)	46
2.	Dalton Hilliard (1982–85)	44
3.	Charles Alexander (1975–78)	40
4.	Terry Robiskie (1973–76)	31
5.	Rondell Mealey (1996–99)	29
6.	Harvey Williams (1986–90)	27
	Garry James (1982–85)	27
8.	LaBrandon Toefield (2000–02)	26
9.	Billy Cannon (1957–59)	24
10.	Herb Tyler (1995–98)	23

100-Yard Games

	Player	Games
1.	Kevin Faulk (1995–98)	22
2.	Dalton Hilliard (1982–85)	20
3.	Charles Alexander (1975–78)	16
4.	Harvey Williams (1986–90)	8
5.	LaBrandon Toefield (2000–02)	7
	Rondell Mealey (1996–99)	7
	Steve Van Buren (1941–43)	7
8.	Justin Vincent (2003–06)	6
	Joseph Addai (2001–05)	6
10.	Domanick Davis (1999–2002)	5
	Terry Robiskie (1973–76)	5
	Don Schwab (1963–65)	5

Passing

Yards

	Player	Yards	Opponent
1.	Rohan Davey	528 (35 of 44)	Alabama, 11/3/2001
2.	Tommy Hodson	438 (31 of 49)	Tennessee, 10/28/1989
3.	Jesse Daigle	394 (25 of 44)	Miss. State, 11/16/1991
4.	Rohan Davey	383 (27 of 38)	Kentucky, 10/13/2001
5.	Tommy Hodson	381 (18 of 30)	Ole Miss, 11/4/1989
6.	Jeff Wickersham	368 (33 of 51)	Miss. State, 11/12/1983
7.	Rohan Davey	359 (19 of 33)	Arkansas, 11/23/2001
8.	Rohan Davey	356 (21 of 43)	Tennessee, 9/21/2001
	Jamie Howard	356 (15 of 23)	Rice, 9/23/1995
10.	Matt Flynn	353 (24 of 44)	Alabama, 11/3/2007

Completions

	Player	Comp.	Opponent
1.	Rohan Davey	35 (44 att.)	Alabama, 11/3/2001
2.	Jeff Wickersham	33 (51 att.)	Miss. State, 11/12/1983
3.	Tommy Hodson	31 (49 att.)	Tennessee, 10/28/1989
	Jeff Wickersham	31 (42 att.)	Notre Dame, 11/23/1985
5.	Josh Booty	29 (58 att.)	Auburn, 9/18/1999
	Jeff Wickersham	29 (42 att.)	Florida, 9/8/1984
7.	Chad Loup	28 (43 att.)	Arkansas, 11/27/1993
8.	Rohan Davey	27 (38 att.)	Kentucky, 10/13/2001
9.	Rohan Davey	26 (37 att.)	Middle Tenn., 11/10/2001
10.	Jesse Daigle	25 (44 att.)	Miss. State, 11/16/1991
	Alan Risher	25 (34 att.)	Miss. State, 11/13/1982

Attempts

Player	Att.	Opponent
1. Josh Booty	58 (29 comp.)	Auburn, 9/18/1999
2. Jeff Wickersham	51 (33 comp.)	Miss. State, 11/12/1983
3. Tommy Hodson	49 (31 comp.)	Tennessee, 10/28/1989
4. Marcus Randall	45 (19 comp.)	Texas, 1/1/2003
Josh Booty	45 (19 comp.)	Georgia, 10/2/1999
Jamie Howard	45 (17 comp.)	Florida, 10/7/1995
Tommy Hodson	45 (25 comp.)	Ohio State, 9/26/1987
8. Rohan Davey	44 (35 comp.)	Alabama, 11/3/2001
Jesse Daigle	44 (25 comp.)	Miss. State, 11/16/1991
10. Rohan Davey	43 (21 comp.)	Tennessee, 9/29/2001
Jamie Howard	43 (23 comp.)	Southern Miss, 11/12/1994
Chad Loup	43 (28 comp.)	Arkansas, 11/27/1993

Completion Percentage

(min. 5 att.)	1.000	Fred Haynes vs. Baylor, 1968 (9 of 9)
	1.000	Matt Flynn vs. North Texas, 10/29/2005 (7 of 7)
(min. 10 att.)	1.000	Rohan Davey vs. Western Carolina, 9/2/2000 (11 of 11)
(min. 20 att.)	.900	JaMarcus Russell vs. Miss. State, 9/30/2006 (18 of 20)
	.900	Matt Mauck vs. Louisiana Tech, 11/1/2003 (18 of 20)

Consecutive Completions (in one game)

1. 14 JaMarcus Russell vs. Miss. State, 9/30/2006
   Matt Mauck vs. Louisiana Tech, 11/1/2003 (first 14 attempts)
   Chad Loup vs. Arkansas, 11/27/1993 (first 14 attempts)
3. 12 Tommy Hodson at Tennessee, 9/17/1988
   Jeff Wickersham at Tulane, 11/30/1985
   Alan Risher vs. Rice, 9/26/1981
6. 11 Rohan Davey vs. Western Carolina, 9/2/2000

Consecutive Passes without an Interception (in one game)

1. 49 Tommy Hodson vs. Tennessee, 10/28/1989
2. 44 Jesse Daigle vs. Miss. State, 11/16/1991
3. 43 Rohan Davey vs. Tennessee, 9/29/2001
4. 40 Tommy Hodson at Ohio State, 9/24/1988
5. 39 Marcus Randall vs. Texas, 1/1/2003
   Tommy Hodson at Ole Miss, 11/1/1986

Touchdowns

Player	TDs	Opponent
1. Matt Flynn	4	Ohio State, 1/7/2008
Matt Mauck	4	Western Illinois, 9/13/2003
Matt Mauck	4	Louisiana Tech, 11/1/2003
Matt Mauck	4	Arkansas, 11/28/2003
Rohan Davey	4	Tennessee, 9/30/2000
Josh Booty	4	Alabama, 11//4/2000
Herb Tyler	4	Akron, 9/27/1997
Jamie Howard	4	Rice, 9/23/1995
Tommy Hodson	4	Ohio, 10/28/1989
Tommy Hodson	4	Tennessee, 9/24/1989
Steve Ensminger	4	Rice, 9/24/1977
12. 44 players	3	Last: Matt Flynn vs. Arkansas, 11/23/2007

Longest Pass

Play	Yards	Opponent
1. Steve Ensminger to Carlos Carson	82	Georgia, 10/14/1978*
2. Jamie Howard to Brett Bech	81	Ole Miss, 10/29/1994
3. Josh Booty to Reggie Robinson	80	W. Carolina, 9/21/2000*
Tommy Hodson to Sammy Martin	80	Rice, 9/19/1987*
Jeff Wickersham to Eric Martin	80	Alabama, 11/5/1983*
Norm Stevens to Al Doggett	80	Kentucky, 10/11/1952*
Y. A. Tittle to Dan Sandifer	80	Georgia Tech, 10/19/1946*
8. Chad Loup to Todd Kinchen	79	Texas A&M, 9/29/1990*
9. Jamie Howard to Brett Bech	76	Auburn, 9/17/1994*
Alan Risher to Orlando McDaniel	76	Florida State, 10/24/1981*

*Touchdown

Yards

Player	Yards	Att.	Comp.	Pct.	TDs	Games
1. Rohan Davey (2001)	3,347	367	217	59.1	18	12
2. JaMarcus Russell (2006)	3,129	342	232	67.8	28	13
3. Matt Mauck (2003)	2,825	358	229	64.0	28	14
4. Tommy Hodson (1989)	2,655	317	183	57.7	22	11
5. Jeff Wickersham (1983)	2,542	337	193	57.3	7	11
6. JaMarcus Russell (2005)	2,443	311	188	60.5	15	12
7. Matt Flynn (2007)	2,407	359	202	56.3	21	12
8. Tommy Hodson (1986)	2,261	288	175	60.8	19	11
9. Jeff Wickersham (1984)	2,165	312	178	57.1	12	11
10. Jeff Wickersham (1985)	2,145	346	209	60.4	5	11

Completions

Player	Comp.	Att.	Pct.	TDs	Yards	Games
1. JaMarcus Russell (2006)	232	342	67.8	28	3,129	13
2. Matt Mauck (2003)	229	358	64.0	28	2,825	14
3. Rohan Davey (2001)	217	367	59.1	18	3,347	12
4. Jeff Wickersham (1985)	209	346	60.4	5	2,145	11
5. Matt Flynn (2007)	202	359	56.3	21	2,407	12
6. Jeff Wickersham (1983)	193	337	57.3	7	2,542	11
7. JaMarcus Russell (2005)	188	311	60.5	15	2,443	12
8. Tommy Hodson (1989)	183	317	57.7	22	2,655	11
9. Jeff Wickersham (1984)	178	312	57.1	12	2,165	11
10. Tommy Hodson (1986)	175	288	60.8	19	2,261	11

Attempts

Player	Att.	Comp.	Pct.	TDs	Yard	Games
1. Rohan Davey (2001)	367	217	59.1	18	3,347	12
2. Matt Flynn (2007)	359	202	56.3	21	2,407	12
3. Matt Mauck (2003)	358	229	64.0	28	2,825	14
4. Jeff Wickersham (1985)	346	209	60.4	5	2,145	11
5. JaMarcus Russell (2006)	342	232	67.8	28	3,129	13
6. Jeff Wickersham (1983)	337	193	57.3	7	2,542	11
7. Josh Booty (1999)	333	162	48.6	7	1,830	10
8. Tommy Hodson (1989)	317	183	57.7	22	2,655	11
9. Jeff Wickersham (1984)	312	178	57.1	12	2,165	11
10. JaMarcus Russell (2005)	311	188	60.5	15	2,443	12

Completion Percentage (min. 50 att.)

Player	Pct.	Att.	Comp.	TDs	Yards	Games
1. JaMarcus Russell (2006)	67.8	342	232	28	3,129	13
2. Herb Tyler (1995)	65.2	69	45	5	589	4
3. Rohan Davey (2000)	64.4	59	38	7	577	4
4. Matt Mauck (2003)	64.0	358	229	28	2,825	14
Nelson Stokley (1965)	64.0	50	32	3	468	10
6. Alan Risher (1982)	63.7	234	149	17	1,834	11
7. Marcus Randall (2004)	63.0	162	102	9	1,269	12
Alan Risher (1981)	63.0	238	150	5	1,780	11
9. Herb Tyler (1998)	61.2	250	153	18	2,018	10
10. Tommy Hodson (1987)	61.1	265	162	15	2,125	11

Touchdowns

	Player	TDs	Att.	Comp.	Pct.	Yards	Games
1.	JaMarcus Russell (2006)	28	342	232	67.8	3,129	13
	Matt Mauck (2003)	28	358	229	64.0	2,825	14
3.	Tommy Hodson (1989)	22	317	183	57.7	2,655	11
4.	Matt Flynn (2007)	21	359	202	56.3	2,407	12
5.	Tommy Hodson (1986)	19	288	175	60.8	2,261	11
6.	Rohan Davey (2001)	18	367	217	59.1	3,347	12
	Herb Tyler (1998)	18	250	153	61.2	2,018	10
8.	Josh Booty (2000)	17	290	145	50.0	2,121	10
	Alan Risher (1982)	17	234	149	63.7	1,834	11
10.	JaMarcus Russell (2005)	15	311	188	60.5	2,443	12
	Tommy Hodson (1987)	15	265	162	61.1	2,125	11

CAREER

Yards

	Player	Yards	Comp.	Att.	Pct.	TDs
1.	Tommy Hodson (1986–89)	9,115	674	1,163	58.0	69
2.	Jeff Wickersham (1982–85)	6,921	587	1,005	58.4	25
3.	JaMarcus Russell (2004–06)	6,625	493	797	61.9	52
4.	Jamie Howard (1992–95)	6,158	459	934	49.1	34
5.	Herb Tyler (1995–98)	5,876	434	715	60.7	40
6.	Alan Risher (1980–82)	4,585	381	615	62.0	31
7.	Rohan Davey (1998–2001)	4,415	478	286	59.8	29
8.	Josh Booty (1999–2000)	3,951	307	623	49.3	24
9.	Matt Mauck (2001–03)	3,831	310	529	58.6	37
10.	Bert Jones (1970–72)	3,225	220	418	52.6	28

Completions

	Player	Comp.	Att.	Pct.	TDs	Yards
1.	Tommy Hodson (1986–89)	674	1,163	58.0	69	9,115
2.	Jeff Wickersham (1982–85)	587	1,005	58.4	25	6,921
3.	JaMarcus Russell (2004–06)	493	797	61.9	52	6,625
4.	Jamie Howard (1992–95)	459	934	49.1	34	6,158
5.	Herb Tyler (1995–98)	434	715	60.7	40	5,876
6.	Alan Risher (1980–82)	381	615	62.0	31	4,585
7.	Matt Mauck (2001–03)	310	529	58.6	37	3,831
8.	Josh Booty (1999–2000)	307	623	49.3	24	3,951
9.	Rohan Davey (1998–2001)	286	478	59.8	29	4,415
10.	Chad Loup (1990–93)	267	468	57.1	15	3,167

Attempts

	Player	Att.	Comp.	Pct.	TDs	Yards
1.	Tommy Hodson (1986–89)	1,163	674	58.0	69	9,115
2.	Jeff Wickersham (1982–85)	1,005	587	58.4	25	6,921
3.	Jamie Howard (1992–95)	934	459	49.1	34	6,158
4.	JaMarcus Russell (2004–06)	797	493	61.9	52	6,625
5.	Herb Tyler (1995–98)	715	434	60.7	40	5,876
6.	Josh Booty (1999–2000)	623	307	49.3	24	3,951
7.	Alan Risher (1980–82)	615	381	62.0	31	4,585
8.	Matt Mauck (2001–03)	529	310	58.6	37	3,831
9.	Rohan Davey (1998–2001)	478	286	59.8	29	4,415
10.	Chad Loup (1990–93)	468	267	57.1	15	3,167

Completion Percentage (min. 400 att.)

	Player	Pct.	Att.	Comp.	TDs	Yards
1.	Alan Risher (1980–82)	62.0	615	381	31	4,585
2.	JaMarcus Russell (2004–06)	61.9	797	493	52	6,625
3.	Herb Tyler (1995–98)	60.7	715	434	40	5,876
4.	Rohan Davey (1998–2001)	59.8	478	286	29	4,415
5.	Matt Mauck (2001–03)	58.6	529	310	37	3,831
6.	Jeff Wickersham (1982–85)	58.4	1,005	587	25	6,921
7.	Tommy Hodson (1986–89)	58.0	1,163	674	69	9,115
8.	Chad Loup (1990–93)	57.1	468	267	15	3,167
9.	Matt Flynn (2004–07)	56.1	437	245	31	3,096
10.	Bert Jones (1970–72)	52.6	418	220	28	3,225

Touchdowns

	Player	TDs	Att.	Comp.	Pct.	Yards
1.	Tommy Hodson (1986–89)	69	1,163	674	58.0	9,115
2.	JaMarcus Russell (2004–06)	52	797	493	61.9	6,625
3.	Herb Tyler (1995–98)	40	715	434	60.7	5,876
4.	Matt Mauck (2001–03)	37	529	310	58.6	3,831
5.	Jamie Howard (1992–95)	34	934	459	49.1	6,158
6.	Matt Flynn (2004–07)	31	437	245	56.1	3,096
	Alan Risher (1980–82)	31	615	381	62.0	4,585
8.	Rohan Davey (1998–2001)	29	478	286	59.8	4,415
9.	Bert Jones (1970–72)	28	418	220	52.6	3,225
10.	Jeff Wickersham (1982–85)	25	1,005	587	58.4	6,921

Wins by a Starting Quarterback

1. Tommy Hodson (1986–89) 31–14–1
2. Herb Tyler (1995–98) 27–11
3. JaMarcus Russell (2004–06) 25–4
   Warren Rabb (1957–59) 25–7
5. Y. A. Tittle (1944–47) 23–11–3

Consecutive Passes without an Interception

1. 137 Alan Risher, 1982
2. 125 Rohan Davey, 2000–01
3. 124 Marcus Randall, 2002–03
4. 105 Tommy Hodson, 1987–88

Receiving

Receptions

Player	Rec.	Yards	Opponent
1. Josh Reed	19*	293	Alabama, 11/3/2001
Wendell Davis	14	208	Ole Miss, 11/1/1986
3. Jerel Myers	13	153	Auburn, 9/18/1999
4. Michael Clayton	12	130	Alabama, 11/15/2003
5. Wendell Davis	11	123	Georgia, 10/10/198
Charles Alexander	11	94	Kentucky, 10/21/1978
Tommy Morel	11	152	Miss. State, 11/18/1967
8. Josh Reed	10	146	Miss. State, 10/20/2001
Josh Reed	10	186	Auburn, 12/1/2001
Josh Reed	10	113	Miss. State, 10/21/2000
Reggie Robinson	10	103	Miss. State, 10/21/2000
Larry Foster	10	111	Auburn, 9/19/1998
Abram Booty	10	116	Arkansas, 11/28/1997
Alvin Lee	10	128	Tennessee, 9/17/1988
Andy Hamilton	10	165	Baylor, 10/3/1970
Tommy Morel	10	103	Tulane, 11/23/1968

*SEC record

Yards

Player	Yards	Rec.	Opponent
1. Josh Reed	293*	19	Alabama, 11/3/2001
2. Todd Kinchen	248	9	Miss. State, 11/16/1991
3. Eric Martin	209	8	Alabama, 11/5/1983
4. Wendell Davis	208	14	Ole Miss, 11/1/1986
5. Sheddrick Wilson	201	9	Rice, 9/23/1995
Carlos Carson	201	5	Rice, 9/24/1977
7. Eddie Kennison	195	6	Utah State, 10/2/1993

Player	Yards	Rec.	Opponent
8. Josh Reed	186	10	Auburn, 12/1/2001
9. Wendell Davis	184	9	North Carolina, 10/25/1986
10. Josh Reed	183	7	Arkansas, 11/23/2001

*SEC record

Yards per Reception (min. 5 catches)

1. 40.2 Devery Henderson at Kentucky, 11/9/2002 (5 for 201)
   Carlos Carson vs. Rice, 9/24/1977 (5 for 201)
3. 32.5 Eddie Kennison vs. Utah State, 10/2/1993 (6 for 195)
4. 27.6 Todd Kinchen vs. Miss. State, 11/16/1991 (9 for 248)
5. 27.4 Josh Reed vs. Western Carolina, 9/2/2000 (5 for 137)
   Larry Foster vs. Kentucky, 10/17/1998 (5 for 137)

Touchdowns

Player	TDs	Opponent
1. Carlos Carson	5	Rice, 9/24/1977
2. Tony Moss	4	Ohio University, 9/30/1989
3. Dwayne Bowe	3	Kentucky, 10/14/2006
Devery Henderson	3	Kentucky, 11/9/2002
Josh Reed	3	Tennessee, 9/30/2000
Sheddrick Wilson	3	Rice, 9/23/1995
Wendell Davis	3	Ole Miss, 10/31/1987
Wendell Davis	3	South Carolina, 12/31/1987
Wendell Davis	3	Tulane, 11/29/1986
Gerald Keigley	3	Auburn, 10/14/1972
Andy Hamilton	3	Notre Dame, 11/20/1971
Tommy Morel	3	Miss. State, 11/18/1967

Receptions

Player	Rec.	Yards
1. Josh Reed (2001)	94	1,740
2. Wendell Davis (1986)	80	1,244
3. Michael Clayton (2003)	78	1,079
4. Wendell Davis (1987)	72	993
5. Josh Reed (2000)	65	1,127
Dwayne Bowe (2006)	65	990
7. Jerel Myers (1999)	64	854
8. Sheddrick Wilson (1995)	60	845
9. Tony Moss (1989)	59	934
Early Doucet (2006)	59	772

Player	Yards	Rec.
6. Wendell Davis (1987)	993	72
7. Dwayne Bowe (2006)	990	65
8. Tony Moss (1988)	957	55
9. Tony Moss (1989)	934	59
10. Andy Hamilton (1970)	870	39

*SEC record

Yards

Player	Yards	Rec.
1. Josh Reed (2001)	1,740*	94
2. Wendell Davis (1986)	1,244	80
3. Josh Reed (2000)	1,127	65
4. Michael Clayton (2003)	1,079	78
5. Eric Martin (1983)	1,064	52

Yards per Reception

(min. 25 catches) 22.3 Andy Hamilton, 1970 (39 for 870)
(min. 50 catches) 20.5 Eric Martin, 1983 (52 for 1,064)
(min. 75 catches) 18.5 Josh Reed, 2001 (94 for 1,740)

Yards per Game

1. 145.0* Josh Reed, 2001 (1,740 in 12 games)
2. 113.1 Wendell Davis, 1986 (1,244 in 11 games)
3. 102.5 Josh Reed, 2000 (1,127 in 11 games)
4. 97.0 Eric Martin, 1983 (1,064 in 11 games)

*SEC record

Touchdowns

Player	TDs
1. Dwayne Bowe (2006)	12
2. Devery Henderson (2003)	11
Wendell Davis (1986)	11
4. Michael Clayton (2003)	10
Josh Reed (2000)	10
Carlos Carson (1977)	10
7. Dwayne Bowe (2005)	9
Eddie Fuller (1989)	9
Tony Moss (1989)	9
Andy Hamilton (1971)	9

100-Yard Games

Player	Games
1. Josh Reed (2001)	11
2. Josh Reed (2000)	6
Wendell Davis (1987)	6
Wendell Davis (1986)	6
5. Tony Moss (1988)	5
Andy Hamilton (1971)	5
7. Michael Clayton (2003)	4
Todd Kinchen (1990)	4
Tony Moss (1989)	4
Eric Martin (1983)	4
Eric Martin (1982)	4
Andy Hamilton (1970)	4
Tommy Morel (1968)	4

CAREER

Receptions

Player	Rec.	Yards
1. Wendell Davis (1984–87)	183	2,708
2. Michael Clayton (2001–03)	182	2,582
3. Josh Reed (1999–2001)	167	3,001
4. Early Doucet (2004–07)	160	2,046
5. Dwayne Bowe (2003–06)	154	2,403
6. Eric Martin (1981–84)	152	2,625
7. Jerel Myers (1999–2002)	149	1,843
8. Craig Davis (2003–06)	141	2,107
9. Tony Moss (1986–89)	132	2,196
10. Larry Foster (1996–99)	125	1,747

Yards

Player	Yards	Rec.
1. Josh Reed (1999–2001)	3,001	167
2. Wendell Davis (1984–87)	2,708	183
3. Eric Martin (1981–84)	2,625	152
4. Michael Clayton (2001–03)	2,582	182
5. Dwayne Bowe (2003–06)	2,403	154
6. Tony Moss (1986–89)	2,196	132
7. Craig Davis (2003–06)	2,107	141
8. Early Doucet (2004–07)	2,046	160
9. Andy Hamilton (1969–71)	1,995	100
10. Todd Kinchen (1988–91)	1,911	112

Touchdowns

Player	TDs
1. Dwayne Bowe (2003–06)	26
2. Michael Clayton (2001–03)	21
3. Early Doucet (2004–07)	20
4. Devery Henderson (2000–03)	19
Wendell Davis (1984–87)	19
6. Andy Hamilton (1969–71)	18
7. Josh Reed (1999–2001)	17
Ken Kavanaugh, Sr. (1937–39)	17

Player	TDs
9. Tony Moss (1986–89)	16
10. Eddie Fuller (1986–89)	15

100-Yard Games

Player	Games
1. Josh Reed (1999–2001)	18
2. Wendell Davis (1984–87)	13
3. Eric Martin (1981–84)	10
4. Tony Moss (1986–89)	9
Andy Hamilton (1969–71)	9
6. Todd Kinchen (1989–91)	8
7. Michael Clayton (2001–03)	7
8. Abram Booty (1997–99)	5
Tommy Morel (1966–68)	5
10. Dwayne Bowe (2003–06)	4
Devery Henderson (2000–03)	4
Jerel Myers (1999–2002)	4
Eddie Kennison (1993–95)	4
Brett Bech (1992–94)	4
Carlos Carson (1977–79)	4

Quarterback-Receiver TD Combinations

1. JaMarcus Russell–Dwayne Bowe	23
2. Tommy Hodson–Wendell Davis	21
3. Tommy Hodson–Tony Moss	14
Matt Mauck–Devery Henderson	14
4. Tommy Hodson–Eddie Fuller	13
Rohan Davey–Josh Reed	13

Total Offense

Plays

1. 61 Josh Booty vs. Auburn, 1999 (3 rush, 58 pass)
2. 56 Matt Flynn vs. Arkansas, 2007 (9 rush, 47 pass)
   Marcus Randall vs. Texas, 2003 (11 rush, 45 pass)
4. 55 Tommy Hodson vs. Tennessee, 1989 (6 rush, 49 pass)
5. 54 Matt Flynn vs. Alabama, 2007 (10 rush, 44 pass)
6. 53 Herb Tyler at Ole Miss, 1998 (14 rush, 39 pass)
   Jeff Wickersham vs. Miss. State, 1983 (2 rush, 51 pass)
8. 51 Chad Loup vs. Arkansas, 1993 (8 rush, 43 pass)
   Jesse Daigle vs. Miss. State, 1991 (7 rush, 44 pass)
10. 50 Jamie Howard vs. Southern Miss, 1994 (7 rush, 43 pass)
   Chad Loup at Florida, 1990 (8 rush, 42 pass)

Total Yards

	Player	Rush	Pass	Total	Opponent
1.	Rohan Davey	12	528	540*	Alabama, 2001
2.	Tommy Hodson	-5	438	433	Tennessee, 1989
3.	Jesse Daigle	6	394	400	Miss. State, 1991
4.	Tommy Hodson	-1	381	380	Ole Miss, 1989
5.	Matt Flynn	19	353	372	Alabama, 2007
6.	Jeff Wickersham	-2	368	366	Miss. State, 1983
7.	Rohan Davey	-21	383	362	Kentucky, 2001
8.	Jamie Howard	0	356	356	Rice, 1995
9.	Rohan Davey	-6	359	353	Arkansas, 2001
10.	JaMarcus Russell	21	332	348	Notre Dame, 2006

*SEC record

Plays

1. 459 Matt Flynn, 2007 (100 rush, 359 pass)
2. 437 Matt Mauck, 2003 (79 rush, 358 pass)
3. 414 Jeff Wickersham, 1985 (68 rush, 346 pass)
4. 405 Rohan Davey, 2001 (38 rush, 367 pass)
5. 395 Jeff Wickersham, 1983 (58 rush, 337 pass)
6. 394 JaMarcus Russell, 2006 (52 rush, 342 pass)
7. 373 Tommy Hodson, 1989 (56 rush, 317 pass)
8. 372 JaMarcus Russell, 2005 (61 rush, 311 pass)
9. 360 Josh Booty, 1999 (27 rush, 333 pass)
10. 355 Alan Risher, 1981 (117 rush, 238 pass)

Total Yards

	Player (year)	Rush	Pass	Total
1.	Rohan Davey (2001)	4	3,347	3,351
2.	JaMarcus Russell (2006)	142	3,129	3,271
3.	Matt Mauck (2003)	97	2,825	2,922
4.	Matt Flynn (2007)	215	2,407	2,622
5.	Tommy Hodson (1989)	-51	2,655	2,604
6.	Jeff Wickersham (1983)	-106	2,542	2,436
7.	JaMarcus Russell (2005)	-22	2,443	2,421
8.	Tommy Hodson (1986)	-42	2,261	2,219
9.	Herb Tyler (1998)	182	2,018	2,200
10.	Josh Booty (2000)	0	2,121	2,121

Plays

1. 1,307 Tommy Hodson, 1986–89 (144 rush, 1,163 pass)
2. 1,181 Jeff Wickersham, 1982–85 (176 rush, 1,005 pass)
3. 1,063 Jamie Howard, 1992–95 (129 rush, 934 pass)
4. 1,006 Herb Tyler, 1995–98 (291 rush, 715 pass)
5. 992 Alan Risher, 1980–82 (377 rush, 615 pass)

Total Yards

	Player, Position (years)	Rush	Pass	Total
1.	Tommy Hodson, QB (1986–89)	-177	9,115	8,938
2.	Jeff Wickersham, QB (1982–85)	-216	6,921	6,705

	Position (years)	Rush	Pass	Total
3.	JaMarcus Russell, QB (2004–06)	79	6,625	6,704
4.	Herb Tyler, QB (1995–98)	778	5,876	6,654
5.	Jamie Howard, QB (1992–95)	-598	6158	5,560
6.	Alan Risher, QB (1980–82)	542	4,585	5,127
7.	Rohan Davey, QB (1998–2001)	77	4,415	4,492
8.	Matt Mauck, QB (2001–03)	345	3,831	4,176
9.	Charles Alexander, TB (1975–78)	4,035	17	4,052
10.	Dalton Hilliard, RB (1982–85)	4,040	0	4,050

All-Purpose

Total Yards

	Player	Rush	Rec.	PR	KOR	Total	Opponent
1.	Kevin Faulk	246	8	106	16	376	Houston, 1996
2.	Josh Reed	0	293	5	40	338	Alabama, 2001
3.	Cecil Collins	232	11	0	57	300	Auburn, 1997
4.	Devery Henderson	10	201	0	87	298	Kentucky, 2002
5.	Domanick Davis	122	0	128	36	286	Miss. St., 2002
6.	Kevin Faulk	212	43	0	17	272	Kentucky, 1997

Player	Rush	Rec.	PR	KOR	Total	Opponent
7. Kevin Faulk	234	4	0	33	271	Michigan St., 1995
8. Domanick Davis	99	15	89	63	266	Ole Miss, 2001
Kevin Faulk	180	12	74	0	266	Ark. St., 1998
10. Kevin Faulk	178	50	3	37	265	Idaho, 1998
Kevin Faulk	138	24	48	55	265	Kentucky, 1996

SEASON

Total Yards

Player	Rush	Rec.	PR	KOR	Total
1. Domanick Davis (2002)	31	130	499	560	2,120
2. Kevin Faulk (1998)	1,279	287	265	278	2,109
3. Kevin Faulk (1996)	1,282	134	375	313	2,104
4. Josh Reed (2001)	7	1,740	5	108	1,860
5. Charles Alexander (1977)	1,686	80	0	0	1,766
6. Kevin Faulk (1997)	1,144	93	192	217	1,646
7. Dalton Hilliard (1984)	1,268	204	0	143	1,472
8. Eddie Kennison (1995)	86	739	253	371	1,449
9. Dalton Hilliard (1985)	1,134	313	0	0	1,447
10. Domanick Davis (2000)	45	120	298	572	1,435
Charles Alexander (1978)	1,172	263	0	0	1,435

CAREER

Total Yards

Player	Rush	Rec.	PR	KOR	Total
1. Kevin Faulk (1995–98)	4,557	600	844	844	6,833*
2. Domanick Davis (1999–2002)	2,056	393	1,126	2,168	5,743
3. Dalton Hilliard (1982–85)	4,050	1,133	0	143	5,326
4. Charles Alexander (1975–78)	4,035	431	0	47	4,513
5. Harvey Williams (1986–90)	2,860	674	0	532	4,066
6. Eric Martin (1981–84)	357	2,625	0	851	3,833
7. Eddie Kennison (1993–95)	140	1,554	947	1,178	3,819
8. Garry James (1982–85)	2,225	1,003	1	56	3,798
9. Billy Cannon (1957–59)	1,867	522	349	616	3,354
10. Sammy Martin (1984–87)	1,359	873	0	1,066	3,298

*SEC record

Scoring Records

GAME

Player	Points	Opponent (date)
1. Kevin Faulk	30 (5 rush TDs)	Kentucky (11/1/1997)
Carlos Carson	30 (5 rec. TDs)	Rice (9/24/1977)
3. Harvey Williams	26 (4 rush TDs, 1 2-pt. conv.)	Miami (Ohio) (9/15/1990)
Wendell Harris	26 (3 rush TDs, FG, 2 PATs)	Tulane (11/24/1961)

Points by Kicking

1. 17 David Browndyke at Miss. State, 11/15/1986 (4 FGs, 5 PATs)
2. 16 Colt David vs. Louisiana Tech, 11/10/2007 (3 FGs, 7 PATs)
3. 15 John Corbello vs. Miami (Ohio), 9/14/2002 (4 FGs, 3 PATs)
   David Browndyke at Ohio State, 9/24/1988 (4 FGs, 3 PATs)
5. 14 Colt David vs. Middle Tenn., 9/15/2007 (3 FGs, 5 PATs)
   André Lafleur at Auburn, 9/17/1994 (4 FGs, 2 PATs)
   David Browndyke at Georgia, 10/10/1987 (4 FGs, 2 PATs)

Longest Scoring Plays

100 Eddie Kennison, punt return vs. Miss. State (9/10/1994)
100 Greg Jackson, interception return at Miss. State (11/12/1988)
100 Eric Martin, kickoff return vs. Kentucky (10/17/1981)
100 Sammy Grezaffi, kickoff return at Tennessee (10/28/1967)
100 White Graves, interception return at Kentucky (10/17/1964)
100 Ken Kavanaugh, fumble return vs. Rice (10/9/1937)

Player, Position (year)	Pts.
1. Colt David, PK (2007)	147 (1 TD, 26 FGs, 63 PATs)
2. LaBrandon Toefield, TB (2001)	114 (19 rush TDs)
3. Charles Alexander, TB (1977)	104 (17 rush TDs, 1 2-pt. con.)
4. Kevin Faulk, TB (1998)	102 (11 rush TDs, 3 rec. TDs, 2 TD returns)
5. Steve Van Buren, HB (1943)	98 (13 rush TDs, 1 TD return, 14 PAT)
6. Dalton Hilliard, RB (1982)	96 (11 rush TDs, 5 rec. TDs)
Charles Alexander, TB (1978)	96 (16 rush TDs)
8. Wendell Harris, HB (1961)	94 (6 rush TDs, 2 rec. TDs, 6 FGs, 26 PATs, 1 2-pt. con.)
9. Kevin Faulk, TB (1997)	90 (9 rush TDs)
10. Jimmy Taylor, FB (1957)	86 (12 rush TDs, 14 PATs)

Points by Kicking

1. 141 Colt David, 2007 (26 FGs, 63 PATs)
2. 85 John Corbello, 2002 (17 FGs, 34 PATs)
3. 83 David Browndyke, 1987 (14 FGs, 41 PATs)
4. 77 Juan Betanzos, 1982 (10 FGs, 47 PATs)
   David Browndyke, 1988 (19 FGs, 20 PATs)

Player, Position	Years	Points
1. Kevin Faulk, TB	1995–98	318 (53 TDs)
2. Dalton Hilliard, RB	1982–85	302 (50 TDs, 1 2-pt. con.)
3. David Browndyke, PK	1986–89	292 (61 FGs, 109 PATs)
4. John Corbello, PK	1999–2002	279 (50 FGs, 129 PATs)
5. Colt David, PK	2005–07	278 (1 TD, 38 FGs, 158 PATs)
6. Charles Alexander, TB	1975–78	254 (42 TDs, 1 2-pt. con.)
7. Rondell Mealey, TB	1996–99	198 (33 TDs)

Player, Position	Years	Points
Juan Betanzos, PK	1982–84	198 (36 FGs, 90 PATs)
9. André Lafleur, PK	1993–95	189 (37 FGs, 78 PATs)
10. Mike Conway, K	1975–78	187 (33 FGs, 88 PATs)

Points by Kicking

1. 292 David Browndyke, 1986–89 (61 FGs, 109 PATs)
2. 279 John Corbello, 1999–2002 (33 FGs, 95 PATs)
3. 272 Colt David, 2005–07 (38 FGs, 158 PATs)
4. 198 Juan Betanzos, 1982–84 (36 FGs, 90 PATs)
5. 187 Mike Conway, 1975–78 (33 FGs, 88 PATs)

Punt Return Records

Punt Returns

7 Eddie Kennison vs. Kentucky (10/15/1994)
7 Norman Jefferson vs. Miami (Ohio) (9/20/1986)
7 Norman Jefferson at Ole Miss (10/29/1983)
7 Sammy Grezaffi at Ole Miss (11/4/1967)
7 Young Bussey at Tulane (12/2/1939)

Punt Return Yards

Player	Ret.	Yards	Opponent
1. Norman Jefferson	7	169	Ole Miss (10/29/1983)
2. Joe Labruzzo	3	145	Rice (9/25/1965)
3. Eddie Kennison	3	141	Miss. State (9/10/1994)
Tommy Casanova	3	141	Ole Miss (12/5/1970)
5. Domanick Davis	4	128	Miss. State (9/28/2002)

Longest Punt Returns

Player	Yards	Opponent
1. Eddie Kennison	100*	Miss. State (9/10/1994)
2. Craig Burns	90	Miss. State (11/14/1970)
3. Billy Cannon	89	Ole Miss (10/31/1959)
4. Pinky Rohm	86	Loyola (10/30/1937)
5. Norman Hodgins	84	Rice (10/2/1971)
6. Joe Labruzzo	83	Texas A&M (9/21/1963)
7. Joe Labruzzo	82	Rice (9/25/1965)
8. Steve Van Buren	81	Georgia 9/25/1943)
9. Skyler Green	80	Florida (10/11/2003)
Sammy Grezaffi	80	Kentucky (10/15/1966)

*NCAA record

Punt Returns

1. 41 Sammy Grezaffi, 1967 (369 yards)
2. 37 Young Bussey, 1937 (465 yards)
3. 36 Domanick Davis, 2002 (499 yards)
       Eddie Kennison, 1994 (438 yards)
       Todd Kinchen, 1991 (339 yards)

Punt Return Yards (since 1937)

	Player	Att.	Yards	TDs
1.	Pinky Rohm (1937)	35	539	3
2.	Domanick Davis (2002)	36	499	1
3.	Young Bussey (1937)	37	465	0
4.	Skyler Green (2003)	25	462	2
5.	Eddie Kennison (1994)	36	438	1
6.	Kevin Faulk (1996)	24	375	1
7.	Sammy Grezaffi (1967)	41	369	0
8.	Skyler Green (2005)	27	359	1
9.	Todd Kinchen (1991)	36	339	2
	Craig Burns (1970)	21	339	2

Punt Returns

1. 94 Domanick Davis, 1999–2002 (1,126 yards)
2. 79 Sammy Grezaffi, 1965–67 (905 yards)
3. 77 Skyler Green, 2002–05 (1,064 yards)

Punt Return Yards (since 1963)

	Player	Att.	Yards	TDs
1.	Domanick Davis (1999–2002)	94	1,126	2
2.	Skyler Green (2002–05)	77	1,064	4

	Player	Att.	Yards	TDs
3.	Eddie Kennison (1993–95)	75	947	1
4.	Sammy Grezaffi (1965–67)	79	905	2
5.	Kevin Faulk (1995–98)	61	832	2
6.	Joe Labruzzo (1963–65)	48	687	2
7.	Norman Jefferson (1983–86)	78	597	1
8.	Craig Burns (1968–70)	42	570	2
9.	Tommy Casanova (1968–70)	44	517	3
10.	Todd Kinchen (1989–91)	57	475	2

Kickoff Return Records

Kickoff Returns

1. 6 Eddie Kennison at Texas A&M (9/2/1995)
2. 5 Domanick Davis vs. Alabama (11/16/2002)
      Domanick Davis vs. Arkansas (11/23/2001)
      Robert Dow vs. Vanderbilt (10/9/1976)

Kickoff Return Yards

	Player	Ret.	Yards	Opponent
1.	Eddie Kennison	6	155	Texas A&M (9/2/1995)
2.	Eric Martin	2	145	Kentucky (10/17/1981)
3.	Hokie Gajan	3	137	Wyoming (12/2/1978)
4.	J. W. Brodnax	3	133	Florida (10/26/1957)
5.	Billy Cannon	2	123	Texas Tech (10/5/1957)
6.	Rondell Mealey	3	121	Arkansas (11/27/1998)
	Sammy Grezaffi	2	121	Tennessee 10/28/1967)
8.	Eric Martin	3	119	Tennessee (10/9/1982)
9.	Trindon Holliday	2	117	Ole Miss (11/17/2007)
10.	Eddie Kennison	2	116	Michigan St. (12/29/1995)

Longest Kickoff Returns

	Player	Yards	Opponent
1.	Eric Martin	100*	Kentucky (10/17/1981)
	Sammy Grezaffi	100*	Tennessee (10/28/1967)
3.	Hokie Gajan	99	Wyoming (12/2/1978)
	J. W. Brodnax	99	Florida (10/26/1957)
5.	Trindon Holliday	98	Ole Miss (11/17/2007)
	Jerry Stovall	98	Georgia Tech (10/6/1962)
7.	Billy Cannon	97	Texas Tech (10/5/1957)
8.	Joe May	95	Kentucky (9/17/1955)
9.	Pinky Rohm	93	La. Normal (11/20/1937)
10.	Trindon Holliday	92	Arkansas (11/24/2006)
	Eddie Kennison	92	Michigan St. (12/29/1995)
	Robert Dow	92	Utah (11/30/1974)

*NCAA record

Kickoff Returns

1. 25 Domanick Davis, 1999 (618 yards)
2. 24 Domanick Davis, 2002 (560 yards)
      Domanick Davis, 2000 (572 yards)
4. 23 Robert Dow, 1975 (598 yards)

Kickoff Return Yards (since 1937)

Player	Att.	Yards	TDs
1. Domanick Davis (1999)	25	618	0
2. Robert Dow (1975)	23	598	0
3. Domanick Davis (2000)	24	572	0
4. Domanick Davis (2002)	24	560	0
5. David Butler (1992)	21	531	0
6. Eric Martin (1981)	18	526	1
7. Robert Dow (1976)	20	499	1
8. Trindon Holliday (2007)	19	498	1
9. Sammy Martin (1987)	17	459	0
10. Domanick Davis (2001)	22	418	0

Kickoff Returns

Player	Att.	Yards	TDs
1. Domanick Davis (1999–2002)	95	2,168	0
2. Robert Dow (1973–76)	70	1,780	1
3. Eddie Kennison (1993–95)	51	1,178	0
4. Sammy Martin (1984–87)	43	1,066	0
5. Sammy Grezaffi (1965–67)	30	899	1
6. Hokie Gajan (1977–80)	38	890	1
7. David Butler (1992–96)	35	863	0
8. Eric Martin (1981–84)	32	851	1
9. Kevin Faulk (1995–98)	34	844	1
10. Skyler Green (2002–05)	38	792	0

Kicking Records

Field Goals Made

1. 4 John Corbello vs. Miami (Ohio) (9/14/2002)
      André Lafleur at Auburn (9/17/1994)
      David Browndyke at Ohio State (9/24/1988)
      David Browndyke at Georgia (10/10/1987)
      David Browndyke at Miss. State (11/15/1986)
      David Browndyke vs. Ole Miss (11/1/1986)
      Mike Conway at Kentucky (10/21/1978)

Points After Touchdown Made

1. 10 Bobby Moreau vs. Rice (9/24/1977)
2. 9 Wade Richey vs. New Mexico State (9/28/1996)
3. 8 Colt David vs. North Texas (10/29/2005)
      David Browndyke vs. Cal State–Fullerton (9/12/1987)
      Mike Conway vs. Oregon (10/22/1977)
      Mark Lumpkin vs. Ole Miss (12/5/1970)

Longest Field Goal Made

Player	Yards	Opponent
1. Wade Richey	54	Kentucky (10/19/1996)
Ron Lewis	54	North Carolina (9/14/1985)
3. Chris Jackson	53	Arkansas (11/26/2004)
4. David Browndyke	52	Ole Miss (11/1/1986)
Juan Roca	52	Florida (10/6/1973)
6. Chris Jackson	51	Ole Miss (11/20/2004)

Player	Yards	Opponent
André Lafleur	51	Miss. State (9/9/1995)
Pedro Suarez	51	Ole Miss (11/3/1990)
Pedro Suarez	51	Ole Miss (11/3/1990)
Juan Carlos Betanzos	51	Rice (9/25/1982)

Longest Punt

Player	Yards	Opponent
1. Donnie Jones	86	Kentucky (11/9/2002)
2. Matt DeFrank	71	Notre Dame (11/22/1986)
3. Donnie Jones	69	UAB (9/23/2000)
4. Donnie Jones	68	Kentucky (10/13/2001)
5. Donnie Jones	67	Auburn (10/25/2003)
Matt DeFrank	67	Kentucky (10/17/1987)
Clay Parker	67	South Carolina (10/23/1982)
8. Chad Kessler	66	Vanderbilt (10/4/1997)
Mitch Worley	66	Miami (10/1/1966)
10. Scott Holstein	65	Texas A&M (9/4/1993)
Rusty Jackson	65	Texas A&M (9/21/1974)
Gerald Brown	65	Tulane (11/20/1965)
Danny Neumann	65	Rice (9/28/1963)

Field Goals Made

Player	Made	Att.
1. Colt David (2007)	26	33
2. David Browndyke (1988)	19	23
3. John Corbello (2002)	17	24
4. Pedro Suarez (1990)	15	17
5. John Corbello (2001)	14	23
André Lafleur (1993)	14	17
David Browndyke (1989)	14	14
David Browndyke (1987)	14	20
David Browndyke (1986)	14	18
Juan Betanzos (1983)	14	18
Mike Conway (1978)	14	15

Field Goals Attempted

Player	Att.	Made
1. Colt David (2007)	33	26
2. John Corbello (2002)	24	17
3. John Corbello (2001)	23	14
David Browndyke (1988)	23	19
5. Doug Moreau (1964)	21	13
6. David Browndyke (1987)	20	14
Juan Betanzos (1984)	20	12
8. Chris Jackson (2005)	19	10
André Lafleur (1995)	19	13
Pedro Suarez (1991)	19	13

Field Goal Pct. (min. 5 attempts)

Player	Pct.
1. David Browndyke (1989)	1.000 (14 of 14)
2. Mike Conway (1978)	.933 (14 of 15)
3. Pedro Suarez (1990)	.882 (15 of 17)
4. David Johnston (1981)	.833 (10 of 12)
5. David Browndyke(1988)	.826 (19 of 23)
6. André Lafleur (1993)	.824 (14 of 17)
7. Mike Conway (1975)	.800 (4 of 5)
8. Colt David (2007)	.787 (26 of 33)
9. David Browndyke(1986)	.778 (14 of 18)
Juan Betanzos (1983)	.778 (14 of 18)

Points After Touchdown

Player	PATs
1. Colt David (2007)	63
2. Colt David (2006)	50
3. Juan Betanzos (1982)	48
4. Colt David (2005)	45
5. Wade Richey (1996)	42
6. John Corbello (2001)	41
David Browndyke (1987)	41
8. Jay Michaelson (1971)	39
9. Mark Lumpkin (1969)	38
10. Ryan Gaudet (2003)	36

Consecutive PATs Made

1.	63	Colt David (2007)
2.	43	Juan Betanzos (1982)
3.	42	Colt David (2006)
4.	41	David Browndyke (1987)
5.	35	Colt David (2005)
6.	34	John Corbello (2002)
		André Lafleur (1995)
8.	27	Ronnie Lewis (1985)
		André Lafleur (1994)

Punts

Player	Punts	Avg.
1. Al Doggett (1952)	81	38.9
2. Jim Barton (1951)	75	36.0
3. Steve Jackson (1975)	73	40.0
4. James Wagner (1981)	67	40.0
5. David Johnston (1980)	66	39.0
6. Donnie Jones (2003)	65	42.4
7. Donnie Jones (2002)	64	44.0
Wayne Dickinson (1970)	64	37.5
Jerry Stovall (1960)	64	42.1
10. Eddie Ray (1969)	63	41.0

Punting Yardage

Player	Yards	Punts
1. Al Doggett (1952)	3,147	81
2. Steve Jackson (1975)	2,936	73
3. Donnie Jones (2002)	2,813	64
4. Donnie Jones (2003)	2,757	65
5. Jerry Stovall (1960)	2,696	64
Jim Barton (1951)	2,696	75
7. James Wagner (1981)	2,682	67
8. Patrick Fisher (2007)	2,627	59
9. Donnie Jones (2001)	2,618	60
10. Eddie Ray (1969)	2,581	63

Punting Average

Player	Avg.	Punts
1. Chad Kessler (1997)	50.28*	39
2. Patrick Fisher (2007)	44.52	59
3. Chad Kessler (1995)	44.09	47
4. Rene Bourgeois (1989)	43.97	39
5. Donnie Jones (2002)	43.95	64
6. Corey Gibbs (1998)	43.71	28
7. Donnie Jones (2001)	43.70	47
8. Corey Gibbs (1999)	43.02	57
9. Eddie Ray (1967)	42.85	52
10. Donnie Jones (2003)	42.42	65

* NCAA record

Field Goals Made

Player	Made	Att.
1. David Browndyke (1986–89)	61	75
2. John Corbello (1999–2002)	50	77
3. Colt David (2005–07)	38	51
4. André Lafleur (1993–95)	37	50
5. Juan Betanzos (1982–84)	36	55
6. Mike Conway (1975–78)	33	48
7. Pedro Suarez (1990–92)	33	45
8. Chris Jackson (2003–06)	26	44
9. Mark Lumpkin (1968–70)	21	43
10. Doug Moreau (1963–65)	20	36

Field Goal Attempts

Player	Att.	Made
1. John Corbello (1999–2002)	77	50
2. David Browndyke (1986–89)	75	61
3. Juan Betanzos (1982–84)	55	36
4. Colt David (2005–07)	51	38
5. André Lafleur (1993–95)	50	37
6. Mike Conway (1975–78)	48	33
7. Pedro Suarez (1990–92)	45	33
8. Chris Jackson (2003–06)	44	26
9. Mark Lumpkin (1968–70)	43	21
10. Ron Lewis (1984–87)	36	15
Juan Roca (1972–74)	36	10
Doug Moreau (1963–65)	36	20

Field Goal Percentage (min. 10 attempts)

Player	Pct.
1. David Browndyke (1986–89)	.813 (61 of 75)
2. David Johnston (1980–81)	.800 (16 of 20)
3. Colt David (2005–07)	.745 (38 of 51)
4. André Lafleur (1993–95)	.740 (37 of 50)
5. Pedro Suarez (1990–92)	.733 (33 of 45)

Points After Touchdown

Player	PATs
1. Colt David (2005–07)	158
2. John Corbello (1999–2002)	129
3. David Browndyke (1986–89)	109
4. Mark Lumpkin (1968–70)	92
5. Juan Betanzos (1982–84)	91
6. Mike Conway (1975–78)	88
7. Rusty Jackson (1972–74)	81
8. André Lafleur (1993–95)	78
9. Wade Richey (1994–97)	77
10. Ryan Gaudet (2003–06)	54

Consecutive PATs Made

1.	109	David Browndyke (1986–89)
2.	77	Colt David (2005–06)
3.	72	Colt David (2006–07)
4.	69	André Lafleur (1993–95)
5.	47	John Corbello (1999–02)

Total Punts

Player	Punts	Avg.
1. Donnie Jones (2000–03)	233	42.1
2. Chad Kessler (1994–97)	186	42.9
3. Clay Parker (1981–84)	180	40.6
4. Rusty Jackson (1972–74)	167	39.5
5. Jerry Stovall (1960–62)	165	39.3
6. Al Doggett (1951–54)	160	38.1
7. Eddie Ray (1967–69)	153	41.2
8. Chris Jackson (2003–06)	140	41.0
9. Brian Griffith (1988–91)	136	40.5
10. Steve Jackson (1975–76)	132	37.9

Punting Average

Player	Avg.	Punts
1. Patrick Fisher (2004–07)	44.1	65
2. Chad Kessler (1994–97)	42.9	39
3. Donnie Jones (2000–03)	42.1	47
4. Clay Parker (1981–84)	41.4	39
5. Eddie Ray (1967–69)	41.2	64
6. Chris Jackson (2003–06)	41.0	140
7. Brian Griffith (1988–91)	40.5	28
Matt DeFrank (1984–87)	40.5	47
9. Rusty Jackson (1972–74)	39.6	57
10. Jerry Stovall (1960–62)	39.0	52

Defensive Records

Tackles

1. 21 Al Richardson vs. South Carolina (10/23/1982)
2. 20 Rudy Harmon at Florida (10/1/1988)
   Toby Caston vs. Georgia (10/11/1986)

Sacks

1. 4 Chuck Wiley vs. South Carolina (9/30/1995)
2. 3 Many times (last: Gabe Northern vs. North Texas, 10/21/1995)

Interceptions

3 Craig Steltz at Miss. State (8/30/2007)
Corey Webster vs. Florida (10/12/2002)
Chris Williams at Rice (9/30/1978)
Clinton Burrell vs. Tulane (11/22/1975)
Craig Burns vs. Ole Miss (12/5/1970)
Jerry Joseph vs. Kentucky (10/16/1965)
Kenny Konz at Tulane (1/26/1949)

Tackles

Player	No.
1. Bradie James (2002)	154
2. Al Richardson (1981)	150
3. Lawrence Williams (1981)	144
4. Al Richardson (1980)	129
5. Lawrence Williams (1982)	123
6. Steve Cassidy (1975)	122
7. Al Richardson (1982)	121
8. Trev Faulk (2001)	119
Lawrence Williams (1980)	119
10. Bradie James (2001)	113
Trev Faulk (2000)	113
Shawn Burks (1985)	113

Tackles for Losses

Player	No.
1. Gabe Northern (1994)	23
2. Kenny Bordelon (1975)	21
3. Anthony McFarland (1998)	18
4. Marcus Spears (2004)	17
Jarvis Green (1998)	17
6. Chad Lavalais (2003)	16

Player	No.
Michael Brooks (1985)	16
John Adams (1978)	16
9. Chuck Wiley (1995)	15
10. Several	14

Sacks

Player	No.
1. Oliver Lawrence (1989)	12
2. Gabe Northern (1994)	11
3. Rydell Malancon (1981)	10
4. Melvin Oliver (2005)	9
Marcus Spears (2004)	9
Gabe Northern (1995)	9
Ron Sancho (1987)	9
8. Tyson Jackson (2006)	8.5
9. Kirston Pittman (2007)	8
Anthony McFarland (1998)	8
Jarvis Green (1998)	8
Oliver Lawrence (1989)	8
Michael Brooks (1985)	8
Michael Brooks (1984)	8
Rydell Malancon (1982)	8
Lyman White (1980)	8

Interceptions

Player	No.
1. Chris Williams (1978)	8
Craig Burns (1970)	8
3. Corey Webster (2003)	7
Corey Webster (2002)	7
Cedric Donaldson (1997)	7
Greg Jackson (1988)	7
7. Craig Steltz (2007)	6
Chris Carrier (1986)	6
Liffort Hobley (1984)	6
Chris Williams (1980)	6
Jerry Joseph (1965)	6

Passes Broken Up

Player	No.
1. Travis Daniels (2003)	25
2. Corey Webster (2003)	23
3. Chevis Jackson (2007)	21
4. Demetrius Hookfin (2002)	17
Corey Webster (2002)	17

Tackles

Player	No.
1. Al Richardson (1979–82)	452
2. Bradie James (1999–2002)	418
3. Lawrence Williams (1979–82)	386
4. Steve Cassidy (1972–75)	346
5. Shawn Burks (1983–85)	336
6. Lyman White (1977–80)	316
7. LaRon Landry (2003–06)	315
Ryan Clark (1998–01)	315
9. Toby Caston (1983–86)	305
10. Trev Faulk (1999–01)	300
Ron Sancho (1985–88)	300

Tackles for Losses

Player	No.
1. Anthony McFarland (1995–98)	55
2. Chuck Wiley (1994–97)	43
3. Gabe Northern (1992–95)	40
4. Jarvis Green (1998–2001)	39
5. Michael Brooks (1983–86)	38
6. Ron Sancho (1985–88)	37
7. Marcus Spears (2001–04)	34.5
8. Chad Lavalais (2000–03)	32.5
9. Kenny Bordelon (1972–75)	30
10. Rydell Malancon (1980–83)	28

Sacks

Player	No.
1. Rydell Malancon (1980–83)	25
2. Ron Sancho (1985–88)	23
3. Gabe Northern (1992–95)	21
4. Melvin Oliver (2002–05)	20
Jarvis Green (1998–2001)	20
6. Marcus Spears (2001–04)	19
Chuck Wiley (1994–97)	19
8. James Gillyard (1992–95)	18
Michael Brooks (1983–86)	18
10. Anthony McFarland (1995–98)	17

Interceptions

Player	No.
1. Chris Williams (1977–80)	20
2. Corey Webster (2001–03)	16
3. LaRon Landry (2003–06)	12
Craig Burns (1968–79)	12
Charles Oakley (1951–53)	12
6. Craig Steltz (2004–07)	11
Tory James (1992–95)	11
Greg Jackson (1985–88)	11
9. Chris Carrier (1984–87)	10
Kevin Guidry (1984–87)	10
Norman Jefferson (1983–86)	10
Liffort Hobley (1980–84)	10
Willie Teal (1976–79)	10

Passes Broken Up

Player	No.
1. Corey Webster (2001–04)	49
2. Chevis Jackson (2004–07)	44
3. LaRon Landry (2003–06)	40
4. Jonathan Zenon (2004–07)	34
Travis Daniels (2001–04)	34
6. Demetrius Hookfin (1999–2002)	29
7. Ryan Clark (1998-2001)	27
8. Craig Steltz (2004–07)	26
Ronnie Prude (2002–05)	26
10. Randall Gay (2001–04)	24

Career Starts

Player	No.
1. Andrew Whitworth (2002–05)	52
2. LaRon Landry (2003–06)	48
Rodney Reed (2000–03)	48
Jerel Myers (1999–2002)	48

Consecutive Starts

Player	No.
1. Andrew Whitworth (2002–05)	52
2. LaRon Landry (2003–06)	48
Rodney Reed (2000–03)	48

200-Yard Rushing Games

Player	Opponent	Yards	Player	Opponent	Yards
Alley Broussard	Ole Miss, 2004	250 (26 att.)	Kevin Faulk	Kentucky, 1997	212 (28 att.)
Kevin Faulk	Houston, 1996	246 (21 att.)	Justin Vincent	Georgia, 2003	201 (18 att.)
Charles Alexander	Oregon, 1977	237 (31 att.)	Kevin Faulk	Alabama, 1998	201 (30 att.)
Kevin Faulk	Michigan State, 1995*	234 (25 att.)	*Bowl game		
Charles Alexander	Wyoming, 1977	233 (43 att.)			
Cecil Collins	Auburn, 1997	232 (27 att.)			
Rondell Mealey	Notre Dame, 1997*	222 (34 att.)			
Harvey Williams	Kentucky, 1990	214 (28 att.)			
Terry Robiskie	Rice, 1976	214 (30 att.)			

100-Yard Rushing Games

Player	Opponent	Yards	Player	Opponent	Yards
Charles Alexander	Tulane, 1977	199 (41 att.)	Dalton Hilliard	Arizona, 1984	145 (29 att.)
Harvey Williams	Rice, 1987	196 (10 att.)	Jim Dousay	Tulane, 1967	145 (29 att.)
Billy Baggett	Ole Miss, 1950	192 (11 att.)	Charles Alexander	Indiana, 1978	144 (32 att.)
LaBrandon Toefield	Utah State, 2001	183 (27 att.)	Charles Alexander	Rice, 1978	144 (24 att.)
Dalton Hilliard	Florida State, 1982	183 (36 att.)	Steve Van Buren	Georgia, 1943	144 (25 att.)
Charles Alexander	Vanderbilt, 1977	183 (26 att.)	Brad Davis	Alabama, 1973	143 (17 att.)
Harvey Williams	Tulane, 1987	181 (19 att.)	Jermaine Sharp	Tulane, 1994	142 (15 att.)
Kevin Faulk	Arkansas State, 1998	180 (17 att.)	Kenny Konz	Tulane, 1949	142 (12 att.)
Cecil Collins	Akron, 1997	179 (20 att.)	Lee Hedges	Tulane, 1949	142 (12 att.)
Kevin Faulk	Idaho, 1998	178 (13 att.)	Alvin Dark	Ole Miss, 1942	142 (11 att.)
Dalton Hilliard	Tulane, 1985	174 (39 att.)	Charles Alexander	Utah, 1976	141 (22 att.)
LaBrandon Toefield	Arkansas, 2001	173 (30 att.)	Odell Beckham	Tulane, 1991	140 (23 att.)
Kevin Faulk	Ole Miss, 1997	172 (25 att.)	Billy Cannon	Alabama, 1957	140 (8 att.)
Cecil Collins	Miss. State, 1997	172 (22 att.)	Paul Lyons	Wisconsin, 1971	139 (19 att.)
Kevin Faulk	Miss. State, 1995	171 (23 att.)	Kevin Faulk	Arkansas, 1997	138 (28 att.)
Jimmy Taylor	Tulane, 1957	171 (19 att.)	Kevin Faulk	Kentucky, 1996	138 (21 att.)
Kevin Faulk	Miss. State, 1996	170 (32 att.)	Charles Alexander	Ole Miss, 1976	138 (16 att.)
Dalton Hilliard	East Carolina, 1985	170 (26 att.)	Jeff Burkett	Georgia Navy, 1942	138 (14 att.)
Dalton Hilliard	Kentucky, 1984	170 (31 att.)	Charles Alexander	Miss. State, 1977	136 (29 att.)
Charles Alexander	Florida, 1977	170 (31 att.)	Don Schwab	Florida, 1964	136 (19 att.)
Jimmy Taylor	Arkansas, 1956	170 (20 att.)	Kevin Faulk	Vanderbilt, 1997	135 (31 att.)
Kevin Faulk	Alabama, 1997	168 (27 att.)	Robert Davis	Texas A&M, 1992	134 (15 att.)
Dalton Hilliard	Wichita State, 1984	166 (17 att.)	Harvey Williams	Georgia, 1986	133 (24 att.)
Garry James	Tulane, 1982	166 (18 att.)	Dalton Hilliard	Tulane, 1984	133 (24 att.)
Harvey Williams	Ole Miss, 1987	165 (14 att.)	Dalton Hilliard	Oregon State, 1982	133 (18 att.)
Rondell Mealey	Houston, 1996	161 (14 att.)	Carl Trimble	Colorado, 1974	133 (8 att.)
Kevin Faulk	North Texas, 1995	160 (19 att.)	Harvey Williams	Georgia, 1990	132 (24 att.)
Kevin Faulk	Ole Miss, 1995	159 (23 att.)	Steve Van Buren	Louisiana Army, 1943	132 (43 att.)
Rondell Mealey	San José State, 1999	158 (24 att.)	Rondell Mealey	Kentucky, 1997	131 (13 att.)
Joseph Addai	Florida, 2005	156 (32 att.)	Joseph Addai	Miami, 2005*	130 (24 att.)
Harvey Williams	Tulane, 1990	156 (27 att.)	Jermaine Sharp	South Carolina, 1994	130 (23 att.)
Charles Alexander	Tulane, 1978	156 (28 att.)	Dan Sandifer	Texas A&M, 1945	130 (11 att.)
Charles Alexander	Florida, 1978	156 (40 att.)	Jermaine Sharp	Miss. State, 1994	129 (23 att.)
Brad Davis	South Carolina, 1973	156 (25 att.)	Terry Robiskie	Ole Miss, 1976	129 (24 att.)
Don Schwab	Tulane, 1963	154 (20 att.)	LaBrandon Toefield	Kentucky, 2001	128 (28 att.)
Dalton Hilliard	Vanderbilt, 1984	152 (25 att.)	Dalton Hilliard	Florida State, 1983	128 (20 att.)
Jessie Myles	Florida, 1980	148 (21 att.)	Garry James	Oregon State, 1982	128 (12 att.)
Charles Alexander	Ole Miss, 1978	147 (28 att.)	Dalton Hilliard	Florida, 1982	128 (20 att.)

Player	Opponent	Yards	Player	Opponent	Yards
Justin Vincent	Auburn, 2003	127 (14 att.)	Levi Johns	Arkansas, 1955	114 (15 att.)
Jacob Hester	Arkansas, 2007	126 (28 att.)	Steve Van Buren	Texas A&M, 1943	114 (43 att.)
Keiland Williams	Virginia Tech, 2007	126 (7 att.)	Domanick Davis	South Carolina, 2002	113 (26 att.)
Terry Robiskie	Kentucky, 1976	126 (24 att.)	Art Cantrelle	Texas A&M, 1970	113 (26 att.)
Adrian Dodson	Holy Cross, 1940	126 (26 att.)	Dan Sandifer	Miami, 1946	113 (11 att.)
Kevin Faulk	Arkansas, 1996	125 (36 att.)	Bill Montgomery	Ole Miss, 1945	113 (11 att.)
James Jacquet	Ole Miss, 1991	125 (13 att.)	Steve Van Buren	Rice, 1943	113 (43 att.)
Levi Johns	Ole Miss, 1953	125 (16 att.)	Justin Vincent	Arkansas, 2003	112 (18 att.)
Shyrone Carey	Western Illinois, 2003	124 (21 att.)	Domanick Davis	North Texas, 1998	112 (17 att.)
Dalton Hilliard	Miss. State, 1985	124 (22 att.)	Vincent Gonzales	Florida, 1955	112 (23 att.)
Kevin Faulk	Miss. State, 1998	123 (24 att.)	LaBrandon Toefield	Miami (Ohio), 2002	111 (17 att.)
Dalton Hilliard	Ole Miss, 1982	123 (23 att.)	Jermaine Sharp	Arkansas, 1994	111 (9 att.)
Charles Alexander	Wake Forest, 1978	123 (31 att.)	Levi Johns	Texas Tech, 1954	111 (21 att.)
Leroy Labat	Miss. State, 1951	123 (29 att.)	James Roshto	Alabama, 1951	111 (9 att.)
Gene Knight	Ole Miss, 1945	123 (13 att.)	Eddie Fuller	Ohio, 1989	110 (8 att.)
Domanick Davis	Illinois, 2002*	122 (28 att.)	Charles Alexander	Alabama, 1977	110 (22 att.)
Domanick Davis	Miss. State, 2002	122 (18 att.)	Steve Van Buren	Georgia, 1943	110 (22 att.)
Garry James	Wichita State, 1984	122 (21 att.)	Joseph Addai	Arizona State, 2005	109 (16 att.)
Billy Cannon	Tennessee, 1959	122 (22 att.)	Alley Broussard	Iowa, 2004*	109 (13 att.)
Rondell Mealey	New Mexico State, 1996	121 (12 att.)	Sam Martin	Georgia, 1986	109 (11 att.)
			Terry Robiskie	South Carolina, 1975	109 (26 att.)
Dalton Hilliard	Notre Dame, 1984	121 (13 att.)	Joe Labruzzo	TCU, 1963	109 (12 att.)
Dalton Hilliard	South Carolina, 1983	121 (24 att.)	Sal Nicolo	Rice, 1952	109 (4 att.)
Dalton Hilliard	Washington, 1983	121 (21 att.)	Alley Broussard	South Carolina, 2003	108 (19 att.)
Ebert Van Buren	Texas A&M, 1949	121 (14 att.)	Kevin Faulk	Notre Dame, 1998	108 (31 att.)
Jacob Hester	Tennesssee, 2007	120 (23 att.)	Earl Gros	Miss. State, 1961	108 (14 att.)
LaBrandon Toefield	Auburn, 2001	120 (29 att.)	Billy Cannon	Kentucky, 1958	108 (12 att.)
I aBrandon Toefield	Tennessee, 2000	120 (15 att.)	Keiland Williams	Notre Dame, 2006*	107 (14 att.)
LaBrandon Toefield	Miss. State, 2000	119 (26 att.)	Joseph Addai	Ole Miss, 2004	107 (14 att.)
Rondell Mealey	North Texas, 1999	119 (13 att.)	Terry Robiskie	Vanderbilt, 1976	107 (17 att.)
Chris Dantin	Rice, 1972	119 (23 att.)	Jacob Hester	Florida, 2007	106 (23 att.)
Dalton Hilliard	Tulane, 1983	118 (28 att.)	Alley Broussard	Louisiana Tech, 2003	106 (16 att.)
Hokie Gajan	Rice, 1979	118 (19 att.)	Domanick Davis	Ole Miss, 2000	106 (25 att.)
Tommy Allen	Kentucky, 1967	118 (9 att.)	Steve Rogers	Tulane, 1974	106 (22 att.)
Steve Van Buren	TCU, 1943	118 (43 att.)	Bill Schroll	Rice, 1947	106 (10 att.)
Justin Vincent	Oklahoma, 2004*	117 (16 att.)	Jabbo Stell	Loyola, 1937	106 (11 att.)
Kevin Faulk	Ole Miss, 1996	117 (28 att.)	Joseph Addai	Auburn, 2005	105 (24 att.)
Gene Lang	Miss. State, 1980	117 (11 att.)	Justin Vincent	Ole Miss, 2003	105 (22 att.)
Brad Davis	Tulane, 1974	117 (23 att.)	Kevin Faulk	Notre Dame, 1997	105 (26 att.)
Art Cantrelle	Ole Miss, 1970	117 (5 att.)	Jerry Murphree	Florida, 1977	105 (25 att.)
Billy Cannon	Tulane, 1958	117 (15 att.)	Joe Labruzzo	Miss. State, 1965	105 (15 att.)
Jimmy Taylor	Ole Miss, 1957	117 (15 att.)	Jerry Marchand	Arkansas, 1953	105 (21 att.)
Albin Collins	Miss. State, 1947	117 (17 att.)	Jay Johnson	Ole Miss, 1993	104 (15 att.)
Eddie Fuller	Tennessee, 1988	116 (18 att.)	Hokie Gajan	Kentucky, 1979	104 (20 att.)
Garry James	Florida State, 1982	116 (20 att.)	Don Schwab	Tulane, 1964	104 (20 att.)
Jacob Hester	Louisiana Tech, 2007	115 (11 att.)	Jimmy Taylor	Oklahoma A&M, 1956	104 (12 att.)
Chris Dantin	Wisconsin, 1972	115 (27 att.)	Rondell Mealey	Akron, 1997	103 (15 att.)
Johnny Robinson	Tennessee, 1959	115 (17 att.)	Gene Knight	Miami, 1946	103 (18 att.)
Jerry Marchand	Tulane, 1952	115 (13 att.)	Bill Montgomery	Georgia Tech, 1945	103 (17 att.)
Kevin Faulk	Vanderbilt, 1996	114 (21 att.)	Joseph Addai	Vanderbilt, 2005	102 (24 att.)
Eddie Fuller	Ole Miss, 1988	114 (21 att.)	Justin Vincent	Arkansas State, 2004	102 (13 att.)
Nelson Stokley	Kentucky, 1965	114 (15 att.)	Kendall Cleveland	Arkansas, 1995	102 (24 att.)
Lynn Amedee	Tulane, 1961	114 (12 att.)	Jim Dousay	Miss. State, 1967	102 (19 att.)

Player	Opponent	Yards		Player	Opponent	Yards
Don Schwab	Miss. State, 1964	102 (22 att.)		Billy Baggett	Vanderbilt, 1950	101 (19 att.)
Don Schwab	TCU, 1963	102 (16 att.)		Steve Van Buren	Georgia Tech, 1943	101 (14 att.)
Danny LeBlanc	Kentucky, 1963	102 (23 att.)		Sulcer Harris	Louisiana Tech, 1941	101 (9 att.)
O. K. Ferguson	Florida, 1955	102 (24 att.)		Harvey Williams	Florida State, 1990	100 (22 att.)
Zollie Toth	Ole Miss, 1949	102 (18 att.)		Dalton Hilliard	Kentucky, 1982	100 (24 att.)
Charles Scott	Tulane, 2006	101 (15 att.)		Joe Labruzzo	Kentucky, 1965	100 (14 att.)
Herb Tyler	Ole Miss, 1997	101 (17 att.)		Vincent Gonzales	Texas Tech, 1954	100 (18 att.)
Arthur Cantrelle	Wisconsin, 1971	101 (11 att.)		Bill Montgomery	Georgia, 1945	100 (11 att.)
Edward Campbell	North Carolina, 1961	101 (10 att.)		*Bowl game		

500/400/300-Yard Passing Games

500-Yard Passing Games

Player	Opponent	Yards
Rohan Davey	Alabama, 2001	528

400-Yard Passing Games

Player	Opponent	Yards
Rohan Davey	Illinois, 2002*	444
Tommy Hodson	Tennessee, 1989	438

300-Yard Passing Games

Player	Opponent	Yards
Jesse Daigle	Miss. State, 1991	394
Rohan Davey	Kentucky, 2001	383
Tommy Hodson	Ole Miss, 1989	381
Jeff Wickersham	Miss. State, 1983	368
Rohan Davey	Arkansas, 2001	359
Rohan Davey	Tennessee, 2001	356
Jamie Howard	Rice, 1995	356
Matt Flynn	Alabama, 2007	353
Jeff Wickersham	Alabama, 1983	344
Jamie Howard	Florida, 1995	339
Chad Loup	Arkansas, 1993	336
JaMarcus Russell	Notre Dame, 2006*	332
JaMarcus Russell	Miss. State, 2006	330
Marcus Randall	Troy, 2004	328
Matt Flynn	Auburn, 2007	319
Rohan Davey	Middle Tenn., 2001	318
Rohan Davey	Tennessee, 2000	318
Jamie Howard	Southern Miss, 1994	314
Matt Mauck	Louisiana Tech, 2003	311
Alan Risher	Miss. State, 1982	308
Matt Mauck	Western Illinois, 2003	305

*Bowl game

200-Yard Receiving Games

Player	Opponent	Yards
Josh Reed	Alabama, 2001	293 (19 rec.)
Todd Kinchen	Miss. State, 1991	248 (9 rec.)
Josh Reed	Illinois, 2002*	239 (14 rec.)

Player	Opponent	Yards
Eric Martin	Alabama, 1983	209 (8 rec.)
Wendell Davis	Ole Miss, 1986	208 (9 rec.)
Devery Henderson	Kentucky, 2002	201 (5 rec.)
Sheddrick Wilson	Rice, 1995	201 (9 rec.)
Carlos Carson	Rice, 1977	201 (5 rec.)

*Bowl game

100-Yard Receiving Games

Player	Opponent	Yards
Eddie Kennison	Utah State, 1993	195 (6 rec.)
Josh Reed	Auburn, 2001	186 (10 rec.)
Wendell Davis	North Carolina, 1986	184 (9 rec.)
Josh Reed	Arkansas, 2001	183 (7 rec.)
Josh Reed	Ole Miss, 2000	173 (8 rec.)
Orlando McDaniel	Miss. State, 1979	172 (3 rec.)
Josh Reed	Auburn, 2000	167 (8 rec.)
Andy Hamilton	Iowa State, 1971*	165 (6 rec.)
Andy Hamilton	Baylor, 1970	165 (10 rec.)
Michael Clayton	Western Illinois, 2003	162 (11 rec.)
Andy Hamilton	Tulane, 1971	161 (6 rec.)
Josh Reed	Kentucky, 2001	160 (8 rec.)
Orlando McDaniel	Florida State, 1981	155 (5 rec.)
Reggie Robinson	Arkansas, 1999	154 (5 rec.)
Jerel Myers	Auburn, 1999	153 (13 rec.)
Abram Booty	Notre Dame, 1998	153 (8 rec.)
Andy Hamilton	Notre Dame, 1971	153 (7 rec.)
Michael Clayton	UL–Monroe, 2003	152 (6 rec.)
Tommy Morel	Miss. State, 1967	152 (11rec.)
Wendell Davis	Cal St. Fullerton, 1987	151 (8 rec.)
Brett Bech	Ole Miss, 1994	149 (6 rec.)
Andy Hamilton	Ole Miss, 1971	148 (9 rec.)
Josh Reed	Miss. State, 2001	146 (10 rec.)
Josh Reed	Tennessee, 2000	146 (7 rec.)
Andy Hamilton	Nebraska, 1971*	146 (9 rec.)
Todd Kinchen	Miami (Ohio), 1990	145 (5 rec.)
Demetrius Byrd	Alabama, 2007	144 (6 rec.)
Eric Martin	Kentucky, 1983	143 (7 rec.)
Warren Virgets	Vanderbilt, 1950	143 (4 rec.)

Player	Opponent	Yards	Player	Opponent	Yards
Josh Reed	Western Carolina, 2000	137 (5 rec.)	Dwayne Bowe	Kentucky, 2006	111 (6 rec.)
Larry Foster	Kentucky, 1998	137 (5 rec.)	Larry Foster	Auburn, 1998	111 (10 rec.)
Eric Martin	Washington, 1983	137 (7 rec.)	Eric Martin	Florida, 1984	111 (9 rec.)
Josh Reed	Tulane, 2001	135 (6 rec.)	Tommy Morel	Miss. State, 1968	111 (6 rec.)
Carlos Carson	Georgia, 1978	135 (5 rec.)	Brett Bech	Arkansas, 1994	110 (5 rec.)
Brett Bech	Arkansas, 1993	134 (9 rec.)	Lonny Myles	Kentucky, 1969	110 (7 rec.)
Todd Kinchen	Texas A&M, 1990	133 (5 rec.)	Tommy Morel	Ole Miss, 1968	110 (6 rec.)
Tony Moss	Alabama, 1988	133 (6 rec.)	Devery Henderson	Florida, 2003	109 (5 rec.)
Wendell Davis	Ole Miss, 1987	133 (6 rec.)	Michael Clayton	Arizona, 2003	109 (6 rec.)
Wendell Davis	South Carolina, 1987*	132 (9 rec.)	Eric Martin	Kentucky, 1982	109 (6 rec.)
Wendell Davis	Texas A&M, 1986	132 (9 rec.)	Abner Wimberly	Ole Miss, 1948	109 (2 rec.)
Michael Clayton	Alabama, 2003	130 (12 rec.)	Abram Booty	Idaho, 1998	108 (7 rec.)
Josh Reed	Alabama, 2000	129 (8 rec.)	Sheddrick Wilson	Florida, 1995	108 (7 rec.)
Eddie Kennison	South Carolina, 1995	129 (9 rec.)	Todd Kinchen	Ole Miss, 1989	108 (5 rec.)
Andy Hamilton	Wisconsin, 1971	129 (5 rec.)	Alvin Lee	Ohio State, 1988	108 (6 rec.)
Dan Sandifer	Tulane, 1944	129 (4 rec.)	Wendell Davis	Georgia, 1986	108 (8 rec.)
Tony Moss	Ole Miss, 1988	128 (6 rec.)	Eric Martin	Tennessee, 1982	108 (6 rec.)
Alvin Lee	Tennessee, 1988	128 (10 rec.)	Lee Hedges	Pacific, 1950	108 (3 rec.)
Michael Clayton	Alabama, 2001	126 (7 rec.)	Dwayne Bowe	Fresno State, 2006	106 (4 rec.)
Brandon LaFell	Virginia Tech, 2007	125 (7 rec.)	Eric Martin	Florida, 1983	106 (5 rec.)
Josh Reed	Tennessee, 2001	125 (7 rec.)	Michael Clayton	Kentucky, 2001	105 (9 rec.)
Scott Ray	Florida, 1992	125 (8 rec.)	Tony Moss	Miss. State, 1989	105 (3 rec.)
Carlos Carson	Alabama, 1978	125 (5 rec.)	Carlos Carson	Rice, 1979	105 (6 rec.)
Josh Reed	Utah State, 2001	124 (5 rec.)	Brett Bech	Auburn, 1994	104 (3 rec.)
Jerel Myers	Ole Miss, 1999	124 (9 rec.)	Chris Hill	Southern Miss, 1994	104 (5 rec.)
Eddie Kennison	Michigan State, 1995*	124 (5 rec.)	Herman Fontenot	Vanderbilt, 1984	104 (6 rec.)
Josh Reed	Florida, 2001	123 (6 rec.)	Dwayne Bowe	Oregon State, 2004	103 (5 rec.)
Larry Foster	Texas–El Paso, 1997	123 (7 rec.)	Skyler Green	Louisiana Tech, 2003	103 (9 rec.)
Tony Moss	Ohio University, 1989	123 (7 rec.)	Todd Kinchen	Kentucky, 1994	103 (4 rec.)
Wendell Davis	Georgia, 1987	123 (11 rec.)	Rogie Magee	Ohio State, 1987	103 (5 rec.)
Eric Martin	Miss. State, 1984	123 (6 rec.)	Gerald Keigley	Auburn, 1972	103 (5 rec.)
Wendell Davis	Notre Dame, 1986	121 (7 rec.)	Andy Hamilton	Miss. State, 1970	103 (2 rec.)
Eric Martin	Florida State, 1982	121 (3 rec.)	Andy Hamilton	Texas A&M, 1970	103 (4 rec.)
Michael Clayton	Illinois, 2001*	120 (8 rec.)	Lonny Myles	Miss. State, 1969	103 (8 rec.)
Josh Reed	Middle Tenn., 2001	120 (9 rec.)	Tommy Morel	Florida State, 1968*	103 (6 rec.)
Terrance Toliver	Louisiana Tech, 2007	119 (3 rec.)	Tommy Morel	Tulane, 1968	103 (10 rec.)
Wendell Davis	Alabama, 1985	119 (3 rec.)	Reggie Robinson	Miss. State, 2000	102 (10 rec.)
Todd Kinchen	Florida State, 1991	118 (7 rec.)	Eddie Fuller	Ole Miss, 1989	102 (5 rec.)
Jerel Myers	West Carolina, 2000	117 (6 rec.)	Wendell Davis	Miss. State, 1986	102 (6 rec.)
Sheddrick Wilson	Auburn, 1995	117 (8 rec.)	Wendell Davis	Florida, 1987	102 (8 rec.)
Tony Moss	Florida State, 1989	117 (6 rec.)	Early Doucet	Alabama, 2006	101 (7 rec.)
Tony Moss	Ohio State, 1988	117 (6 rec.)	Craig Davis	Miss. State, 2006	101 (6 rec.)
Abram Booty	Arkansas State, 1998	116 (7 rec.)	Devery Henderson	Auburn, 2003	101 (6 rec.)
Abram Booty	Arkansas, 1997	116 (10 rec.)	Abram Booty	Florida, 1997	101 (4 rec.)
Early Doucet	Notre Dame, 2006*	115 (8 rec.)	Todd Kinchen	Alabama, 1991	101 97 rec.)
Tony Moss	Miami, 1988	115 (7 rec.)	Tony Moss	Tulane, 1989	101 (5 rec.)
Devery Henderson	Miss. State, 2003	114 (7 rec.)	Wendell Davis	Alabama, 1987	101 (9 rec.)
Jerel Myers	Houston, 1999	114 (8 rec.)	Doug Moreau	Texas A&M, 1964	101 (6 rec.)
Josh Reed	Miss. State, 2000	113 (10 rec.)	Dilton Richmond	Louisiana Normal, 1942	101 (3 rec.)
Eddie Kennison	Rice, 1995	113 (4 rec.)	Josh Reed	Houston, 1999	100 (5 rec.)
Tony Moss	Tulane, 1988	112 (5 rec.)	Todd Kinchen	Georgia, 1990	100 (6 rec.)
Eric Martin	Miss. State, 1982	112 (5 rec.)	Ken Kavanaugh	Vanderbilt, 1939	100 (5 rec.)
Malcolm Scott	Florida State, 1981	112 (8 rec.)	*Bowl game		

TEAM RECORDS

Rushing

Rushes
Game:	83	vs. Wyoming, 1977 (487 yards)
	82	vs. Florida, 1977 (385 yards)
	79	at Florida, 1978 (315 yards)
Season:	675	1973 (2,622 yards)
	674	1977 (3,352 yards)
	663	1976 (3,041 yards)

Yards Gained
Game:	503	vs. Oregon, 1977 (69 att.)
	502	vs. Rice, 1977 (72 att.)
	487	vs. Wyoming, 1977 (83 att.)
Season:	3,352	1977 (674 att.)
	3,041	1976 (663 att.)
	2,823	1997 (521 att.)

Yards Gained per Rush
Game:	10.1	vs. Rice, 1987 (43 for 436)
Season:	6.8	1945

Yards Gained per Game
Season:	304.7	1977 (3,352 yards)
	274.5	1976 (3,041 yards)
	256.6	1997 (2,823 yards)

Touchdowns by Rushing
Game:	8	vs. Tulane, 1961
	8	at Kentucky, 1997
Season:	35	2007
	35	1977
	34	1997
	33	1996
	30	1969

Passing

Passes Attempted
Game:	69	vs. Auburn, 1999 (33 comp.)
	56	at Tulane, 1979 (26 comp.)
	52	vs. Florida, 1995 (20 comp.)
Season:	442	2007 (256 comp.)
	411	2001 (238 comp.)
	405	1999 (200 comp.)
	401	2003 (255 comp.)
	368	2006 (245 comp.)

Passes Completed
Game:	35	at Alabama, 2001 (44 att.)
	33	vs. Miss. State, 1983 (51 att.)
	33	vs. Auburn, 1999 (69 att.)
	31	at Notre Dame, 1985 (42 att.)
	31	vs. Tennessee, 1989 (51 att.)
Season:	256	2007 (442 att.)
	255	2003 (401 att.)
	245	2006 (368 att.)
	238	2001 (411 att.)
	220	1985 (366 att.)

Completion Percentage, Game:
(min. 10 att.)	.846	at Tulane, 1945 (11 of 13)
	.842	vs. Akron, 1997 (16 of 19)
(min. 20 att.)	.857	vs. Alabama, 2006 (18 of 21)
	.857	vs. North Texas, 2005 (24 of 28)
(min. 30 att.)	.813	at South Carolina, 2003 (26 of 32)
	.806	vs. Louisiana Tech, 2003 (25 of 31)

Most Passes without an Interception, Game:
49	vs. Tennessee, 1989
44	vs. Miss. State, 1991
43	at Tennessee, 2001
40	at Ohio State, 1988
40	vs. Ole Miss, 1998

Passes Intercepted
Game:	6	at Auburn, 1994
	6	vs. Tennessee, 1939
Season:	25	1999
	21	1994
	19	5 times

Yards Gained Passing
Game:	528	at Alabama, 2001
	485	vs. Western Carolina, 2000
	456	vs. Rice, 1995
	438	vs. Tennessee, 1989
Season:	3,578	2001 (238 of 411)
	3,272	2006 (245 of 268)
	3,257	2003 (255 of 401)
	3,154	2007 (256 of 442)
	2,912	2005 (216 of 360)

Yards per Game Passing
Season:	298.2	2001 (3,578 yards)
	258.1	1989 (2,839 yards)
	245.3	2000 (2,698 yards)
	240.7	2006 (3,272 yards)
	238.5	1986 (2,623 yards)

Touchdown Passes
Game:	7	vs. Ohio, 1989
	5	vs. Tulane, 1946
	5	vs. Rice, 1977
	5	vs. Cal State–Fullerton, 1987
	5	vs. Akron, 1997
	5	vs. Western Carolina, 2000
Season:	30	2006
	30	2003
	29	2007
	26	1989
	24	2000

Scoring

Points
Game:	93	vs. Louisiana–Lafayette, 1936
	77	vs. Rice, 1977
	70	vs. Arkansas State, 1991
	66	vs. Wyoming, 1977
	63	vs. Baylor, 1969
	63	vs. New Mexico State, 1996
	63	at Kentucky, 1997

Season: 541 2007
475 2003
438 2006
383 2005
375 1977

Points per Game
Season: 38.6 2007
34.9 1969
34.1 1977
33.9 2003
33.7 2006

Total Touchdowns
Game: 11 vs. Rice, 1977
9 several occasions (last at Kentucky, 1997)
Season: 66 2007
63 2003
59 2006
51 1977
48 1997

Points After Touchdown, Kicking
Game: 11 vs. Rice, 1977
9 several occasions
Season: 63 2007
57 2006
57 2003
47 1982
45 2005

Field Goals
Game: 4 vs. Miami (Fla.), 2005
4 at Auburn, 1994
4 at Georgia, 1987
4 at Miss. State, 1986
4 vs. Ole Miss, 1986
4 at Kentucky, 1978
Season: 26 2007
19 1986
17 2004
17 2002
17 1988

Punting

Most Punts
Game: 17 at Tennessee, 1942
17 vs. Miss. State, 1940
Season: 104 1941

Yards Punting
Game: 664 vs. Miss. State, 1940
Season: 4,010 1941

Yards per Punt
Game:
(min. 5 punts) 53.2 at Miss. State, 1997 (5 for 266 yards)
51.3 at Ole Miss, 1957 (7 for 359 yards)
(min. 10 punts) 47.3 at Ole Miss, 1960 (10 for 473 yards)
Season: 46.0 1997 (54 for 2,486 yards)

Kickoff Returns

Returns
Game: 8 vs. Florida, 1993 (166 yards)
at Florida, 1994 (141 yards)
Season: 47 1989

Yards
Game: 178 vs. Alabama, 1983
Season: 1,179 1948 (46 returns)

Punt Returns

Returns
Game: 13 at Tulane, 1937
Season: 72 1937

Yards Returned
Game: 205 vs. Ole Miss, 1970
Season: 1,004 1937

Total Defense

Fewest Yards Allowed
Game: 26 vs. Mercer, 1940
Season: 1,236 1937

Fewest Yards Allowed per Game
Season: 123.6 1937

Rushing Defense

Fewest Yards Allowed
Game: -50 vs. Ole Miss, 1982
-43 vs. Mercer, 1940
Season: 389 1969
574 1970

Fewest Yards Allowed per Game
Season: 38.9 1969
52.2 1970

Passing Defense

Fewest Yards Allowed
Game: 0 vs. Alabama, 1971
0 vs. Ole Miss, 1958
0 at Alabama, 1958
0 vs. Texas Tech, 1954
0 vs. Ole Miss, 1942
0 vs. Louisiana Normal, 1942
0 vs. Auburn, 1939
0 vs. Texas, 1937
0 vs. Florida, 1937
Season: 524 1959

Fewest Yards Allowed per Game
Season: 52.4 1959

Most Interceptions
Game: 8 vs. Villanova, 1951
Season: 27 1984

Most Interceptions Returned for TDs
Game: 3   vs. Arkansas State, 1991
Season: 4   1991

Most Defensive TDs
Game: 3   vs. Arkansas State, 1991
Season: 7   2003

Most Sacks
Season: 44   2003

Scoring Defense

Fewest Points Allowed
Game: 0   vs. many opponents, most recent: vs. Middle
                   Tenn., 2007 (44–0)
Season: 27   1937
           29   1959

Fewest Points Allowed per Game
Season: 2.7   1937

Fewest Touchdowns Allowed
Season: 3   1959

Most Shutouts
Season: 6   1937

Plays

Game: 99   vs. Tulane, 1969
          98   vs. Tulane, 1968
Season: 1,054   2007 (6,152 total yards)
        994   2003 (5,857 total yards)
        883   2002 (4,550 total yards)
        882   1985 (4,284 total yards)
        872   1977 (4,542 total yards)

Yards Gained
Game: 746   vs. Rice, 1977
        680   vs. Western Carolina, 2000
        664   vs. Rice, 1987
        653   vs. Louisiana Tech, 2003
Season: 6,152   2007 (1,054 plays)
     5,857   2003 (994 plays)
     5,427   2006 (818 plays)
     5,418   2001 (862 plays)
     4,863   2005 (869 plays)

Yards Gained per Play
Game: 11.1   vs. Kentucky, 2006
    10.06   vs. Rice, 1987
Season: 6.7   1945
      6.6   2006
      6.3   2001

Yards Gained per Game
Season: 451.5   2001
     440.3   1987
     439.4   2007
     418.4   2003
     417.5   2006

Most First Downs
Game: 35   vs. Miss. State, 1969
Season: 316   2007
      298   2003

Most Yards Penalized
Game: 184   at Florida, 1961
Season: 880   2007
      790   1989

Most Fumbles Lost
Game: 6   at Rice, 1974
        6   vs. Georgia, 1952
        6   vs. Texas, 1952
        6   vs. Rice, 1951
Season: 29   1974

MISCELLANEOUS RECORDS

	W–L–T
LSU vs. No. 1	2–7–1
LSU as No. 1	14–3
LSU on TV	114–101–2
LSU in Homecoming games	55–25–3
LSU in season openers	81–28–5
LSU in home openers	70–14–3

LSU's longest winning streak: 19 (started with 7–6 win over Tulane, 11/30/57; ended with 14–13 loss at Tennessee, 11/7/59).

LSU vs. All Opponents

Opponent	Series Record	First, Last Played	Opponent	Series Record	First, Last Played
Akron	1–0–0	1997	Mississippi	55–37–4	1894, 2007
Alabama	23–43–5	1895, 2007	Miss. College	9–0–1	1910, 1923
Appalachian State	1–0–0	2005	Miss. State	65–33–3	1896, 2007
Arizona	3–0–0	1984, 2006	Missouri	0–1–0	1978
Arizona State	1–0–0	2005	Nebraska	0–5–1	1971, 1987
Arkansas	33–18–2	1901, 2007	New Mexico State	1–0–0	1996
Arkansas State	3–0–0	1991, 2004	North Carolina	5–1–0	1948, 1986
Army	0–1–0	1931	Northwestern State	10–0–0	1911, 1942
Auburn	22–19–1	1901, 2007	Notre Dame	5–5–0	1970, 2007
Baylor	8–3–0	1907, 1985	North Texas	2–0–0	1995, 2005
Boston College	2–0–0	1947, 1953	Ohio	1–0–0	1989, 1989
Cal State–Fullerton	1–0–0	1987	Ohio State	1–1–1	1987, 2008
Centenary	3–1–1	1895, 1933	Oklahoma	1–1–0	1950, 2004
Chattanooga	1–0–0	1954	Oklahoma State	1–0–0	1956
Cincinnati	0–1–0	1897	Oregon	2–1–0	1932, 1977
Citadel	1–0–0	2002	Oregon State	4–0–0	1976, 2004
Clemson	2–0–0	1959, 1996	Pacific	3–0–0	1950, 1972
Colorado	5–1–0	1962, 1980	Penn State	0–1–0	1974
Colorado State	1–1–0	1985, 1992	Rice	37–13–5	1915, 1995
Cumberland	0–1–0	1903	Rutgers	0–1–0	1922
Duke	1–1–0	1929, 1958	San José State	1–0–0	1999
East Carolina	1–0–0	1985	Santa Clara	0–2–0	1937, 1938
Florida	23–28–3	1937, 2007	Sewanee	3–6–0	1899, 1932
Florida State	2–7–0	1968, 1991	South Carolina	15–2–1	1930, 2007
Fordham	2–0–0	1942, 1946	South Dakota Wesleyan	1–0–0	1930
Fresno State	1–0–0	2006	Southeastern La.	1–0–0	1949
George Washington	1–0–0	1934	Southern Cal	1–1–0	1979, 1984
Georgia	14–11–1	1928, 2005	Southern Methodist	0–1–1	1922, 1934
Georgia Tech	6–12–0	1915, 2000	Southern Miss.	1–1–0	1951, 1994
Hardin-Simmons	1–0–0	1958	Southwestern (Tenn.)	1–0 0	1908
Haskell	1–1–0	1908, 1914	Southwestern Texas	1–0–0	1911
Havana University	1–0–0	1907	Spring Hill	8–0–0	1920, 1932
Holy Cross	2–1–0	1939, 1941	Stanford	0–1–0	1977
Houston	2–1–0	1996, 2000	Syracuse	1–1–0	1965, 1989
Howard	1–0–0	1907	TCU	5–2–1	1931, 1968
Idaho	1–0–0	1998	Tennessee	7–20–3	1925, 2007
Illinois	1–0–0	2002	Texas	7–9–1	1896, 2004
Indiana	2–1–0	1924, 1978	Texas A&M	26–20–3	1899, 1995
Iowa	0–1–0	2004	Texas–El Paso	1–0–0	1997
Iowa State	1–0–0	1971	Texas Tech	2–0–0	1954, 1957
Jefferson College	6–0–0	1913, 1920	Transylvania	1–0–0	1909
Kansas State	1–0–0	1980	Troy	1–0–0	2004
Kentucky	38–16–1	1949, 2007	Tulane	67–22–7	1893, 2007
Louisiana College	2–0–0	1928, 1929	UAB	0–1–0	2000
Louisiana–Lafayette	21–0–0	1902, 2006	Utah	2–0–0	1974, 1976
Louisiana–Monroe	1–0–0	2003	Utah State	2–0–0	1993, 2001
Louisiana Tech	17–1–0	1901, 2007	Vanderbilt	20–7–1	1902, 2005
Loyola	4–1–0	1922, 1939	Virginia Tech	1–1–0	2002, 2007
Manhattan	1–0–0	1935	Wake Forest	3–0–0	1960, 1979
Maryland	0–3–0	1951, 1955	Washington	1–0–0	1983
Mercer	1–0–0	1940	Western Carolina	1–0–0	2000
Miami (Fla.)	9–3–0	1946, 2005	Western Illinois	1–0–0	2003
Miami (Ohio)	2–1–0	1986, 2002	Wichita State	1–0–0	1984
Michigan State	1–0–0	1995	Wisconsin	2–0–0	1971, 1972
Middle Tennessee	2–0–0	2001, 2007	Wyoming	3–0–0	1968, 1978
Millsaps	2–1–0	1900, 1933			

Top Ten Tiger Stadium Crowds

	Attendance	Opponent	Date	Score		Attendance	Opponent	Date	Score
1.	92,910	Florida	10/6/07	LSU, 28–24	6.	92,588	Alabama	11/11/06	LSU, 28–14
2.	92,739	Virginia Tech	9/6/07	LSU, 48–7	7.	92,530	South Carolina	9/22/07	LSU, 28–16
3.	92,664	Auburn	10/22/05	LSU, 20–17 (OT)	8.	92,512	Louisiana Tech	11/10/07	LSU, 58–10
4.	92,630	Auburn	10/20/07	LSU, 30–24	9.	92,449	Ole Miss	11/18/06	LSU, 23–20 (OT)
5.	92,606	Arkansas	11/23/07	Arkansas, 50–48 (3 OT)	10.	92,407	Middle Tenn.	9/15/07	LSU, 44–0

LSU Coaching Records

No.	Name	Alma Mater	Tenure	Yrs.	W–L–T	Pct.
1.	Dr. Charles E. Coates	Johns Hopkins	1893	1	0–1–0	.000
2.	Albert P. Simmons	Yale	1894–95	2	5–1–0	.833
3.	Allen W. Jeardeau	Harvard	1896–97	2	7–1–0	.875
4.	Edmond A. Chavanne	LSU	1898, 1900	2	3–2–0	.600
5.	John P. Gregg	Wisconsin	1899	1	1–4–0	.200
6.	W. S. Borland	Allegheny	1901–03	3	15–7–0	.681
7.	D. A. Killian	Michigan	1904–06	3	8–6–2	.563
8.	Edgar R. Wingard	Susquehanna	1907–08	2	17–3–0	.850
9.	Joe G. Pritchard	Vanderbilt	1909	1	4–1–0	.800
10.	John W. Mayhew	Brown	1910	1	3–6–0	.333
11.	James K. "Pat" Dwyer	Penn	1911–13	3	16–7–2	.680
12.	E. T. McDonald	Colgate	1914–16	3	14–7–1	.659
13.	Dana X. Bible	Carson-Newman	1916	1	1–0–2	.667
14.	Wayne Sutton	Washington State	1917	1	3–5–0	.375
15.	Irving R. Pray	MIT	1916, 1922	3	11–9–0	.550
16.	Branch Bocock	Georgetown	1920–21	2	11–4–2	.706
17.	Mike Donahue	Yale	1923–27	5	23–19–3	.544
18.	Russ Cohen	Vanderbilt	1928–31	4	23–13–1	.635
19.	Lawrence "Biff" Jones	Army	1932–34	3	20–5–6	.741
20.	Bernie Moore	Carson-Newman	1935–47	13	83–39–6	.671
21.	Gaynell "Gus" Tinsley	LSU	1948–54	7	35–34–6	.507
22.	Paul Dietzel	Miami (Ohio)	1955–61	7	46–24–3	.651
23.	Charles McClendon	Kentucky	1962–79	18	137–59–7	.692
24.	Robert "Bo" Rein*	Ohio State	(11/30/79–1/10/80)			
25.	Jerry Stovall	Missouri Baptist	1980–83	4	22–21–2	.511
26.	Bill Arnsparger	Miami (Ohio)	1984–86	3	26–8–2	.750
27.	Mike Archer	Miami (Fla.)	1987–90	4	27–18–1	.598
28.	Hudson "Curley" Hallman	Texas A&M	1991–94	4	16–28–0	.364
29.	Gerry DiNardo	Notre Dame	1995–99	5	32–24–1	.570
30.	Hal Hunter	Northwestern	1999 (interim)	0	1–0–0	1.00
31.	Nick Saban	Kent State	2000–04	5	48–16–0	.750
32.	Les Miles	Michigan	2005–	3	34–6–0	.850
Totals			114 seasons		692–380–47	.639

*Rein died in an airplane crash on January 10, 1980, shortly after being named LSU's head coach.

Year-by-Year Results

Season results from left to right: LSU's AP ranking (after
  1935), date, opponent's ranking, opponent, win/loss/tie,
  score (overtime), TV network.
*Denotes SEC game
HC: Homecoming

Number in parentheses after opponent indicates one of the
following neutral or off-campus sites:

(1) Jackson, La.	(12) Houston
(2) Vicksburg, Miss.	(13) Shreveport
(3) New Orleans	(14) Dallas
(4) Meridian, Miss.	(15) Galveston, Tex.
(5) Mobile, Ala.	(16) San Antonio, Tex.
(6) Little Rock, Ark.	(17) New York City
(7) Alexandria, La.	(18) Montgomery, Ala.
(8) Memphis, Tenn.	(19) Indianapolis
(9) Birmingham, Ala.	(20) Jackson, Miss.
(10) Columbus, Miss.	(21) Monroe
(11) Gulfport, Miss.	(22) Columbus, Ga.

1893   Record: 0-1-0   SIAA: 0-1-0
Coach: Dr. Charles E. Coates
Captain: Ruffin G. Pleasant (QB)

Nov. 25	at Tulane	L	0–34

1894   Record: 2-1-0   SIAA: 0-1-0
Coach: Albert P. Simmons
Captain: Samuel Marmaduke Dinwidie Clark (FB)

Nov. 30	at Natchez AC	W	26 0
Dec. 3	Ole Miss	L	6–26
Dec. 21	Centenary	W	30–0

1895   Record: 3-0-0   SIAA: 2-0-0
Coach: Albert P. Simmons
Captain: J. E. Snyder (QB)

Oct. 26	Tulane	W	8–4
Nov. 2	at Centenary (1)	W	16–6
Nov. 18	Alabama	W	12–6

1896   Record: 6-0-0   SIAA: 3-0-0
Coach: Allen W. Jeardeau
Captain: Edwin Allen "Ned" Scott (T)

Oct. 10	Centenary	W	46–0
Oct. 24	at Tulane	W	6–0
Nov. 13	at Ole Miss (2)	W	12–4
Nov. 16	Texas	W	14–0
Nov. 20	Miss. State	W	52–0
Nov. 28	at Southern AC (3)	W	6–0

1897   Record: 1-1-0   SIAA: 0-0-0
Coach: Allen W. Jeardeau
Captain: Edwin Allen "Ned" Scott (T)

Dec. 20	Montgomery AC	W	28–6
Jan. 8	Cincinnati	L	0–26

1898   Record: 1-0-0   SIAA: 1-0-0
Coach: Edmond A. Chavanne
Captain: Edmond A. Chavanne (T)

Dec. 14	Tulane	W	37–0

1899   Record: 1-4-0   SIAA: 1-2-0
Coach: John P. Gregg
Captain: Hulette F. Aby (T)

Nov. 3	at Ole Miss (4)	L	0–11
Nov. 10	Lake Charles HS (exhib.)	W	48–0
Nov. 12	Sewanee	L	0–34
Nov. 30	at Texas	L	0–29
Dec. 2	at Texas A&M	L	0–52
Dec. 8	Tulane	W	38–0

1900   Record: 2-2-0   SIAA: 0-1-0
Coach: Edmond A. Chavanne
Captain: I. H. Schwing (QB)

Nov. 11	Millsaps	W	70–0
Nov. 17	at Tulane	L	0–29
Nov. 30	at Millsaps	L	5–6
Dec. 5	LSU Alumni	W	10–0

1901   Record: 5-1-0   SIAA: 2-1-0
Coach: W. S. Borland
Captain: E. L. Gorham (HB)

Oct. 28	at Louisiana Tech	W	57–0
Nov. 7	Ole Miss	W	46–0
Nov. 16	at Tulane	W	11–0
Nov. 20	Auburn	L	0–28
Nov. 28	YMCA–N.O.	W	38–0
Dec. 5	Arkansas	W	15–0

1902   Record: 6-1-0   SIAA: 4-1-0
Coach: W. S. Borland
Captain: Henry E. Landry (FB)

Oct. 16	at Southwestern La.	W	42–0
Oct. 18	Texas (16)	W	5–0
Oct. 27	Auburn	W	5–0
Nov. 8	Ole Miss (3)	W	6–0
Nov. 17	Vanderbilt	L	5–27
Nov. 27	at Miss. State	W	6–0
Nov. 29	at Alabama	W	11–0

1903   Record: 4-5-0   SIAA: 0-4-0
Coach: W. S. Borland
Captain: J. J. Coleman (HB)

Oct. 14	LSU Alumni	W	16–0
Oct. 24	Eagles–N.O.	W	33–0
Oct. 30	at Louisiana Tech	W	16–0
Oct. 31	at Shreveport AC	W	5–0
Nov. 7	at Miss. State	L	0–11
Nov. 9	at Alabama	L	0–18
Nov. 11	at Auburn	L	0–12
Nov. 16	Cumberland	L	0–41
Nov. 21	Ole Miss (3)	L	0–11

1904   Record: 3–4–0   SIAA: 1–2–0
Coach: Dan A. Killian
Captain: E. L. Klock (T)

Oct. 16	Louisiana Tech	W	17–0
Oct. 22	at Shreveport AC	L	0–16
Oct. 23	at Louisiana Tech	L	0–6
Nov. 5	Ole Miss	W	5–0
Nov. 10	Nashville Med.	W	16–0
Nov. 19	at Tulane	L	0–5
Dec. 1	Alabama	L	0–11

1905   Record: 3–0–0   SIAA: 2–0–0
Coach: Dan A. Killian
Captain: Frank M. Edwards (G)

Nov. 18	Louisiana Tech	W	16–0
Nov. 25	at Tulane	W	5–0
Dec. 1	Miss. State	W	15–0

1906   Record: 2–2–2   SIAA: 0–1–1
Coach: Dan A. Killian
Captain: E. E. Weil (FB)

Oct. 10	Monroe AC	W	5–0
Oct. 20	Ole Miss	L	0–9
Oct. 27	at Miss. State	T	0–0
Nov. 9	Louisiana Tech	W	17–0
Nov. 19	Texas A&M	L	12–21
Nov. 29	Arkansas	T	6–6

1907   Record: 7–3–0   SIAA: 2–1–0
Coach: Edgar R. Wingard
Captain: Solle W. Brannon (QB)

Oct. 11	Louisiana Tech	W	28–0
Oct. 19	at Texas	L	5–12
Oct. 21	at Texas A&M	L	5–11
Oct. 28	Howard	W	57–0
Nov. 6	Arkansas	W	17–12
Nov. 9	Miss. State	W	23–11
Nov. 16	at Ole Miss (20)	W	23–0
Nov. 23	at Alabama (5)	L	4–6
Nov. 30	Baylor	W	48–0
Dec. 25	at Havana, Cuba	W	56–0

National Champion (National Championship Foundation)
1908   Record: 10–0–0 SIAA: 2–0–0
Coach: Edgar R. Wingard
Captain: Marshall H. "Cap" Gandy (T)

Oct. 3	YMGC–N.O.	W	41–0
Oct. 11	Jackson Barracks –N.O.	W	81–5
Oct. 17	Texas A&M (3)	W	26–0
Oct. 26	Southwestern, Tenn.	W	55–0
Oct. 31	at Auburn	W	10–2
Nov. 7	Miss. State	W	50–0
Nov. 10	Baylor	W	89–0
Nov. 16	at Haskell (3)	W	32–0
Nov. 23	at Louisiana Tech	W	22–0
Nov. 26	at Arkansas (6)	W	36–4

1909   Record: 6–2–0   SIAA: 3–1–0
Coaches: Joe G. Pritchard, John W. Mayhew
Captain: R. L. "Big" Stovall (C)

Oct. 2	Jackson Barracks–N.O.	W	70–0
Oct. 9	Ole Miss	W	10–0
Oct. 16	Miss. State	W	15–0
Oct. 30	Sewanee (3)	L	6–15
Nov. 4	at Louisiana Tech (7)	W	23–0
Nov. 13	at Arkansas (8)	L	0–16
Nov. 18	Transylvania	W	52–0
Nov. 25	at Alabama (9)	W	12–6

1910   Record: 1–5–0   SIAA: 0–3–0
Coach: John W. Mayhew
Captain: Bill Seip (E)

Oct. 15	Miss. College	W	40–0
Oct. 21	at Miss. State (10)	L	0–3
Oct. 29	Sewanee (3)	L	5–31
Nov. 5	at Vanderbilt	L	0–22
Nov. 19	at Texas	L	0–12
Nov. 24	at Arkansas (6)	L	0–51

1911   Record: 6–3–0   SIAA: 1–1–0
Coach: James K. "Pat" Dwyer
Captain: Arthur J. "Tommy" Thomas (G)

Oct. 7	Southwestern La.	W	42–0
Oct. 14	Louisiana Normal	W	46–0
Oct. 20	Miss. College	W	40–0
Oct. 28	Meteor AC	W	40–0
Nov. 4	at Baylor	W	6–0
Nov. 12	at Miss. State (11)	L	0–6
Nov. 18	at Southwest Texas (12)	L	6–17
Nov. 30	at Arkansas (6)	L	0–11
Dec. 9	Tulane	W	6–0

1912   Record: 4–3–0   SIAA: 1–3–0
Coach: James K. "Pat" Dwyer
Captain: Charles S. Reiley (T)

Oct. 5	Southwestern La.	W	85–3
Oct. 11	Miss. College	W	45–0
Oct. 19	Ole Miss	L	7–10
Nov. 2	Miss. State	L	0–7
Nov. 9	at Auburn (5)	L	0–7
Nov. 16	at Arkansas (6)	W	7–6
Nov. 28	Tulane	W	21–3

1913   Record: 6–1–2   SIAA: 1–1–1
Coach: James K. "Pat" Dwyer
Captain: T. W. "Tom" Dutton (C)

Oct. 4	at Louisiana Tech	W	20–2
Oct. 11	at Southwestern La.	W	26–0
Oct. 18	Jefferson College	W	45–6
Oct. 23	Baylor	W	50–0
Nov. 1	at Auburn (5)	L	0–7
Nov. 8	Arkansas (13)	W	12–7
Nov. 15	at Miss. State	T	0–0
Nov. 22	Tulane	W	40–0
Nov. 27	at Texas A&M (12)	T	7–7

1914   Record: 4–4–1   SIAA: 0–1–1
Coach: E. T. McDonald
Captain: George B. Spencer (T)

Sept. 27	Southwestern La.	W	54–0
Oct. 3	Louisiana Tech	W	60–0
Oct. 10	Miss. College	W	14–0
Oct. 17	Ole Miss	L	0–21
Oct. 24	Jefferson College	W	14–13
Oct. 31	at Texas A&M (14)	L	9–63
Nov. 7	Arkansas (13)	L	12–20
Nov. 14	at Haskell (3)	L	0–31
Nov. 26	at Tulane	T	0–0

1915   Record: 6–2–0   SIAA: 3–1–0
Coach: E. T. McDonald
Captain: Alfred J. Reid (FB)

Oct. 1	Jefferson College	W	42–0
Oct. 8	Miss. College	W	14–0
Oct. 15	at Ole Miss	W	28–0
Oct. 22	Georgia Tech (3)	L	7–36
Oct. 29	Miss. State	W	10–0
Nov. 5	Arkansas (13)	W	13–7
Nov. 17	at Rice	L	0–6
Nov. 25	Tulane	W	12–0

1916   Record: 7–1–2   SIAA: 2–1–1
Coaches: E. T. McDonald, I. R. Pray, D. X. Bible
Captain: Phillip Cooper (T)

Sept. 30	at Southwestern La.	W	24–0
Oct. 7	Jefferson College	W	59–0
Oct. 14	at Texas A&M (15)	W	13–0
Oct. 21	Miss. College	W	50–7
Oct. 28	Sewanee (3)	L	0–7
Nov. 5	at Arkansas (13)	W	17–7
Nov. 12	at Miss. State	W	13–3
Nov. 19	Ole Miss	W	41–0
Nov. 24	Rice	T	7–7
Nov. 30	at Tulane	T	14–14

1917   Record: 3–5–0   SIAA: 1–3–0
Coach: Wayne Sutton
Captain: Arthur "Mickey" O'Quinn (E)

Oct. 6	Southwestern La.	W	20–6
Oct. 13	at Ole Miss	W	52–7
Oct. 20	Sewanee (3)	L	0–3
Oct. 27	at Texas A&M (16)	L	0–27
Nov. 3	at Arkansas (13)	L	0–14
Nov. 10	Miss. College	W	34–0
Nov. 17	Miss. State	L	0–9
Nov. 29	Tulane	L	6–28

1918
No Team (World War I)

1919   Record: 6–2–0   SIAA: 2–2–0
Coach: Irving R. Pray
Captain: T. W. Dutton (C)

Oct. 4	Southwestern La.	W	39–0
Oct. 11	Jefferson College	W	38–0
Oct. 18	Ole Miss	W	13–0
Oct. 25	at Arkansas (13)	W	20–0
Nov. 1	at Miss. State	L	0–6
Nov. 8	Miss. College	W	24–0
Nov. 15	Alabama	L	0–23
Nov. 22	at Tulane	W	27–6

1920   Record: 5–3–1   SIAA: 0–3–0
Coach: Branch Bocock
Captain: Roy L. Benoit (QB)

Oct. 2	Jefferson College	W	81–0
Oct. 2	Louisiana Normal	W	34–0
Oct. 9	Spring Hill	W	40–0
Oct. 16	at Texas A&M	T	0–0
Oct. 23	Miss. State	L	7–12
Oct. 30	Miss. College	W	41–9
Nov. 6	at Arkansas (13)	W	3–0
Nov. 13	at Alabama	L	0–21
Nov. 25	Tulane	L	0–21

1921   Record: 6–1–1   SIAA: 2–1–1
Coach: Branch Bocock
Captain: F. L. "Fritz" Spence (E)

Oct. 8	Louisiana Normal	W	78–0
Oct. 15	Texas A&M	W	6–0
Oct. 22	Spring Hill	W	41–7
Oct. 29	Alabama (3)	T	7–7
Nov. 5	at Arkansas (13)	W	10–7
Nov. 12	Ole Miss	W	21–0
Nov. 19	at Tulane	L	0–21
Dec. 3	at Miss. State	W	17–14

1922   Record: 3–7–0   SIAA: 1–2–0
Coach: Irving R. Pray
Captain: E. L. "Tubby" Ewen (E)

Sept. 30	Louisiana Normal	W	13–0
Oct. 7	Loyola	L	0–7
Oct. 14	at SMU	L	0–51
Oct. 20	at Texas A&M	L	0–47
Oct. 28	at Arkansas (13)	L	6–40
Nov. 2	Spring Hill	W	25–7
Nov. 7	at Rutgers (17)	L	0–25
Nov. 10	at Alabama	L	3–47
Nov. 18	Miss. State	L	0–7
Nov. 30	Tulane (HC)	W	25–14

1923   Record: 3–5–1   SIC: 0–3–0
Coach: Mike Donahue
Captain: E. L. "Tubby" Ewen (E)

Sept. 29	Louisiana Normal	W	40–0
Oct. 6	Southwestern La.	W	7–3
Oct. 13	Spring Hill	W	33–0
Oct. 20	Texas A&M	L	0–28
Oct. 27	at Arkansas (13)	L	13–26
Nov. 2	at Miss. College (2)	T	0–0
Nov. 16	at Alabama (18)	L	3–30
Nov. 24	at Tulane	L	0–20
Dec. 1	at Miss. State	L	7–14

1924   Record: 5–4–0   SIC: 0–3–0
Coach: Mike Donahue
Captain: C. C. "Cliff" Campbell (T)

Sept. 27	Spring Hill	W	7–6
Oct. 4	Southwestern La.	W	31–7
Oct. 11	at Indiana (19)	W	20–14
Oct. 18	at Rice	W	12–0
Oct. 25	at Auburn (9)	L	0–3
Nov. 1	at Arkansas (13)	L	7–10
Nov. 8	at Georgia Tech	L	7–28
Nov. 15	Louisiana Normal	W	40–0
Nov. 25	Tulane (HC)†	L	0–13

† First game in Tiger Stadium

1925   Record: 5–3–1   SIC: 0–2–1
Coach: Mike Donahue
Captain: Jonathan Edward Steele (G)

Sept. 26	Louisiana Normal	W	27–0
Oct. 3	Southwestern La.	W	38–0
Oct. 10	Alabama (HC)	L	0–42
Oct. 17	LSU Freshmen	W	6–0
Oct. 24	at Tennessee	T	0–0
Oct. 31	at Arkansas (13)	L	0–12
Nov. 7	Rice	W	6–0
Nov. 14	at Loyola	W	13–0
Nov. 21	Tulane	L	0–16

1926   Record: 6–3–0   SIC: 3–3–0
Coach: Mike Donahue
Captain: L. T. "Babe" Godfrey (HB)

Sept. 25	Louisiana Normal	W	47–0
Oct. 2	Southwestern La.	W	34–0
Oct. 9	Tennessee	L	7–14
Oct. 16	at Auburn (18)	W	10–0
Oct. 23	at Miss. State (20)	L	6–7
Oct. 30	at Alabama	L	0–24
Nov. 6	at Arkansas (13)	W	14–0
Nov. 13	Ole Miss	W	3–0
Nov. 25	at Tulane	W	7–0

1927   Record: 4–4–1   SIC: 2–3–1
Coach: Mike Donahue
Captain: L. T. "Babe" Godfrey (HB)

Sept. 24	Louisiana Tech	W	45–0
Oct. 1	Southwestern La.	W	52–0
Oct. 8	at Alabama (9)	T	0–0
Oct. 15	at Auburn (18)	W	9–0
Oct. 22	at Miss. State (20)	W	9–7
Oct. 29	at Arkansas (13)	L	0–28
Nov. 5	at Ole Miss	L	7–12
Nov. 12	at Georgia Tech	L	0–23
Nov. 24	Tulane	L	6–13

1928   Record: 6–2–1   SIC: 3–1–1
Coach: Russ Cohen
Captain: Jess Tinsley (T)

Oct. 6	Southwestern La.	W	46–0
Oct. 13	Louisiana College	W	41–0
Oct. 20	at Miss. State (20)	W	31–0
Oct. 27	Spring Hill	W	30–7
Nov. 3	at Arkansas (13)	L	0–7
Nov. 10	Ole Miss (HC)	W	19–6
Nov. 17	at Georgia	W	13–12
Nov. 29	at Tulane	T	0–0
Dec. 8	at Alabama (9)	L	0–13

1929   Record: 6–3–0   SIC: 3–1–0
Coach: Russ Cohen
Captain: Frank Ellis (T)

Sept. 28	Louisiana College	W	58–0
Oct. 5	Southwestern La.	W	58–0
Oct. 12	Sewanee (HC)	W	27–14
Oct. 19	at Miss. State (20)	W	31–6
Oct. 26	Louisiana Tech	W	53–7
Nov. 2	at Arkansas (13)	L	0–32
Nov. 9	at Duke	L	6–32
Nov. 16	Ole Miss	W	13–6
Nov. 28	Tulane	L	0–21

1930   Record: 6–4–0   SIC: 2–3–0
Coach: Russ Cohen
Captain: Walter "Dobie" Reeves (HB)

Sept. 20	S. Dakota Wesleyan	W	76–0
Sept. 27	Louisiana Tech	W	71–0
Oct. 4	Southwestern La.	W	85–0
Oct. 11	at South Carolina	L	6–7
Oct. 18	at Miss. State (20)	L	6–8
Oct. 25	Sewanee (HC)	W	12–0
Nov. 1	at Arkansas (13)	W	27–12
Nov. 8	Ole Miss	W	6–0
Nov. 15	at Alabama (18)	L	0–33
Nov. 27	at Tulane	L	7–12

1931   Record: 5–4–0   SIC: 2–2–0
Coach: Russ Cohen
Captain: Edward Khoury (T)

Sept. 26	at TCU	L	0–3
Oct. 3	Spring Hill††	W	35–0
Oct. 10	South Carolina (HC)	W	19–12
Oct. 17	Miss. State	W	31–0
Oct. 24	at Arkansas (13)	W	13–6
Oct. 31	Sewanee	L	6–12
Nov. 7	at Army	L	0–20
Nov. 14	at Ole Miss (20)	W	26–3
Nov. 28	at Tulane	L	7–34

†† First night game in Tiger Stadium

1932   Record: 6–3–1   SIC: 3–0–0
Coach: Lawrence M. "Biff" Jones
Captain: Walter Fleming (E)

Sept. 24	TCU	T	3–3
Oct. 1	at Rice	L	8–10
Oct. 8	Spring Hill	W	80–0
Oct. 15	at Miss. State (21)	W	24–0
Oct. 22	at Arkansas (13)	W	14–0
Oct. 29	Sewanee (HC)	W	38–0
Nov. 5	at South Carolina	W	6–0
Nov. 12	at Centenary	L	0–6
Nov. 26	Tulane	W	14–0
Dec. 17	Oregon	L	0–12

1933   Record: 7–0–3   SEC: 3–0–2

Coach: Lawrence M. "Biff" Jones
Captain: Jack Torrance (T)

Sept. 30	Rice	W	13–0
Oct. 7	Millsaps	W	40–0
Oct. 14	Centenary	T	0–0
Oct. 21	at Arkansas (13)	W	20–0
Oct. 28	*Vanderbilt (HC)	T	7–7
Nov. 4	South Carolina	W	30–7
Nov. 18	*Ole Miss	W	31–0
Nov. 25	*at Miss. State (21)	W	21–6
Dec. 2	*at Tulane	T	7–7
Dec. 9	*Tennessee	W	7–0

1934   Record: 7–2–2   SEC: 4–2–0

Coach: Lawrence M. "Biff" Jones
Captain: Bert Yates (HB)

Sept. 29	at Rice	T	9–9
Oct. 6	SMU	T	14–14
Oct. 13	*Auburn (HC)	W	20–6
Oct. 20	at Arkansas (13)	W	16–0
Oct. 27	*at Vanderbilt	W	29–0
Nov. 3	*Miss. State	W	25–3
Nov. 10	at George Wash.	W	6–0
Nov. 17	*at Ole Miss (20)	W	14–0
Dec. 1	*Tulane	L	12–13
Dec. 8	*at Tennessee	L	13–19
Dec. 15	Oregon	W	14–13

National Champion (Williamson)
SEC Champion

1935   Record: 9–2–0   SEC: 5–0–0

Coach: Bernie H. Moore
Captain: W. J. Barrett (E)

Sept. 28	Rice	L	7–10	
Oct. 5	Texas	W	18–6	
Oct. 12	at Manhattan	W	32–0	
Oct. 19	at Arkansas (13)	W	13–7	
Oct. 26	*at Vanderbilt	W	7–2	
Nov. 2	*Auburn (HC)	W	6–0	
Nov. 9	*Miss. State	W	28–13	
Nov. 16	*at Georgia	W	13–0	
Nov. 23	Southwestern La.	W	56–0	
Nov. 30	*at Tulane	W	41–0	

Sugar Bowl, New Orleans

Jan. 1	TCU	L	2–3	5,000

National Champion (Williamson, Sagarin)
SEC Champion

1936   Record: 9–1–1   SEC: 6–0–0

Final ranking: No. 2 (AP)
Coach: Bernie H. Moore
Captain: Bill May (QB/FB)

	Sept. 26	Rice	W	20–7
	Oct. 3	at Texas	T	6–6
	Oct. 10	*Georgia	W	47–7
	Oct. 17	*Ole Miss	W	13–0
#13	Oct. 24	at Arkansas (13)	W	19–7
#8	Oct. 31	*at Vanderbilt	W	19–0
#7	Nov. 7	*Miss. State (HC)	W	12–0
#7	Nov. 14	*at Auburn (9)	W	19–6
#5	Nov. 21	Southwestern La.	W	93–0
#2	Nov. 28	*#19 Tulane	W	33–0

Sugar Bowl, New Orleans

#2	Jan. 1	#6 Santa Clara	L	14–21

1937   Record: 9–2–0   SEC: 5–1–0

Final ranking: No. 8 (AP)
Coach: Bernie H. Moore
Captain: Art "Slick" Morton (HB/TB)

	Sept. 25	*Florida	W	19–0
	Oct. 2	Texas	W	9–0
	Oct. 9	at Rice	W	13–0
	Oct. 16	*Ole Miss	W	13–0
#6	Oct. 23	*at #20 Vanderbilt	L	6–7
#17	Oct. 30	Loyola	W	52–6
#18	Nov. 6	*Miss. State (HC)	W	41–0
#12	Nov. 13	*#14 Auburn	W	9–7
#8	Nov. 20	Louisiana Normal	W	52–0
#10	Nov. 27	*at Tulane	W	20–0

Sugar Bowl, New Orleans

#8	Jan. 1	#9 Santa Clara	L	0–6

1938   Record: 6–4–0   SEC: 2–4–0

Coach: Bernie H. Moore
Captain: Ben Friend (T)

Sept. 24	*Ole Miss	L	7–20
Oct. 1	at Texas	W	20–0
Oct. 8	Rice	W	3–0
Oct. 15	Loyola	W	47–0
Oct. 22	*#16 Vanderbilt (HC)	W	7–0
Oct. 29	*at #8 Tennessee	L	6–14
Nov. 5	*Miss. State	W	32–7
Nov. 12	*at Auburn (9)	L	6–28
Nov. 19	Southwestern La.	W	32–0
Nov. 26	*Tulane	L	0–14

1939   Record: 4–5–0   SEC: 1–5–0

Coach: Bernie H. Moore
Captain: Young Bussey (HB)

	Sept. 30	*Ole Miss	L	7–14
	Oct. 7	at Holy Cross	W	26–7
	Oct. 14	Rice	W	7–0
	Oct. 21	Loyola	W	20–0
	Oct. 28	*at Vanderbilt	W	12–6
#18	Nov. 4	*#1 Tennessee (HC)	L	0–20
	Nov. 11	*Miss. State	L	12–15
	Nov. 18	*Auburn	L	7–21
	Dec. 2	*at #5 Tulane	L	20–33

1940   Record: 6–4–0   SEC: 3–3–0

Coach: Bernie H. Moore
Captain: Charles Anastasio (HB)

Sept. 21	Louisiana Tech	W	39–7
Sept. 28	*Ole Miss	L	6–19
Oct. 5	Holy Cross	W	25–0
Oct. 12	at Rice	L	0–23
Oct. 19	Mercer	W	20–0
Oct. 26	*Vanderbilt (HC)	W	7–0
Nov. 2	*at #7 Tennessee	L	0–28

Nov. 9	*#19 Miss. State	L	7–22
Nov. 16	*at Auburn (9)	W	21–13
Nov. 30	*Tulane	W	14–0

1941   Record: 4–4–2   SEC: 2–2–2
Coach: Bernie H. Moore
Captain: Leo Bird (HB)

Sept. 20	Louisiana Tech	W	25–0
Sept. 27	Holy Cross	L	13–19
Oct. 4	at Texas	L	0–34
Oct. 11	*#19 Miss. State	T	0–0
Oct. 18	Rice	W	27–0
Oct. 25	*Florida	W	10–7
Nov. 1	*Tennessee (HC)	L	6–13
Nov. 8	*#16 Ole Miss	L	12–13
Nov. 15	*Auburn	T	7–7
Nov. 29	*at Tulane	W	19–0

1942   Record: 7–3–0   SEC: 3–2–0
Coach: Bernie H. Moore
Captain: Willie Miller (G)

	Sept. 19	Louisiana Normal	W	40–0
	Sept. 26	Texas A&M	W	16–7
	Oct. 3	at Rice	L	14–27
	Oct. 10	*Miss. State	W	16–6
	Oct. 17	*Ole Miss (HC)	W	21–7
	Oct. 24	Georgia Navy	W	34–0
#19	Oct. 31	at *#20 Tennessee	L	0–26
	Nov. 7	at Fordham	W	26–13
	Nov. 14	*at Auburn (9)	L	7–25
	Nov. 26	*Tulane	W	18–6

1943   Record: 6–3–0   SEC: 2–2–0
Coach: Bernie H. Moore
Captain: Steve Van Buren (HB)

	Sept. 25	*Georgia	W	34–27
	Oct. 2	Rice	W	20–7
#17	Oct. 9	Texas A&M	L	13–28
	Oct. 16	Louisiana Army (STU)	W	28–7
	Oct. 23	*at Georgia (22)	W	27–6
	Oct. 30	TCU	W	14–0
#20	Nov. 6	*at Georgia Tech	L	7–42
	Nov. 20	*at Tulane	L	0–27

Orange Bowl, Miami
| Jan. 1 | Texas A&M | W | 19–14 |

1944   Record: 2–5–1   SEC: 2–3–1
Coach: Bernie H. Moore
Captain: Al Cavigga (G)

Sept. 30	*Alabama	T	27–27
Oct. 7	at Rice	L	13–14
Oct. 14	Texas A&M	L	0–7
Oct. 21	*Miss. State	L	6–13
Oct. 28	*at Georgia	W	15–7
Nov. 4	*#16 Tennessee (HC)	L	0–13
Nov. 18	*#9 Georgia Tech	L	6–14
Nov. 30	*Tulane	W	25–6

1945   Record: 7–2–0   SEC: 5–2–0
Final ranking: No. 15 (AP)
Coach: Bernie H. Moore
Captain: Andy Kosmac (QB)

	Sept. 29	Rice	W	42–0
	Oct. 6	*Alabama	L	7–26
	Oct. 13	#17 Texas A&M	W	31–12
	Oct. 20	*at #12 Georgia	W	32–0
#13	Oct. 27	*Vanderbilt	W	39–7
#17	Nov. 3	*Ole Miss	W	32–13
#14	Nov. 10	*Miss. State (HC)	L	20–27
	Nov. 17	*at Georgia Tech	W	9–7
	Dec. 1	*at Tulane	W	33–0

1946   Record: 9–1–1   SEC: 5–1–0
Final ranking: No. 8 (AP)
Coach: Bernie H. Moore
Captain: Dilton Richmond (E)

	Sept. 28	at Rice	W	7–6
	Oct. 5	*Miss. State	W	13–6
#13	Oct. 12	Texas A&M	W	33–9
#12	Oct. 19	*Georgia Tech (HC)	L	7–26
	Oct. 26	*at Vanderbilt	W	14–0
	Nov. 2	*Ole Miss	W	34–21
#19	Nov. 9	*Alabama	W	31–21
#11	Nov. 15	at Miami (Fla.)	W	20–7
#9	Nov. 23	Fordham	W	40–0
#9	Nov. 30	*Tulane	W	41–27

Cotton Bowl, Dallas
| #8 | Jan. 1 | #16 Arkansas | T | 0–0 |

1947   Record: 5–3–1   SEC: 2–3–1
Coach: Bernie H. Moore
Captain: Jim Cason (HB)

	Sept. 27	Rice	W	21–14
	Oct. 4	*at Georgia	L	19–35
	Oct. 11	Texas A&M	W	19–13
	Oct. 17	at Boston College	W	14–13
#18	Oct. 25	*#19 Vanderbilt (HC)	W	19–13
#17	Nov. 1	*Ole Miss	L	18–20
	Nov. 15	*Miss. State	W	21–6
	Nov. 22	*at #8 Alabama	L	12–41
	Dec. 6	*at Tulane	T	6–6

1948   Record: 3–7–0   SEC: 1–5–0
Coach: Gaynell Tinsley
Captain: Ed Claunch (C)

Sept. 18	at Texas	L	0–33
Oct. 2	Rice	W	26–13
Oct. 9	Texas A&M	W	14–13
Oct. 16	*#16 Georgia	L	0–22
Oct. 23	at #3 North Carolina	L	7–34
Oct. 30	*Ole Miss (HC)	L	19–49
Nov. 6	*at Vanderbilt	L	7–48
Nov. 13	*Miss. State	L	0–7
Nov. 20	*Alabama	W	26–6
Nov. 27	*#14 Tulane	L	0–46

1949 Record: 8–3–0 SEC: 4–2–0
Final ranking: No. 9 (AP)
Coach: Gaynell Tinsley
Captain: Mel Lyle (E)

	Sept. 24	*Kentucky	L	0–19
	Oct. 1	Rice	W	14–7
	Oct. 8	Texas A&M	W	34–0
	Oct. 14	*at Georgia	L	0–7
	Oct. 22	#6 North Carolina	W	13–7
#17	Oct. 29	*Ole Miss	W	34–7
#17	Nov. 5	*Vanderbilt	W	33–13
#16	Nov. 12	*Miss. State (HC)	W	34–7
#13	Nov. 19	Southeastern La.	W	48–7
#13	Nov. 26	*at #10 Tulane	W	21–0

Sugar Bowl, New Orleans

#9	Jan. 1	#2 Oklahoma	L	0–35

1950 Record: 4–5–2 SEC: 2–3–2
Coach: Gaynell Tinsley
Captain: Ebert Van Buren (HB)

Sept. 23	*at #13 Kentucky	L	0–14
Sept. 30	Pacific	W	19–0
Oct. 7	at Rice	L	20–35
Oct. 14	*Georgia Tech (HC)	L	0–13
Oct. 21	*Georgia	T	13–13
Nov. 4	*Ole Miss	W	40–14
Nov. 11	*at Vanderbilt	W	33–7
Nov. 18	*Miss. State	L	7–13
Nov. 24	Villanova	W	13–7
Dec. 2	*at #20 Tulane	T	14–14
Dec. 9	at #3 Texas	L	6–21

1951 Record: 7–3–1 SEC: 4–2–1
Coach: Gaynell Tinsley
Captains: Ray Potter (T), Chester Freeman (RHB)

Sept. 22	Southern Miss	W	13–0
Sept. 29	*at #9 Alabama (5)	W	13–7
Oct. 6	Rice	W	7–6
Oct. 13	*at #8 Georgia Tech	L	7–25
Oct. 20	*at Georgia	W	7–0
Oct. 27	#5 Maryland	L	0–27
Nov. 3	*Ole Miss (HC)	T	6–6
Nov. 10	*Vanderbilt	L	13–20
Nov. 17	*Miss. State	W	3–0
Nov. 24	Villanova (13)	W	45–7
Dec. 1	*Tulane	W	14–13

1952 Record: 3–7–0 SEC: 2–5–0
Coach: Gaynell Tinsley
Captains: Norm Stevens (QB), Joe Modicut (LG), Bill Lansing (RG), Leroy Labat (HB), Jim Sanford (T), Ralph McLeod (LE)

Sept. 20	#11 Texas	L	14–35
Sept. 27	*Alabama	L	20–21
Oct. 4	at #17 Rice	W	27–7
Oct. 11	*at Kentucky	W	34–7
Oct. 18	*Georgia	L	14–27
Oct. 25	at #2 Maryland	L	6–34
Nov. 1	*at Ole Miss	L	0–28
Nov. 8	*#8 Tennessee (HC)	L	3–22
Nov. 15	*Miss. State	L	14–33
Nov. 29	*at Tulane	W	16–0

1953 Record: 5–3–3 SEC: 2–3–3
Coach: Gaynell Tinsley
Captains: Jerry Marchand (LHB), Charley Oakley (FB)

	Sept. 19	#11 Texas	W	20–7
	Sept. 26	*at #5 Alabama (5)	T	7–7
#19	Oct. 3	Boston College	W	42–6
#14	Oct. 10	*Kentucky	T	6–6
	Oct. 17	*at Georgia	W	14–6
#14	Oct. 24	*at Florida	T	21–21
	Oct. 31	*#18 Ole Miss	L	16–27
	Nov. 7	*at Tennessee	L	14–32
	Nov. 14	*Miss. State (HC)	L	13–26
	Nov. 21	at Arkansas (6)	W	9–8
	Nov. 28	*Tulane	W	32–13

1954 Record: 5–6–0 SEC: 2–5–0
Coach: Gaynell Tinsley
Captain: Sid Fournet (LG)

Sept. 18	at #4 Texas	L	6–20
Sept. 25	*Alabama	L	0–12
Oct. 2	*at Kentucky	L	6–7
Oct. 9	*at Georgia Tech	L	20–30
Oct. 16	#20 Texas Tech	W	20–13
Oct. 23	*#18 Florida	W	20–7
Oct. 30	*#12 Ole Miss (HC)	L	6–21
Nov. 6	Chattanooga	W	26–19
Nov. 13	*Miss. State	L	0–25
Nov. 20	#9 Arkansas (13)	W	7–6
Nov. 27	*Tulane	W	14–13

1955 Record: 3–5–2 SEC: 2–3–1
Coach: Paul Dietzel
Captains: Joe Tuminello (E), O. K. Ferguson (FB)

	Sept. 17	*Kentucky	W	19–7
#16	Sept. 24	at Texas A&M (14)	L	0–28
	Oct. 1	at #11 Rice	T	20–20
	Oct. 8	*#4 Georgia Tech	L	0–7
	Oct. 15	*at Florida	L	14–18
	Oct. 29	*Ole Miss	L	26–29
	Nov. 5	at #1 Maryland	L	0–13
	Nov. 12	*#18 Miss. State (HC)	W	34–7
	Nov. 19	at Arkansas (6)	W	13–7
	Nov. 26	*Tulane	T	13–13

1956 Record: 3–7–0 SEC: 1–5–0
Coach: Paul Dietzel
Captain: Don Scully (G)

Sept. 29	#11 Texas A&M	L	6–9
Oct. 6	at Rice	L	14–23
Oct. 13	*at #3 Georgia Tech	L	7–39
Oct. 20	*at Kentucky	L	0–14
Oct. 27	*Florida (HC)	L	6–21
Nov. 3	*Ole Miss	L	17–46
Nov. 10	Oklahoma A&M	W	13–0
Nov. 17	*Miss. State	L	13–32

Nov. 24	Arkansas (13)	W	21–7	
Dec. 1	*at Tulane	W	7–6	

1957 Record: 5–5–0 SEC: 4–4–0
Coach: Paul Dietzel
Captain: Alvin Aucoin (LT)

	Sept. 21	Rice	L	14–20
	Sept. 28	*Alabama	W	28–0
	Oct. 5	at Texas Tech	W	19–14
	Oct. 12	*#17 Georgia Tech	W	20–13
#17	Oct. 19	*Kentucky (HC)	W	21–0
#10	Oct. 26	*at Florida	L	14–22
	Nov. 2	*at Vanderbilt	L	0–7
	Nov. 9	*at #14 Ole Miss	L	12–14
	Nov. 16	*#12 Miss. State	L	6–14
	Nov. 30	*Tulane	W	25–6

National Champion
SEC Champion
1958 Record: 11–0–0 SEC: 6–0–0
Final ranking: No. 1 (AP, UPI)
Coach: Paul Dietzel
Captain: Billy Hendrix (E)

	Sept. 20	at Rice	W	26–6	
#15	Sept. 27	*at Alabama (5)	W	13–3	
#13	Oct. 4	Hardin-Simmons	W	20–6	
#11	Oct. 10	at Miami (Fla.)	W	41–0	
#9	Oct. 18	*Kentucky	W	32–7	
#3	Oct. 25	*Florida (HC)	W	10–7	
#1	Nov. 1	*#6 Ole Miss	W	14–0	
#1	Nov. 8	Duke	W	50–18	
#1	Nov. 15	*at Miss. State (20)	W	7–6	
#1	Nov. 22	*at Tulane	W	62–0	

Sugar Bowl, New Orleans

#1	Jan. 1	#12 Clemson	W	7–0	NBC

1959 Record: 9–2–0 SEC: 5–1–0
Final ranking: No. 3 (AP, UPI)
Coach: Paul Dietzel
Captain: Lynn LeBlanc (T)

#1	Sept. 19	Rice	W	26–3	NBC
#1	Sept. 26	#9 TCU	W	10–0	
#1	Oct. 3	Baylor (13)	W	22–0	
#1	Oct. 10	Miami (Fla.)	W	27–3	
#1	Oct. 17	*at Kentucky	W	9–0	
#1	Oct. 24	*at Florida	W	9–0	
#1	Oct. 31	*#3 Ole Miss (HC)	W	7–3	
#1	Nov. 7	*at #13 Tennessee	L	13–14	
#3	Nov. 14	*Miss. State	W	27–0	
#3	Nov. 21	*Tulane	W	14–6	

Sugar Bowl, New Orleans

#3	Jan. 1	#2 Ole Miss	L	0–21	NBC

1960 Record: 5–4–1 SEC: 2–3–1
Coach: Paul Dietzel
Captain: Charles "Bo" Strange (C)

	Sept. 17	Texas A&M	W	9–0
	Oct. 1	Baylor	L	3–7
	Oct. 8	*at Georgia Tech	L	2–6

Oct. 15	*at Kentucky	L	0–3	
Oct. 22	*Florida	L	10–13	
Oct. 29	*at #2 Ole Miss	T	6–6	ABC
Nov. 5	South Carolina (HC)	W	35–6	
Nov. 12	*Miss. State	W	7–3	
Nov. 19	Wake Forest	W	16–0	
Nov. 26	*at Tulane	W	17–6	

SEC Champion
1961 Record: 10–1–0 SEC: 6–0–0
Final ranking: No. 3 (UPI), No. 4 (AP)
Coach: Paul Dietzel
Captain: Roy "Moonie" Winston (G)

#5	Sept. 23	at Rice	L	3–16	
	Sept. 30	Texas A&M	W	16–7	
	Oct. 7	*#3 Georgia Tech	W	10–0	
	Oct. 14	at South Carolina	W	42–0	
#10	Oct. 21	*Kentucky (HC)	W	24–14	
#7	Oct. 28	*at Florida	W	23–0	
#6	Nov. 4	*#2 Ole Miss	W	10–7	
#4	Nov. 11	at North Carolina	W	30–0	ABC
#4	Nov. 18	*Miss. State	W	14–6	
#4	Nov. 25	*Tulane	W	62–0	

Orange Bowl, Miami

#4	Jan. 1	#7 Colorado	W	25–7	NBC

National Champion (Berryman)
1962 Record: 9–1–1 SEC: 5–1–0
Final ranking: No. 7 (AP), No. 8 (UPI)
Coach: Charles McClendon
Captain: Fred Miller (RT)

#5	Sept. 22	Texas A&M	W	21–0	
#5	Sept. 29	Rice	T	6–6	
	Oct. 6	*at #5 Georgia Tech	W	10–7	CBS
#6	Oct. 13	Miami (Fla.)	W	17–3	
#4	Oct. 20	*at Kentucky	W	7–0	
#6	Oct. 27	*Florida (HC)	W	23–0	
#4	Nov. 3	*#6 Ole Miss	L	7–15	
#9	Nov. 10	TCU	W	5–0	
#10	Nov. 17	*at Miss. State (20)	W	28–0	
#8	Nov. 24	*at Tulane	W	38–3	

Cotton Bowl, Dallas

#7	Jan. 1	#4 Texas	W	13–0	CBS

1963 Record: 7–4–0 SEC: 4–2–0
Coach: Charles McClendon
Captain: Billy Truax (E)

	Sept. 21	Texas A&M	W	14–6	
	Sept. 28	at Rice	L	12–21	
	Oct. 5	*#7 Georgia Tech	W	7–6	
	Oct. 11	at Miami (Fla.)	W	3–0	
	Oct. 19	*Kentucky (HC)	W	28–7	
	Oct. 26	*at Florida	W	14–0	
	Nov. 2	*#3 Ole Miss	L	3–37	CBS
	Nov. 9	TCU	W	28–14	
	Nov. 16	*Miss. State (20)	L	6–7	
	Nov. 23	*Tulane	W	20–0	

Bluebonnet Bowl, Houston

	Dec. 21	Baylor	L	7–14	CBS

1964   Record: 8–2–1   SEC: 4–2–1
Final ranking: No. 7 (AP, UPI)
Coach: Charles McClendon
Captain: Richard Granier (C)

	Sept. 19	Texas A&M	W	9–6	
	Sept. 26	at Rice	W	3–0	
	Oct. 10	North Carolina	W	20–3	
#9	Oct. 17	*at Kentucky	W	27–7	
#7	Oct. 24	*Tennessee (HC)	T	3–3	NBC
#9	Oct. 31	*Ole Miss	W	11–10	
#8	Nov. 7	*at #3 Alabama (9)	L	9–17	
#9	Nov. 14	*Miss. State	W	14–10	
#8	Nov. 21	*at Tulane	W	13–3	
#7	Dec. 5	*Florida	L	6–20	

Sugar Bowl, New Orleans

#7	Jan. 1	Syracuse	W	13–10	NBC

1965   Record: 8–3–0   SEC: 3–3–0
Final ranking: No. 8 (AP), No. 14 (UPI)
Coach: Charles McClendon
Captains: Billy Ezell (QB), John Aaron (RG)

#8	Sept. 18	Texas A&M	W	10–0	
#7	Sept. 25	Rice	W	42–14	
#5	Oct. 2	*at Florida	L	7–14	
	Oct. 9	at Miami (Fla.)	W	34–27	
	Oct. 16	*Kentucky (HC)	W	31–21	
#9	Oct. 23	South Carolina	W	21–7	
#5	Oct. 30	*at Ole Miss (20)	L	0–23	
	Nov. 6	*#5 Alabama	L	7–31	NBC
	Nov. 13	*Miss. State	W	37–20	
	Nov. 20	*Tulane	W	62–0	

Cotton Bowl, Dallas

	Jan. 1	#2 Arkansas	W	14–7	CBS

1966   Record: 5–4–1   SEC: 3–3–0
Coach: Charles McClendon
Captains: Leonard Neumann (TB), Gawain DiBetta (FB)

	Sept. 17	South Carolina	W	28–12	
	Sept. 24	at Rice	L	15–17	
	Oct. 1	Miami (Fla.)	W	10–8	
	Oct. 8	Texas A&M	T	7–7	
	Oct. 15	*at Kentucky	W	30–0	
	Oct. 22	*#8 Florida (HC)	L	7–28	
	Oct. 29	*Ole Miss	L	0–17	
	Nov. 5	*at #4 Alabama (9)	L	0–21	ABC
	Nov. 12	*Miss. State	W	17–7	ABC
	Nov. 19	*at Tulane†	W	21–7	

† Designated a conference game by the SEC

1967   Record: 7–3–1   SEC: 3–2–1
Coach: Charles McClendon
Captains: Barry Wilson (C), Benny Griffin (LB)

	Sept. 23	Rice	W	20–14	
	Sept. 30	Texas A&M	W	17–6	
	Oct. 7	*at Florida	W	37–6	
	Oct. 14	Miami (Fla.)	L	15–17	
	Oct. 21	*Kentucky (HC)	W	30–7	
	Oct. 28	*at #4 Tennessee	L	14–17	
	Nov. 4	*at Ole Miss (20)	T	13–13	ABC

	Nov. 11	*Alabama	L	6–7	
	Nov. 18	*Miss. State	W	55–0	
	Nov. 25	Tulane	W	41–27	

Sugar Bowl, New Orleans

	Jan. 1	#6 Wyoming	W	20–13	NBC

1968   Record: 8–3–0   SEC: 4–2–0
Final ranking: No. 19 (AP)
Coach: Charles McClendon
Captains: Barton Frye (CB), Jerry Guillot (RG)

#20	Sept. 21	#13 Texas A&M	W	13–12	
#14	Sept. 28	at Rice	W	21–7	
#10	Oct. 5	Baylor	W	48–16	
#8	Oct. 11	at Miami (Fla.)	L	0–30	
#20	Oct. 19	*Kentucky	W	13–3	
#18	Oct. 26	*TCU†† (HC)	W	10–7	
#14	Nov. 2	*Ole Miss	L	24–27	
#20	Nov. 9	*at Alabama (9)	L	7–16	
	Nov. 16	*Miss. State	W	20–16	
	Nov. 23	*at Tulane††	W	34–10	

Peach Bowl, Atlanta

	Dec. 30	#19 Florida State	W	31–27	TVS

†† Designated a conference game by the SEC

1969   Record: 9–1–0   SEC: 4–1–0
Final ranking: No. 7 (UPI), No. 10 (AP)
Coach: Charles McClendon
Captains: George Bevan (LB), Robert "Red" Ryder (OT)

	Sept. 20	Texas A&M	W	35–6	
	Sept. 27	at Rice	W	42–0	
#16	Oct. 4	Baylor	W	63–8	
#14	Oct. 10	at Miami (Fla.)	W	20–0	
#9	Oct. 18	*at Kentucky	W	37–10	
#9	Oct. 25	*#14 Auburn (HC)	W	21–20	ABC
#8	Nov. 1	*at Ole Miss (20)	L	23–26	ABC
#12	Nov. 8	*Alabama	W	20–15	
#12	Nov. 15	*Miss. State	W	61–6	
#10	Nov. 22	Tulane	W	27–0	

SEC Champion
1970   Record: 9–3–0   SEC: 5–0–0
Final ranking: No. 6 (UPI), No. 7 (AP)
Coach: Charles McClendon
Captains: Felix "Buddy" Lee (QB), John Sage (T)

#12	Sept. 19	Texas A&M	L	18–20	
	Sept. 26	Rice	W	24–0	
	Oct. 3	Baylor	W	31–10	
#19	Oct. 10	Pacific	W	34–0	
#15	Oct. 17	*Kentucky (HC)	W	14–7	
#14	Oct. 24	*at #6 Auburn	W	17–9	
#11	Nov. 7	*at #19 Alabama (9)	W	14–9	ABC
#9	Nov. 14	*Miss. State	W	38–7	
#6	Nov. 21	at #4 Notre Dame	L	0–3	
#6	Nov. 28	at Tulane	W	26–14	
#8	Dec. 5	*#16 Ole Miss	W	61–17	NBC

Orange Bowl, Miami

#5	Jan. 1	#3 Nebraska	L	12–17	NBC

1971 Record: 9–3 SEC: 3–2–0
Final ranking: No. 11 (AP), No. 10 (UPI)
Coach: Charles McClendon
Captains: Louis Cascio (LB), Mike Demarie (OG)

#9	Sept. 11	Colorado	L	21–31	
	Sept. 18	Texas A&M	W	37–0	
#18	Sept. 25	at Wisconsin	W	38–28	
#16	Oct. 2	Rice	W	38–3	
#16	Oct. 9	*Florida (HC)	W	48–7	
#12	Oct. 16	*at Kentucky	W	17–13	
#11	Oct. 30	*at Ole Miss (20)	L	22–24	
#18	Nov. 6	*#4 Alabama	L	7–14	ABC
#20	Nov. 13	*at Miss. State (20)	W	28–3	
#14	Nov. 20	#7 Notre Dame	W	28–8	
#10	Nov. 27	Tulane	W	36–7	

Sun Bowl, El Paso, Texas

#11	Dec. 18	Iowa State	W	33–15	

1972 Record: 9–2–1 SEC: 4–1–1
Final ranking: No. 10 (UPI), No 11 (AP)
Coach: Charles McClendon
Captains: Paul Lyons (QB), James "Pepper" Rutland (LB)

#9	Sept. 16	Pacific	W	31–13	
#8	Sept. 23	Texas A&M	W	42–17	
#9	Sept. 30	Wisconsin	W	27–7	
#8	Oct. 7	at Rice	W	12–6	
#8	Oct. 14	*#9 Auburn	W	35–7	
#7	Oct. 21	*Kentucky	W	10–0	
#6	Nov. 4	*Ole Miss	W	17–16	
#6	Nov. 11	*at #2 Alabama (9)	L	21–35	ABC
#8	Nov. 18	*Miss. State (HC)	W	28–14	
#8	Nov. 25	*at Florida	T	3–3	
#11	Dec. 2	at Tulane	W	9–3	

Astro-Bluebonnet Bowl, Houston

#10	Dec. 30	#11 Tennessee	L	17–24	Hughes

1973 Record: 9–3–0 SEC: 5–1–0
Final ranking: No. 13 (AP), No. 14 (UPI)
Coach: Charles McClendon
Captains: Tyler Lafauci (OG/DT), Charles "Binks" Miciotto (DE)

#15	Sept. 15	#10 Colorado	W	17–6	
#11	Sept. 22	Texas A&M	W	28–23	
#10	Sept. 29	Rice	W	24–9	
#10	Oct. 6	*Florida	W	24–3	
#10	Oct. 13	*at Auburn	W	20–6	
#9	Oct. 20	*Kentucky	W	28–21	
#9	Oct. 27	at South Carolina	W	33–29	
#7	Nov. 3	*at Ole Miss (20)	W	51–14	ABC
#7	Nov. 17	*Miss. State (HC)	W	26–7	
#7	Nov. 22	*#2 Alabama	L	7–21	ABC
#8	Dec. 1	at Tulane	L	0–14	

Orange Bowl, Miami

#13	Jan. 1	#6 Penn State	L	9–16	NBC

1974 Record: 5–5–1 SEC: 2–4–0
Coach: Charles McClendon
Captains: Brad Boyd (TE), Steve Lelekacs (LB)

#9	Sept. 14	Colorado	W	42–14	
#7	Sept. 21	Texas A&M	L	14–21	
#17	Sept. 28	at Rice	T	10–10	
	Oct. 5	*at #13 Florida	L	14–24	
	Oct. 12	*Tennessee (HC)	W	20–10	
	Oct. 19	*at Kentucky	L	13–20	
	Nov. 2	*Ole Miss	W	24–0	
	Nov. 9	*at Alabama (9)	L	0–30	ABC
	Nov. 16	*at Miss. State (20)	L	6–7	
	Nov. 23	Tulane	W	24–22	
	Nov. 30	Utah	W	35–10	

1975 Record: 5–6–0 SEC: 2–4–0
Coach: Charles McClendon
Captains: Greg Bienvenu (C), Steve Cassidy (OT)

	Sept. 13	at #6 Nebraska	L	7–10	
	Sept. 20	#11 Texas A&M	L	8–39	
	Sept. 27	Rice (13)	W	16–13	
	Oct. 4	*#20 Florida (HC)	L	6–34	
	Oct. 11	*at #19 Tennessee	L	10–24	
	Oct. 18	*Kentucky	W	17–14	
	Oct. 25	#20 South Carolina	W	24–6	
	Nov. 1	*at Ole Miss (20)	L	13–17	ABC
	Nov. 8	*#5 Alabama	L	10–23	
	Nov. 15	*Miss. State[†††]	W	6–16	
	Nov. 22	at Tulane	W	42–6	

[†††] Forfeited to LSU by NCAA

1976 Record: 7–3–1 SEC: 3–3–0
Coach: Charles McClendon
Captains: Roy Stuart (OG), Alex "Butch" Knight (DE)

	Sept. 11	#1 Nebraska	T	6–6	
#16	Sept. 18	Oregon State	W	28–11	
#15	Sept. 25	Rice	W	31–0	
#11	Oct. 2	*at #19 Florida	L	23–28	
#20	Oct. 9	*Vanderbilt (HC)	W	33–20	
#16	Oct. 16	*at Kentucky	L	7–21	
	Oct. 30	*Ole Miss	W	45–0	
	Nov. 6	*at #15 Alabama (9)	L	17–28	
	Nov. 13	*at Miss. State[†††] (20)	W	13–21	
	Nov. 20	Tulane	W	17–7	
	Nov. 27	Utah	W	35–7	

[†††] Forfeited to LSU by NCAA

1977 Record: 8–4–0 SEC: 4–2–0
Coach: Charles McClendon
Captains: Kelly Simmons (FB), Steve Ripple (LB)

	Sept. 17	at Indiana	L	21–24	
	Sept. 24	Rice	W	77–0	
	Oct. 1	*#9 Florida	W	36–14	
#18	Oct. 8	*at Vanderbilt	W	28–15	
#16	Oct. 15	*#12 Kentucky (HC)	L	13–33	
	Oct. 22	Oregon	W	56–17	
	Oct. 29	*at Ole Miss (20)	W	28–21	ABC
#18	Nov. 5	*#2 Alabama	L	3–24	ABC
	Nov. 12	*Miss. State	W	27–24	
	Nov. 19	at Tulane	W	20–17	
	Nov. 26	Wyoming	W	66–7	

Sun Bowl, El Paso, Texas

	Dec. 31	Stanford	L	14–24	CBS

1978   Record: 8–4–0   SEC: 3–3–0
Coach: Charles McClendon
Captains: Charles Alexander (TB), Thad Minaldi (LB)

#13	Sept. 16	Indiana	W	24–17	
#10	Sept. 23	Wake Forest	W	13–11	
#11	Sept. 30	at Rice	W	37–7	
#11	Oct. 7	*at Florida	W	34–21	
#11	Oct. 14	*Georgia (HC)	L	17–24	
#16	Oct. 21	*at Kentucky	W	21–0	
#12	Nov. 4	*Ole Miss	W	30–8	ABC
#10	Nov. 11	*at #3 Alabama (9)	L	10–31	ABC
#17	Nov. 18	*at Miss. State (20)	L	14–16	
	Nov. 25	Tulane	W	40–21	
	Dec. 2	Wyoming	W	24–17	

Liberty Bowl, Memphis

	Dec. 23	#18 Missouri	L	15–20	ABC

1979   Record: 7–5–0   SEC: 4–2–0
Coach: Charles McClendon
Captains: John Ed Bradley (C), Willie Teal (CB), Rusty Brown (S)

	Sept. 15	at Colorado	W	44–0	
	Sept. 22	Rice	W	47–3	
#20	Sept. 29	#1 Southern California	L	12–17	
#17	Oct. 6	*Florida	W	20–3	
#13	Oct. 13	*at Georgia	L	14–21	
	Oct. 20	*Kentucky	W	23–19	
	Oct. 27	#8 Florida State (HC)	L	19–24	ABC
	Nov. 3	*at Ole Miss (20)	W	28–24	
	Nov. 10	*#1 Alabama	L	0–3	
	Nov. 17	*Miss. State	W	21–3	
	Nov. 24	at #18 Tulane	L	13–24	ABC

Tangerine Bowl, Orlando

	Dec. 22	Wake Forest	W	34–10	Mizlou

1980   Record: 7–4–0   SEC: 4–2–0
Coach: Jerry Stovall
Captains: Hokie Gajan (FB), Lyman White (OLB)

	Sept. 6	#13 Florida State	L	0–16	
	Sept. 13	Kansas State	W	21–0	
	Sept. 20	Colorado	W	23–20	
	Sept. 27	at Rice	L	7–17	
	Oct. 4	*at #19 Florida	W	24–7	
	Oct. 11	*Auburn (HC)	W	21–17	
	Oct. 18	*at Kentucky	W	17–10	
	Nov. 1	*Ole Miss	W	38–16	ABC
	Nov. 8	*at #6 Alabama	L	7–28	
	Nov. 15	*at #19 Miss. State (20)	L	31–55	
	Nov. 22	Tulane	W	24–7	

1981   Record: 3–7–1   SEC: 1–4–1
Coach: Jerry Stovall
Captains: James Britt (CB), Tom Tully (OG)

	Sept. 5	*#4 Alabama	L	7–24	ABC
	Sept. 12	at #4 Notre Dame	L	9–27	USA
	Sept. 19	Oregon State	W	27–24	
	Sept. 26	Rice	W	28–14	
	Oct. 3	*Florida	L	10–24	
	Oct. 10	*at Auburn	L	7–19	
	Oct. 17	*Kentucky	W	24–10	
	Oct. 24	#20 Florida State (HC)	L	14–38	
	Oct. 3	*at Ole Miss (20)	T	27–27	
	Nov. 14	*Miss. State	L	9–17	
	Nov. 28	at Tulane	L	7–48	

1982   Record: 8–3–1   SEC: 4–1–1
Final ranking: No. 11 (AP, UPI)
Coach: Jerry Stovall
Captains: Alan Risher (QB), James Britt (CB)

	Sept. 18	Oregon State	W	45–7	
	Sept. 25	Rice	W	52–13	
	Oct. 2	*at #4 Florida	W	24–13	
#18	Oct. 9	*Tennessee	T	24–24	
#16	Oct. 16	*at Kentucky	W	34–10	
#14	Oct. 23	South Carolina (HC)	W	14–6	
#13	Oct. 30	*Ole Miss	W	45–8	
#11	Nov. 6	*at #8 Alabama (9)	W	20–10	
#6	Nov. 13	*at Miss. State	L	24–27	ABC
#12	Nov. 20	#7 Florida State	W	55–21	
#7	Nov. 27	Tulane	L	28–31	

Orange Bowl, Miami

#13	Dec. 1	#3 Nebraska	L	20–21	NBC

1983   Record: 4–7–0   SEC: 0–6–0
Coach: Jerry Stovall
Captains: John Fritchie (ILB), Mike Gambrell (C)

#13	Sept. 10	#12 Florida State	L	35–40	ABC
	Sept. 17	at Rice	W	24–10	
	Sept. 24	#9 Washington	W	40–14	
#16	Oct. 1	*#12 Florida	L	17–31	
	Oct. 8	*at Tennessee	L	6–20	TBS
	Oct. 15	*Kentucky (HC)	L	13–21	
	Oct. 22	South Carolina	W	20–6	
	Oct. 29	*at Ole Miss (20)	L	24–27	
	Nov. 5	*#19 Alabama	L	26–32	ABC
	Nov. 12	*Miss. State	L	26–45	
	Nov. 19	at Tulane	W	20–7	TBS

1984   Record: 8–3–1   SEC: 4–1–1
Final ranking: No. 15 (AP), No. 16 (UPI)
Coach: Bill Arnsparger
Captains: Gregg Dubroc (OLB), Liffort Hobley (FS), Kevin
    Langford (OG), Jeff Wickersham (QB)

	Sept. 8	*at Florida	T	21–21	TBS
	Sept. 15	Wichita State	W	47–7	
	Sept. 22	Arizona	W	27–26	
	Sept. 29	at #15 Southern Cal	W	23–3	
#12	Oct. 13	*Vanderbilt (HC)	W	34–27	ESPN
#10	Oct. 20	*at #16 Kentucky	W	36–10	ABC
#7	Oct. 27	Notre Dame	L	22–30	ABC
#15	Nov. 3	*Ole Miss	W	32–29	
#12	Nov. 10	*at Alabama (9)	W	16–14	
#9	Nov. 17	*at Miss. State	L	14–16	
#16	Nov. 24	Tulane	W	33–15	

Sugar Bowl, New Orleans

#11	Jan. 1	#5 Nebraska	L	10–28	ABC

1985   Record: 9–2–1   SEC: 4–1–1
Final ranking: No. 20 (AP, UPI)
Coach: Bill Arnsparger
Captains: Shawn Burks (ILB), Dalton Hilliard (RB), Jeff Wicker-
      sham (QB), Karl Wilson (DE)

#12	Sept. 14	at North Carolina	W	23–13	
#9	Sept. 21	Colorado State	W	17–3	
#8	Oct. 5	*#11 Florida	L	0–20	
#20	Oct. 12	*at Vanderbilt	W	49–7	
#17	Oct. 19	*Kentucky (HC)	W	10–0	ESPN
#16	Nov. 2	*at Ole Miss (20)	W	14–0	TBS
#15	Nov. 9	*#20 Alabama	T	14–14	ABC
#19	Nov. 16	*Miss. State	W	17–15	
#17	Nov. 23	at Notre Dame	W	10–7	USA
#13	Nov. 30	at Tulane	W	31–19	
#12	Dec. 7	East Carolina	W	35–15	

Liberty Bowl, Memphis

#12	Dec. 27	Baylor	L	7–21	Katz

SEC Champion
1986   Record: 9–3–0   SEC: 5–1–0
Final ranking: No. 10 (AP), No. 11 (UPI)
Coach: Bill Arnsparger
Captains: Eric Andolsek (OG), Michael Brooks (OLB), John
      Hazard (OT), Karl Wilson (DE)

#14	Sept. 13	#7 Texas A&M	W	35–17	ESPN
#8	Sept. 20	Miami (Ohio)	L	12–21	
#18	Oct. 4	*at Florida	W	28–17	
#16	Oct. 11	*Georgia	W	23–14	
#12	Oct. 18	*at Kentucky	W	25–16	
#12	Oct. 25	North Carolina (HC)	W	30–3	
#12	Nov. 1	*Ole Miss	L	19–21	ABC
#18	Nov. 8	*at #6 Alabama (9)	W	14–10	ESPN
#12	Nov. 15	*at Miss. State (20)	W	47–0	ESPN
#8	Nov. 22	Notre Dame	W	21–19	
#5	Nov. 29	Tulane	W	37–17	

USF&G Sugar Bowl, New Orleans

#5	Jan. 1	#6 Nebraska	L	15–30	ABC

1987   Record: 10–1–1   SEC: 5–1–0
Final ranking: No. 5 (AP, UPI)
Coach: Mike Archer
Captains: Eric Andolsek (OG), Tommy Clapp (DE), Wendell
      Davis (SE), Nicky Hazard (ILB)

#6	Sept. 5	at #15 Texas A&M	W	17–3	ESPN
#6	Sept. 12	Cal State Fullerton	W	56–12	
#4	Sept. 19	Rice	W	49–16	
#4	Sept. 26	#7 Ohio State	T	13–13	CBS
#7	Oct. 3	*#19 Florida	W	13–10	ESPN
#7	Oct. 10	*at #16 Georgia	W	26–23	ESPN
#6	Oct. 17	*Kentucky	W	34–9	TBS
#5	Oct. 31	*at Ole Miss (20)	W	42–13	
#5	Nov. 7	*#13 Alabama	L	10–22	ESPN
#10	Nov. 14	*Miss. State (HC)	W	34–14	
#9	Nov. 21	at Tulane	W	41–36	

Mazda Gator Bowl, Jacksonville, Fla.

#7	Dec. 31	#8 South Carolina	W	30–13	CBS

SEC Champion
1988   Record: 8–4–0   SEC: 6–1–0
Final ranking: No. 19 (AP)
Coach: Mike Archer
Captains: Tommy Hodson (QB), Todd Coutee (C), Ralph Nor-
      wood (OT), Eric Hill (OLB), Greg Jackson(WS)

#18	Sept. 3	#10 Texas A&M	W	27–0	
#9	Sept. 17	*at Tennessee	W	34–9	TBS
#9	Sept. 24	at #18 Ohio State	L	33–36	ABC
#14	Oct. 1	*at #17 Florida	L	6–19	CBS
	Oct. 8	*#4 Auburn	W	7–6	ESPN
#19	Oct. 15	*Kentucky	W	15–12	
#13	Oct. 29	*Ole Miss (HC)	W	31–20	TBS
#13	Nov. 5	*at #18 Alabama	W	19–18	CBS
#12	Nov. 12	*at Miss. State	W	20–3	TBS
#11	Nov. 19	*#3 Miami (Fla.)	L	3–44	ESPN
#16	Nov. 26	Tulane	W	44–14	

Hall of Fame Bowl, Tampa, Fla.

#16	Jan. 2	#17 Syracuse	L	10–23	NBC

1989   Record: 4–7–0   SEC: 2–5–0
Coach: Mike Archer
Captains: Tommy Hodson (QB), Karl Dunbar (DT)

#7	Sept. 2	at Texas A&M	L	16–28	ESPN
#21	Sept. 16	Florida State	L	21–31	ESPN
	Sept. 30	Ohio	W	57–6	
	Oct. 7	*Florida	L	13–16	
	Oct. 14	*at #12 Auburn	L	6–10	CBS
	Oct. 21	*at Kentucky	L	21–27	
	Oct. 28	*#11 Tennessee (HC)	L	39–45	TBS
	Nov. 4	*at Ole Miss	W	35–30	
	Nov. 11	*#4 Alabama	L	16–32	ESPN
	Nov. 18	*Miss. State	W	44–20	
	Nov. 25	at Tulane	W	27–7	

1990   Record: 5–6–0   SEC: 2–5–0
Coach: Mike Archer
Captains: Sol Graves (QB), Marc Boutte (DT)

	Sept. 8	*Georgia	W	18–13	
	Sept. 15	Miami (Ohio)	W	35–7	
	Sept. 22	*at Vanderbilt	L	21–24	TBS
	Sept. 29	#11 Texas A&M	W	17–8	
	Oct. 6	*at #10 Florida	L	8–34	ESPN
	Oct. 20	*Kentucky	W	30–20	
	Oct. 27	at #12 Florida State	L	3–42	TBS
	Nov. 3	*#17 Ole Miss (HC)	L	10–19	
	Nov. 10	*at Alabama	L	3–24	
	Nov. 17	*at Miss. State (20)	L	22–34	
	Nov. 24	Tulane	W	16–13	

1991   Record: 5–6–0   SEC: 3–4–0
Coach: Curley Hallman
Captains: Todd Kinchen (SE), Marc Boutte (DT), Darrell Wil-
      liams (FB)

	Sept. 7	*at Georgia	L	10–31	ABC
	Sept. 14	at #20 Texas A&M	L	7–45	
	Sept. 21	*Vanderbilt	W	16–14	
	Oct. 5	*#13 Florida	L	0–16	
	Oct. 12	Arkansas State	W	70–14	
	Oct. 19	*at Kentucky	W	29–26	TBS

Oct. 26	#1 Florida State	L	16–27	ESPN
Nov. 2	*at Ole Miss (20)	W	25–22	
Nov. 9	*#8 Alabama	L	17–20	ABC
Nov. 16	*Miss. State (HC)	L	19–28	
Nov. 23	at Tulane	W	39–20	

1992   Record: 2–9–0   SEC: 1–7–0
Coach: Curley Hallman
Captains: Darron Landry (OG), Anthony Williams (LB), Carlton Buckels (CB)

Sept. 5	#7 Texas A&M	L	22–31	ABC
Sept. 12	*#22 Miss. State	W	24–3	
Sept. 19	*at Auburn	L	28–30	JP-TV
Sept. 26	Colorado State	L	14–17	
Oct. 3	*#7 Tennessee	L	0–20	ESPN
Oct. 10	*at #23 Florida	L	21–28	
Oct. 17	*Kentucky	L	25–27	
Oct. 31	*at Ole Miss (20)	L	0–32	
Nov. 7	*#3 Alabama	L	11–31	ABC
Nov. 21	Tulane (HC)	W	24–12	
Nov. 27	*at Arkansas	L	6–30	ESPN

1993   Record: 5–6–0   SEC: 3–5–0
Coach: Curley Hallman
Captains: Chad Loup (QB), Anthony Marshall (FS), Scott Holstein (P), Gabe Northern (DE)

Sept. 4	at #5 Texas A&M	L	0–24	ABC
Sept. 11	*at Miss. State	W	18–16	ABC
Sept. 18	*Auburn	L	10–34	
Sept. 25	*at #13 Tennessee	L	20–42	JP-TV
Oct. 2	Utah State	W	38–17	
Oct. 9	*#5 Florida	L	3–58	ESPN
Oct. 16	*at Kentucky	L	17–35	
Oct. 30	*Ole Miss (HC)	W	19–17	
Nov. 6	*at #5 Alabama	W	17–13	JP-TV
Nov. 20	Tulane	W	24–10	
Nov. 27	*Arkansas	L	24–42	ESPN

1994   Record: 4–7–0   SEC: 3–5–0
Coach: Curley Hallman
Captains: Brett Bech (SE), Ivory Hilliard (FS), Jonny Fayard (TE), Troy Twillie (FS)

Sept. 3	#15 Texas A&M	L	13–18	
Sept. 10	*Miss. State	W	44–24	
Sept. 17	*at #11 Auburn	L	26–30	JP-TV
Oct. 1	*South Carolina (HC)	L	17–18	
Oct. 8	*at #1 Florida	L	18–42	JP-TV
Oct. 15	*Kentucky	W	17–13	
Oct. 29	*at Ole Miss	L	21–34	
Nov. 5	*#6 Alabama	L	17–35	ESPN
Nov. 12	Southern Miss	L	18–20	
Nov. 19	at Tulane	W	49–25	
Nov. 26	*at Arkansas (6)	W	30–12	

1995   Record: 7–4–1   SEC: 4–3–1
Final ranking: No. 25 (USA Today/CNN)
Coach: Gerry DiNardo
Captain: Sheddrick Wilson (WR)

Sept. 2	at #3 Texas A&M	L	17–33	ABC
Sept. 9	*at Miss. State	W	34–16	JP-TV

	Sept. 16	*#5 Auburn	W	12–6	
#18	Sept. 23	Rice (HC)	W	52–7	
#14	Sept. 30	*at South Carolina	T	20–20	JP-TV
#21	Oct. 7	*#3 Florida	L	10–28	JP-TV
	Oct. 14	*at Kentucky	L	16–24	
	Oct. 21	North Texas	W	49–7	
	Nov. 4	*at #16 Alabama	L	3–10	ABC
	Nov. 11	*Ole Miss	W	38–9	
	Nov. 18	*#14 Arkansas	W	28–0	ABC

Poulan/Weed Eater Independence Bowl, Shreveport

Dec. 29	Michigan State	W	45–26	ESPN

1996   Record: 10–2   SEC: 6–2
Final ranking: No. 12 (AP), No. 13 (USA Today/CNN)
Coach: Gerry DiNardo
Captains: Ben Bordelon (OT), Allen Stansberry (LB)

#17	Sept. 7	Houston	W	35–34	
#21	Sept. 21	*at #14 Auburn	W	19–15	ESPN
#17	Sept. 28	New Mexico State (HC)	W	63–7	
#14	Oct. 5	*Vanderbilt	W	35–0	
#12	Oct. 12	*at #1 Florida	L	13–56	CBS
#17	Oct. 19	*Kentucky	W	41–14	
#13	Oct. 26	*Miss. State	W	28–20	JP-TV
#11	Nov. 9	*#10 Alabama	L	0–26	ESPN
#17	Nov. 16	*at Ole Miss	W	39–7	
#18	Nov. 23	Tulane	W	35–17	
#19	Nov. 29	*at Arkansas (6)	W	17–7	CBS

Peach Bowl, Atlanta

#17	Dec. 28	Clemson	W	10–7	ESPN

1997   Record: 9–3   SEC: 6–2
Final ranking: No. 13 (AP, USA Today/ESPN)
Coach: Gerry DiNardo
Captains: Adam Perry (OG), Chuck Wiley (DT)

#10	Sept. 6	Texas–El Paso	W	55–3	
#10	Sept. 13	*at Miss. State	W	24–9	ESPN
#10	Sept. 20	*#12 Auburn	L	28–31	ESPN
#13	Sept. 27	Akron (HC)	W	56–0	
#13	Oct. 4	*at Vanderbilt	W	7–6	
#14	Oct. 11	*#1 Florida	W	28–21	ESPN
#8	Oct. 18	*Ole Miss	L	21–36	JP-TV
#16	Nov. 1	*at Kentucky	W	63–28	ESPN2
#14	Nov. 8	*at Alabama	W	27–0	CBS
#11	Nov. 15	Notre Dame	L	6–24	CBS
#17	Nov. 28	*Arkansas	W	31–21	CBS

Poulan/Weed Eater Independence Bowl, Shreveport

#15	Dec. 28	Notre Dame	W	27–9	ESPN

1998   Record: 4–7   SEC: 2–6
Coach: Gerry DiNardo
Captains: Todd McClure (C), Anthony McFarland (NG), Joe Wesley (ILB)

#7	Sept. 12	Arkansas State	W	42–6	
#7	Sept. 19	*at Auburn	W	31–19	ESPN
#6	Sept. 26	Idaho (HC)	W	53–20	
#6	Oct. 3	*#12 Georgia	L	27–28	ESPN
#11	Oct. 10	*at #6 Florida	L	10–22	ESPN
#21	Oct. 17	*Kentucky	L	36–39	ESPN2
	Oct. 24	*#24 Miss. State	W	41–6	ESPN2
	Oct. 31	*at Ole Miss	L	31–37 (OT)	

	Nov. 7	*Alabama	L	16–22	CBS
	Nov. 21	at #10 Notre Dame	L	36–39	NBC
	Nov. 27	*at #13 Arkansas (6)	L	14–41	CBS

1999   Record: 3–8   SEC: 1–7
Coaches: Gerry DiNardo, Hal Hunter (interim, Arkansas game)
Captains: Rondell Mealey (TB), Johnny Mitchell (DT), Charles Smith (ILB)

	Sept. 4	San José State	W	29–21	
	Sept. 11	North Texas (HC)	W	52–0	
	Sept. 18	*Auburn	L	7–41	ESPN
	Oct. 2	*at #10 Georgia	L	22–23	JP-TV
	Oct. 9	*#8 Florida	L	10–31	CBS
	Oct. 16	*at Kentucky	L	5–31	JP-TV
	Oct. 23	*at #12 Miss. State	L	16–17	ESPN2
	Oct. 30	*#25 Ole Miss	L	23–42	
	Nov. 6	*at #12 Alabama	L	17–23	JP-TV
	Nov. 13	Houston	L	7–20	
	Nov. 26	*#17 Arkansas	W	35–10	CBS

2000   Record: 8–4   SEC: 5–3
Final ranking: No. 22 (AP)
Coach: Nick Saban
Captains: Rohan Davey (QB), Trev Faulk (LB), Louis Williams (OT)

	Sept. 2	Western Carolina	W	58–0	
	Sept. 9	Houston	W	28–13	
	Sept. 16	*at #24 Auburn	L	17–34	ESPN
	Sept. 23	UAB (HC)	L	10–13	
	Sept. 30	*#11 Tennessee	W	38–31 (OT)	ESPN
	Oct. 7	*at #12 Florida	L	9–41	JP-TV
	Oct. 14	*Kentucky	W	34–0	
	Oct. 21	*#13 Miss. State	W	45–38 (OT)	ESPN2
	Nov. 4	*Alabama	W	30–28	CBS
	Nov. 11	*at Ole Miss	W	20–9	ESPN2
#24	Nov. 24	*at Arkansas (6)	L	3–14	CBS

Chick-fil-A Peach Bowl, Atlanta

	Dec. 29	#15 Georgia Tech	W	28–14	ESPN

SEC Champion
2001   Record: 10–3   SEC: 5–3
Final ranking: No. 7 (AP), No. 8 (USA Today/ESPN)
Coach: Nick Saban
Captains: Rohan Davey (QB), Trev Faulk (LB), Robert Royal (TE)

#14	Sept. 1	Tulane	W	48–17	
#13	Sept. 8	Utah State	W	31–14	
#14	Sept. 29	*at #7 Tennessee	L	18–26	ESPN
#18	Oct. 6	*#2 Florida	L	15–44	CBS
	Oct. 13	*at Kentucky	W	29–25	
	Oct. 20	*at Miss. State	W	42–0	ESPN2
	Oct. 27	*Ole Miss	L	24–35	ESPN2
	Nov. 3	*at Alabama	W	35–21	CBS
	Nov. 10	Middle Tennessee (HC)	W	30–14	
	Nov. 23	*#24 Arkansas	W	41–38	CBS
#22	Dec. 1	*#25 Auburn	W	27–14	ESPN

SEC Championship Game, Atlanta

#21	Dec. 8	#2 Tennessee	W	31–20	CBS

Nokia Sugar Bowl, New Orleans

#12	Jan. 1	#7 Illinois	W	47–34	ABC

2002   Record: 8–5   SEC: 5–3
Coach: Nick Saban
Captains: Bradie James (LB), LaBrandon Toefield (RB)

#14	Sept. 1	at #16 Virginia Tech	L	8–26	ABC
#24	Sept. 7	The Citadel	W	35–10	
#25	Sept. 14	Miami (Ohio)	W	33–7	
#22	Sept. 28	*Miss. State	W	31–13	
#21	Oct. 5	UL–Lafayette (HC)	W	48–0	
#18	Oct. 12	*at #16 Florida	W	36–7	ESPN
#14	Oct. 19	*South Carolina	W	38–14	ESPN2
#10	Oct. 26	*at Auburn	L	7–31	JP-TV
#16	Nov. 9	*at Kentucky	W	33–30	JP-TV
#14	Nov. 16	*#10 Alabama	L	0–31	ESPN
#21	Nov. 23	*Ole Miss	W	14–13	ESPN2
#17	Nov. 29	*at Arkansas (6)	L	20–21	CBS

SBC Cotton Bowl, Dallas

	Jan. 1	#9 Texas	L	20–35	Fox

National Champion
SEC Champion
2003   Record: 13–1   SEC: 7–1
Final ranking: No. 1 (USA Today/ESPN), No. 2 (AP)
Coach: Nick Saban
Captains: Chad Lavalais (DT), Matt Mauck (QB), Rodney Reed (OT), Michael Clayton (WR)

#14	Aug. 30	UL–Monroe	W	49–7	
#13	Sept. 6	at Arizona	W	59–13	TBS
#12	Sept. 13	Western Illinois	W	35–7	
#11	Sept. 20	*#7 Georgia	W	17–10	CBS
#7	Sept. 27	*at Miss. State	W	41–6	ESPN2
#6	Oct. 11	*Florida	L	7–19	CBS
#10	Oct. 18	*at South Carolina	W	33–7	ESPN2
#9	Oct. 25	*#17 Auburn	W	31–7	ESPN
#7	Nov. 1	Louisiana Tech (HC)	W	49–10	
#4	Nov. 15	*at Alabama	W	27–3	ESPN
#3	Nov. 22	*at #15 Ole Miss	W	17–14	CBS
#3	Nov. 28	*Arkansas	W	55–24	CBS

SEC Championship Game, Atlanta

#3	Dec. 6	#5 Georgia	W	34–13	CBS

Nokia Sugar Bowl (BCS National Championship Game), New Orleans

#2	Jan. 4	#3 Oklahoma	W	21–14	ABC

2004   Record: 9–3   SEC: 6–2
Final ranking: No. 16 (AP, USA Today/ESPN)
Coach: Nick Saban
Captains: Marcus Spears (DE), Marcus Randall (QB), Corey Webster (CB), Andrew Whitworth (OT)

#4	Sept. 4	Oregon State	W	22–21 (OT)	ESPN
#6	Sept. 11	Arkansas State	W	53–3	
#5	Sept. 18	*at #14 Auburn	L	9–10	CBS
#13	Sept. 25	*Miss. State	W	51–0	JP-TV
#13	Oct. 2	*at #3 Georgia	L	16–45	CBS
#24	Oct. 9	*at #12 Florida	W	24–21	ESPN
#18	Oct. 23	Troy State (HC)	W	24–20	
#19	Oct. 30	*Vanderbilt	W	24–7	
#17	Nov. 13	*Alabama	W	26–10	ESPN
#14	Nov. 20	*Ole Miss	W	27–24	
#14	Nov. 26	*at Arkansas (6)	W	43–14	CBS

Capital One Bowl, Orlando

#12	Jan. 1	#11 Iowa	L	25–30	ABC

2005 Record: 11–2 SEC: 7–1
Final ranking: No. 5 (USA Today/ESPN), No. 6 (AP)
Coach: Les Miles
Captains: Joseph Addai (RB), Skyler Green (WR), Andrew
        Whitworth (OT), Kyle Williams (DT)

#5	Sept. 10	at #15 Arizona State	W	35–31	ESPN
#4	Sept. 26	*#10 Tennessee	L	27–30 (OT)	ESPN2
#4	Oct. 1	*at Miss. State	W	37–7	
#11	Oct. 8	*at Vanderbilt	W	34–6	ESPN2
#10	Oct. 15	*#11 Florida	W	21–17	CBS
#7	Oct. 22	*#15 Auburn	W	20–17 (OT)	ESPN
#7	Oct. 29	North Texas	W	56–3	
#6	Nov. 5	Appalachian State (HC)	W	24–0	
#5	Nov. 12	*at #3 Alabama	W	16–13 (OT)	CBS
#4	Nov. 19	*at Ole Miss	W	40–7	ESPN2
#3	Nov. 25	*Arkansas	W	19–17	CBS

SEC Championship Game, Atlanta

#3	Dec. 3	#13 Georgia	L	14–34	CBS

Chick-fil-A Peach Bowl, Atlanta

#10	Dec. 30	#9 Miami	W	40–3	ESPN

2006 Record: 11–2–0 SEC: 6–2
Final ranking: No. 3 (AP, USA Today)
Coach: Les Miles
Captains: JaMarcus Russell (QB), LaRon Landry (FS), Chris
        Jackson (P/PK)

#8	Sept. 2	UL–Lafayette	W	45–3	
#8	Sept. 9	Arizona	W	45–3E	ESPN2
#6	Sept. 16	*at #3 Auburn	L	3–7	CBS
#10	Sept. 23	Tulane (HC)	W	49–7	
#9	Sept. 30	*Miss. State	W	48–17	LFS
#9	Oct. 7	*at #5 Florida	L	10–23	CBS

#14	Oct. 14	*Kentucky	W	49–0	
#14	Oct. 21	Fresno State	W	38–6	ESPN2
#13	Nov. 4	*at #8 Tennessee	W	28–24	CBS
#12	Nov. 11	*Alabama	W	28–14	ESPN
#9	Nov. 18	*Ole Miss	W	23–20 (OT)	
#9	Nov. 24	*at #5 Arkansas (6)	W	31–26	CBS

Allstate Sugar Bowl, New Orleans

#4	Jan. 3	#11 Notre Dame	W	41–14	Fox

National Champion
SEC Champion
2007 Record: 12–2 SEC: 6–2
Final ranking: No. 1 (AP, USA Today)
Coach: Les Miles
Captains: Matt Flynn (QB), Jacob Hester (RB), Glenn Dorsey
        (DT), Craig Steltz (SS), Patrick Fisher (P)

#2	Aug. 30	*at Miss. State	W	45–0	ESPN
#2	Sept. 8	#9 Virginia Tech	W	48–7	ESPN
#2	Sept. 15	Middle Tennessee	W	44–0	
#2	Sept. 22	*#12 South Carolina	W	28–16	CBS
#2	Sept. 29	at Tulane	W	34–9	ESPN2
#1	Oct. 6	*Florida	W	28–24	CBS
#1	Oct. 13	*at #17 Kentucky	L	37–43 (3OT)	CBS
#4	Oct. 20	*#18 Auburn	W	30–24	ESPN
#3	Nov. 3	*#17 Alabama	W	41–34	CBS
#2	Nov. 10	Louisiana Tech	W	58–10	
#1	Nov. 17	*at Ole Miss	W	41–24	CBS
#1	Nov. 23	*Arkansas	L	48–50 (3OT)	CBS

SEC Championship Game, Atlanta

#5	Dec. 1	#14 Tennessee	W	21–14	CBS

Allstate BCS National Championship Game, New Orleans

#2	Jan. 7	#1 Ohio State	W	38–24	Fox

Tigers in Pro Football

(LSU players who were active for at least one regular-season game in the NFL or AFL.)

HOF: Pro Football Hall of Fame

A
Adams, John (B)—Chicago Bears, 1959–62
Addai, Joseph (RB)—Indianapolis Colts, 2006–07
Alexander, Charles (RB)—Cincinnati Bengals, 1979–85
Alexander, Dan (G)—New York Jets, 1977–89
Alexander, Eric (LB)—New England Patriots, 2004–07
Allen, Kenderick (DT)—New Orleans Saints, 2003; New York
    Giants, 2004–05; Green Bay Packers, 2006; Cincinnati Ben-
    gals, 2007
Andolsek, Eric (G)—Detroit Lions, 1988–91
Andrews, Mitch (TE)—Denver Broncos, 1987

B
Baggett, Billy (B)—Dallas Texans, 1952
Barbay, Roland (NT)—Seattle Seahawks, 1987
Barnes, Walter (G)—Philadelphia Eagles, 1948–51
Bishop, Harold (TE)—Tampa Bay Buccaneers, 1994; Cleveland
    Browns, 1995; Baltimore Ravens, 1996; Pittsburgh Steel-
    ers, 1998
Booker, Fred (DB)—New Orleans Saints, 2005
Booty, Josh (QB)—Cleveland Browns, 2001–03
Bordelon, Ben (OG)—San Diego Chargers, 1997

Bordelon, Ken (LB)—New Orleans Saints, 1976–77, 1979–82
Boutte, Marc (DT)—Los Angeles Rams, 1992–93; Washington
    Redskins, 1994–99
Boyd, Danny (PK)—Jacksonville Jaguars, 2002
Branch, Mel (DE)—Dallas Texans/Kansas City Chiefs,
    1960–65; Miami Dolphins, 1966–68
Brazell, Bennie (WR)—Cincinnati Bengals, 2006
Britt, James (DB)—Atlanta Falcons, 1983–87
Brodnax, John "Red" (FB)—Denver Broncos, 1960
Brooks, Michael (LB)—Denver Broncos, 1987–92; New York
    Giants, 1993–95; Detroit Lions, 1996
Burkett, Jeff (E)—Chicago Cardinals, 1947
Burks, Shawn (LB)—Washington Redskins, 1986
Burrell, Clinton (DB)—Cleveland Browns, 1979–84
Bussey, Young (QB)—Chicago Bears, 1940–41

C
Cannon, Billy (RB/TE)—Houston Oilers, 1960–63; Oakland
    Raiders, 1964–69; Kansas City Chiefs, 1970
Capone, Warren (LB)—Dallas Cowboys, 1975; New Orleans
    Saints, 1976

Carson, Carlos (WR)—Kansas City Chiefs, 1980–89; Philadelphia Eagles, 1989

Casanova, Tommy (S)—Cincinnati Bengals, 1972–77

Cason, Jim (HB)—San Francisco 49ers, 1950–52, 1954; Los Angeles Rams, 1955–56

Caston, Toby (LB)—Houston Oilers, 1987–88; Detroit Lions, 1989–93

Champagne, Ed (T)—Los Angeles Rams, 1947–50

Chatman, Ricky (LB)—Indianapolis Colts, 1987

Clapp, Tommy (LB)—Tampa Bay Buccaneers, 1988

Clark, Ryan (S)—New York Giants, 2002–03; Washington Redskins, 2004–05; Pittsburgh Steelers, 2006–07

Clayton, Michael (WR)—Tampa Bay Buccaneers, 2004–07

Coates, Ray (B)—New York Giants, 1948–49

Coffee, Jim (B)—Chicago Cardinals, 1937–38

Collins, Al (B)—Baltimore Colts, 1950; Green Bay Packers, 1951

Collins, Ray (T)—San Francisco 49ers, 1950–52; New York Giants, 1954; Dallas Texans, 1960–61

Crass, Bill (B)—Chicago Cardinals, 1937

D

Dale, Jeff (S)—San Diego Chargers, 1985–86, 1988

Daniel, Eugene (CB)—Indianapolis Colts, 1984–96; Baltimore Ravens, 1997

Daniels, Travis (DB)—Miami Dolphins, 2005–07

Dardar, Ramsey (DT)—St. Louis Cardinals, 1984

Davey, Rohan (QB)—New England Patriots, 2002–04; Arizona Cardinals, 2005

Davidson, Kenny (DE)—Pittsburgh Steelers, 1990–93; Houston Oilers, 1994–95; Cincinnati Bengals, 1996

Davis, Brad (RB)—Atlanta Falcons, 1975–76

Davis, Domanick (RB)—Houston Texans, 2003–05

Davis, Tommy (PK)—San Francisco 49ers, 1959–69

Davis, Wendell (WR)—Chicago Bears, 1988–93; Indianapolis Colts, 1995

Demarie, John (G/T)—Cleveland Browns, 1967–75; Seattle Seahawks, 1976

Duhe, A. J. (DE/LB)—Miami Dolphins, 1977–84

Dunbar, Karl (DE)—New Orleans Saints, 1993; Arizona Cardinals, 1994–95

E

Edwards, Eric (TE)—Arizona Cardinals, 2004–06; Washington Redskins, 2007

Elko, Bill (NT)—San Diego Chargers, 1983–84; Indianapolis Colts, 1987

Estes, Don (G)—San Diego Chargers, 1966

F

Faneca, Alan (G)—Pittsburgh Steelers, 1998–2007

Faulk, Kevin (RB)—New England Patriots, 1999–2007

Faulk, Trev (LB)—Arizona Cardinals, 2002–03; St. Louis Rams, 2004–05

Fontenot, Herman (RB)—Cleveland Browns, 1985–88; Green Bay Packers, 1989–90

Foster, Larry (WR)—Detroit Lions, 2000–02; Arizona Cardinals, 2003

Fournet, Sid (G)—Los Angeles Rams, 1955–56; Pittsburgh Steelers, 1957; Dallas Texans, 1960–61; New York Jets, 1962–63

Fuller, Eddie (RB)—Buffalo Bills, 1991–93

Fussell, Tommy (DE)—Boston Patriots, 1967

G

Gajan, Hokie (FB)—New Orleans Saints, 1982–85

Garlington, John (LB)—Cleveland Browns, 1968–77

Gaubatz, Dennis (LB)—Detroit Lions, 1963–64; Baltimore Colts, 1965–69

Gay, Randall (CB)—New England Patriots, 2004–07

Glamp, Joe (B)—Pittsburgh Steelers, 1947–49

Gorinski, Walt (B)—Pittsburgh Steelers, 1946

Graves, White (S)—Boston Patriots, 1965–67; Cincinnati Bengals, 1968

Green, Howard (DT)—Baltimore Ravens, 2002; New Orleans Saints, 2003–05

Green, Skyler (WR)—Cincinnati Bengals, 2006–07

Green, Jarvis (DE)—New England Patriots, 2002–07

Gros, Earl (RB)—Green Bay Packers, 1962–63; Philadelphia Eagles, 1964–66; Pittsburgh Steelers, 1967–69; New Orleans Saints, 1970

Guidry, Kevin (CB)—Denver Broncos, 1988; Phoenix Cardinals, 1989

H

Haliburton, Ronnie (TE)—Denver Broncos, 1990–91

Hamilton, Andy (WR)—Kansas City Chiefs, 1973–74; New Orleans Saints, 1975

Harris, Bo (LB)—Cincinnati Bengals, 1975–82

Harris, Wendell (DB)—Baltimore Colts, 1962–65; New York Giants, 1966–67

Henderson, Devery (WR)—New Orleans Saints, 2004–07

Hill, Eric (LB)—Phoenix/Arizona Cardinals, 1989–97; St. Louis Rams, 1998; San Diego Chargers, 1999

Hill, Marquise (DE)—New England Patriots, 2004–06

Hill, Raion (DB)— Buffalo Bills, 2000–01

Hilliard, Dalton (RB)—New Orleans Saints, 1986–93

Hobley, Liffort (DB)—St. Louis Cardinals, 1985; Miami Dolphins, 1987–93

Hodgins, Norm (DB)—Chicago Bears, 1974

Hodson, Tommy (QB)—New England Patriots, 1990–92; Miami Dolphins, 1993; Dallas Cowboys, 1994; New Orleans Saints, 1995–96

J

Jackson, Al (G)—Dallas Cowboys, 2000–01

Jackson, Greg (DB)—New York Giants, 1989–93; Philadelphia Eagles, 1994–95; New Orleans Saints, 1996; San Diego Chargers, 1997–2000

Jackson, Rusty (P)—Los Angeles Rams, 1976; Buffalo Bills, 1978–79

Jackson, Steve (DB)—Oakland Raiders, 1977

James, Bradie (LB)—Dallas Cowboys, 2003–07

James, Garry (RB)—Detroit Lions, 1986–88

James, Tory (CB)—Denver Broncos, 1996–99; Oakland Raiders, 2000–02; Cincinnati Bengals, 2003–06

Jean Batiste, Garland (RB)—New Orleans Saints, 1987

Jefferson, Norman (DB)—Green Bay Packers, 1987–88

Joiner, Tim (LB)—Houston Oilers, 1983–84; Denver Broncos, 1987

Jones, Bert (QB)—Baltimore Colts, 1973–81; Los Angeles Rams, 1982

Jones, Donnie (P)—Seattle Seahawks, 2004; Miami Dolphins, 2005–06; St. Louis Rams, 2007

Jones, Reggie (WR)—San Diego Chargers, 2000–01

Jones, Victor (RB)—Houston Oilers, 1990–91; Denver Broncos, 1992; Pittsburgh Steelers, 1993–94; Kansas City Chiefs, 1994

K

Kavanaugh, Ken, Sr. (E)—Chicago Bears, 1940–41, 1945–50

Kennison, Eddie (WR/KR)—St. Louis Rams, 1996–98; New Orleans Saints, 1999; Chicago Bears, 2000; Denver Broncos, 2001; Kansas City Chiefs, 2001–07

Kinchen, Brian (TE)—Miami Dolphins, 1988–90; Cleveland Browns, 1991–95; Baltimore Ravens, 1996–98; Carolina Panthers, 1999–2000; New England Patriots, 2003

Kinchen, Todd (WR)—Los Angeles Rams, 1992–95; Denver Broncos, 1996; Atlanta Falcons, 1997–98

Konz, Ken (DB)—Cleveland Browns, 1953–59

L

LaFleur, David (TE)—Dallas Cowboys, 1997–2000

LaFleur, Greg (TE)—St. Louis Cardinals, 1981–85; Indianapolis Colts, 1986

Lang, Gene (RB)—Denver Broncos, 1984–87; Atlanta Falcons, 1988–90

Lavalais, Chad (DT)—Atlanta Falcons, 2004–05

LeBlanc, Clarence (S)—New York Giants, 2003

Lee, Buddy (QB)—Chicago Bears, 1971

Leggett, Earl (T)—Chicago Bears, 1957–65; Los Angeles Rams, 1966; New Orleans Saints, 1967

LeJeune, Norman (DB)—Miami Dolphins, 2005–06

Livings, Nate (OL)—Cincinnati Bengals, 2006–07

M

Malancon, Rydell (LB)—Atlanta Falcons, 1984; Green Bay Packers, 1987

Marshall, Anthony (DB)—Chicago Bears, 1994–97; Philadelphia Eagles, 1998

Marshall, Leonard (DE)—New York Giants, 1983–92; New York Jets, 1993; Washington Redskins, 1994

Martin, Eric (WR)—New Orleans Saints, 1985–93; Kansas City Chiefs, 1994

Martin, Sammy (WR)—New England Patriots, 1988–91; Indianapolis Colts, 1991

Masters, Billy (TE)—Buffalo Bills, 1967–69; Denver Broncos, 1970–74; Kansas City Chiefs, 1975–76

Mauck, Matt (QB)—Denver Broncos, 2004; Tennessee Titans, 2005–06

Mawae, Kevin (G/C)—Seattle Seahawks, 1995–97; New York Jets, 1998–2005; Tennessee Titans, 2006–07

May, Bill (B)—Chicago Cardinals, 1937–38

Mayes, Adrian (DB)—Arizona Cardinals, 2004–05

Mayes, Mike (CB)—New Orleans Saints, 1989; New York Jets, 1990; Minnesota Vikings, 1991

McClure, Todd (C)—Atlanta Falcons, 2000–07

McCormick, Dave (T)—San Francisco 49ers, 1966; New Orleans Saints, 1967–68

McDaniel, Orlando (WR)—Denver Broncos, 1982

McFarland, Anthony (DT)—Tampa Bay Buccaneers, 1999–2005; Indianapolis Colts, 2006–07

Mealey, Rondell (RB)—Green Bay Packers, 2001–02

Miller, Arnold (DE)—Cleveland Browns, 1999–2000

Miller, Blake (C)—Detroit Lions, 1992

Miller, Fred (DT)—Baltimore Colts, 1963–72

Miller, Nate (G)—Atlanta Falcons, 1997

Miller, Paul (DE)—Los Angeles Rams, 1954–57; Dallas Texans, 1960–61; San Diego Chargers, 1962

Mixon, Kenny (DE)—Miami Dolphins, 1998–2001; Minnesota Vikings, 2002–04

Montgomery, Bill (B)—Chicago Cardinals, 1946

Moreau, Doug (TE)—Miami Dolphins, 1966–69

Morgan, Mike (LB)—Philadelphia Eagles, 1964–67; Washington Redskins, 1968; New Orleans Saints, 1969–70

Myles, Jesse (RB)—Denver Broncos, 1983–84

N

Neal, Ed (G)—Chicago Bears, 1951

Neck, Tommy (HB)—Chicago Bears, 1962–63

Niswanger, Rudy (C)—Kansas City Chiefs, 2006–07

Northern, Gabe (DE)—Buffalo Bills, 1996–99; Minnesota Vikings, 2000

Norwood, Ralph (T)—Atlanta Falcons, 1989

Nunnery, R. B. (DT)—Dallas Texans, 1960

O

Oliver, Melvin (DE)—San Francisco 49ers, 2006–07

P

Peterman, Stephen (OG)—Dallas Cowboys, 2004–05; Detroit Lions, 2006–07

Porter, Tracy (WR)—Detroit Lions, 1981–82; Baltimore Colts, 1983–84

Price, Marcus (OT)—San Diego Chargers, 1997–99; New Orleans Saints, 2000–01; Buffalo Bills, 2002–04; Dallas Cowboys, 2005

Prude, Ronnie (DB)—Baltimore Ravens, 2006–07

Prudhomme, Remi (C/G)—Buffalo Bills, 1966–67, 1972; Kansas City Chiefs, 1968–69; New Orleans Saints, 1971–72

Q

Quinn, Marcus (DB)—Tampa Bay Buccaneers, 1987

R

Rabb, Warren (QB)—Detroit Lions, 1960; Buffalo Bills, 1961–62

Randall, Marcus (LB)—Tennessee Titans, 2005–06

Ray, Eddie (RB/P)—Boston Patriots, 1970; San Diego Chargers, 1971; Atlanta Falcons, 1972–74; Buffalo Bills, 1976

Raymond, Corey (S)—New York Giants, 1992–94; Detroit Lions, 1995–97

Reed, Joe (B)—Chicago Cardinals, 1937, 1939

Reed, Josh (WR)—Buffalo Bills, 2002–07

Rehage, Steve (S)—New York Giants, 987

Reid, Joe (LB)—Los Angeles Rams, 1951

Reynolds, M. C. (QB)—Chicago Cardinals, 1958–59; Washington Redskins, 1960; Buffalo Bills, 1961; Oakland Raiders, 1962

Rice, George (DT)—Houston Oilers, 1966–69

Richards, Bobby (DE)—Philadelphia Eagles, 1962–65; Atlanta Falcons, 1966–67

Richey, Wade (PK)—San Francisco 49ers, 1998–2000; San Diego Chargers, 2001–02; Baltimore Ravens, 2003–04

Risher, Alan (QB)—Tampa Bay Buccaneers, 1985; Green Bay Packers, 1987

Robinson, Johnny (S)—Dallas Texans/Kansas City Chiefs, 1960–71

Robiskie, Terry (RB)—Oakland Raiders, 1977–79; Miami Dolphins, 1980–81

Rogers, Steve (RB)—New Orleans Saints, 1975; New York Jets, 1976

Roman, Mark (DB)—Cincinnati Bengals, 2000–03; Green Bay Packers, 2004–05; San Francisco 49ers, 2006–07

Royal, Robert (TE)—Washington Redskins, 2003–05; Buffalo Bills, 2006–07

Rukas, Justin (T)—Brooklyn Dodgers, 1936

S

Sandifer, Dan (B)—Washington Redskins, 1948–49; Detroit Lions, 1950; San Francisco 49ers, 1950; Philadelphia Eagles, 1950–51; Green Bay Packers, 1952–53; Chicago Cardinals, 1953

Savoie, Nicky (TE)—New Orleans Saints, 1997

Schroll, Charles (B)—Detroit Lions, 1950; Green Bay Packers, 1951

Scott, Malcolm (TE)—New York Giants, 1983; New Orleans Saints, 1987

Shurtz, Hubert (T)—Pittsburgh Steelers, 1948

Smith, Lance (G)—St. Louis/Phoenix Cardinals, 1985–93; New York Giants, 1994–96

Smoot, Raymond (G)—San Diego Chargers, 1993

Spears, Marcus (DE)—Dallas Cowboys, 2005–07

Stovall, Jerry (DB)—St. Louis Cardinals, 1963–71

Sutton, Mike (DL)—Tennessee Oilers, 1998

Sykes, Gene (DB)—Buffalo Bills, 1963–65; Denver Broncos, 1967

T

Tarasovic, George (DE)—Pittsburgh Steelers, 1952–53, 1956–63; Philadelphia Eagles, 1963–65; Denver Broncos, 1967

(HOF) Taylor, Jim (FB)—Green Bay Packers, 1958–66; New Orleans Saints, 1967

Teal, Willie (CB)—Minnesota Vikings, 1980–86; Los Angeles Raiders, 1987

Thomas, Henry (DT)—Minnesota Vikings, 1987–94; Detroit Lions, 1995–96; New England Patriots, 1997–2000

Tinsley, Gaynell (E)—Chicago Cardinals, 1937–38, 1940

Tinsley, Jess (T)—Chicago Cardinals, 1929–33

(HOF) Tittle, Y. A. (QB)—Baltimore Colts, 1950; San Francisco 49ers, 1951–60; New York Giants, 1961–64

Toefield, LaBrandon (RB)—Jacksonville Jaguars, 2003–07

Torrance, Jack (T)—Chicago Bears, 1939–40

Toth, Zollie (RB)—New York Yanks, 1950–51; Baltimore Colts, 1953–54

Truax, Billy (TE)—Los Angeles Rams, 1964–70; Dallas Cowboys, 1971–73

V

Van Buren, Ebert (RB)—Philadelphia Eagles, 1951–53

(HOF) Van Buren, Steve (RB)—Philadelphia Eagles, 1944–51

Vaughn, Cameron (LB)—Denver Broncos, 2006; Atlanta Falcons, 2007

W

Walker, Denard (CB)—Tennessee Oilers/Titans, 1997–2000; Denver Broncos, 2000–02; Minnesota Vikings, 2003–04; Oakland Raiders, 2005

Webster, Corey (CB)—New York Giants, 2005–07

Wesley, Joe (LB)—San Francisco 49ers, 1999–2001

White, James (DE)—Cleveland Browns, 1985

White, Lyman (LB)—Atlanta Falcons, 1981–82

Whitlatch, Blake (LB)—New York Jets, 1978

Whitworth, Andrew (OT)—Cincinnati Bengals, 2006–07

Wiley, Chuck (DT)—Carolina Panthers, 1999; Atlanta Falcons, 2000–01; Minnesota Vikings, 2002–04

Wilkerson, Ben (C)—Cincinnati Bengals, 2005–06; Atlanta Falcons, 2007

Williams, Chris (CB)—Buffalo Bills, 1981–83

Williams, Harvey (RB)—Kansas City Chiefs, 1991–93; Oakland Raiders, 1994–98

Williams, Kyle (DT)—Buffalo Bills, 2006–07

Williams, Louis (OL)—Carolina Panthers, 2001–02

Williams, Mike (CB)—San Diego Chargers, 1975–82; Los Angeles Rams, 1983

Williams, Willie (T)—Phoenix Cardinals, 1991; New Orleans Saints, 1994

Wilson, Karl (DE)—San Diego Chargers, 1987–88; Phoenix Cardinals, 1989; Miami Dolphins, 1990, 1993; Los Angeles Rams, 1991; New York Jets, 1992–93, San Francisco 49ers, 1993; Tampa Bay Buccaneers, 1994; Buffalo Bills, 1995

Wilson, Sheddrick (WR)—Houston Oilers, 1996

Wimberly, Abner (E)—Green Bay Packers, 1950–52

Winey, Brandon (T)—Denver Broncos, 2001; Washington Redskins, 2003; New York Giants, 2004

Winston, Roy "Moonie" (LB)—Minnesota Vikings, 1962–76

Woodley, David (QB)—Miami Dolphins, 1980–83; Pittsburgh Steelers, 1984–85

Wroten, Claude (OT)—St. Louis Rams, 2006–07

Y

Young, Rodney (DB)—New York Giants, 1995–98

Youngblood, George (S)—Chicago Bears, 1969

Z

Zaunbrecher, Godfrey (C)—Minnesota Vikings, 1971–73

Tigers in the AAFC (All-American Football Conference)

(merged with the NFL in 1950)

Cason, Jim (HB)—San Francisco 49ers, 1948–49
Kingery, Wayne (B) —Baltimore Colts, 1949

Land, Fred (T)—San Francisco 49ers, 1948
Tittle, Y. A. (QB)—Baltimore Colts, 1948–49

Tigers in the NFL, AFL Draft

RS: AFL "Redshirt Draft" in 1965 and 1966
EXP: Expansion draft
Number before name indicates overall draft position.

Name (Position)	Round	Team
1936		
Abe Mickal (B)	6	Detroit Lions
1937		
Marvin "Moose" Stewart (C)	2	Chicago Bears
Gaynell "Gus" Tinsley (E)	2	Chicago Cardinals
1939		
Eddie Gatto (T)	5	Cleveland Rams
Dick Gormley (C)	20	Philadelphia Eagles
1940		
Ken Kavanaugh Sr. (E)	2	Chicago Bears
Young Bussey (B)	18	Chicago Bears
1941		
J. W. Goree (G)	12	Pittsburgh Steelers
Leo Barnes (T)	20	Cleveland Rams
1943		
Walt Gorinski (B)	17	Philadelphia Eagles/ Pittsburgh Steelers
Percy Holland (G)	22	Detroit Lions
Bill Edwards (G)	29	Chicago Cardinals
Willie Miller (G)	30	Cleveland Rams
1944		
Steve Van Buren (B)	1	Philadelphia Eagles
Joe Hartley (T)	12	Chicago Bears
Jim Talley (C)	12	Philadelphia Eagles
Reldon Bennett (T)	16	Boston Yanks
Dilton Richmond (E)	21	Boston Yanks
Jim McLeod (E)	29	Cleveland Rams
1945		
Alvin Dark (B)	2	Philadelphia Eagles
Hal Helscher (B)	8	Green Bay Packers
Holley Heard (T)	11	Chicago Cardinals
Bill Montgomery (B)	13	Philadelphia Eagles
Gene "Red" Knight (B)	26	Chicago Cardinals
Felix Trapani (G)	26	Brooklyn Tigers
1946		
Tom Loflin (E)	19	New York Giants
Andy Kosmac (C)	21	Green Bay Packers
Charlie Webb (E)	23	Washington Redskins
1947 NFL		
Gene "Red" Knight (B)	2	Washington Redskins
Hubert Shurtz (T)	15	Philadelphia Eagles
Ed Champagne (T)	16	Los Angeles Rams
Fred Hall (G)	18	Philadelphia Eagles
Charlie Webb (E)	18	Washington Redskins
Shelton Ballard (C)	19	Chicago Cardinals
Clyde Lindsey (E)	28	Chicago Cardinals

Name (Position)	Round	Team
1947 AAFC		
54 Gene "Red" Knight (B)	7	San Francisco 49ers
1948 NFL		
Y. A. Tittle (QB)	1	Chicago Bears
Dan Sandifer (B)	3	Washington Redskins
Jim Cason (B)	5	Chicago Cardinals
Ray Coates (B)	8	New York Giants
Abner Wimberly (E)	10	Boston Yanks
Fred Land (T)	11	Detroit Lions
Bill Schroll (B)	12	Los Angeles Rams
Ed Claunch (C)	18	Philadelphia Eagles
1948 AAFC		
15 Jim Cason (B)	3	San Francisco 49ers
20 Dan Sandifer (B)	4	Baltimore Colts
32 Fred Land (T)	6	San Francisco 49ers
111 Ray Coates (B)	17	Buffalo Bills
125 Abner Wimberly (E)	19	Los Angeles Dons
200 Albin "Rip" Collins (B)	28	New York Yanks
1949 NFL		
Albin "Rip" Collins (B)	6	Boston
1949 AAFC		
21 Albin "Rip" Collins (B)	3	Cleveland Browns
1950		
Ray Collins (T)	3	San Francisco 49ers
Zollie Toth (B)	4	New York Bulldogs
Ebert Van Buren (B)	8	New York Giants
Melvin Lyle (E)	10	New York Bulldogs
Al Hover (G)	14	Chicago Bears
1951		
Kenny Konz (B)	1	Cleveland Browns
Y. A. Tittle (QB)	1	San Francisco 49ers
Ebert Van Buren (B)	1	Philadelphia Eagles
Albin "Rip" Collins (B)	2	Green Bay Packers
Jim Shoaf (G)	10	Detroit Lions
Joe Reid (C)	13	Los Angeles Rams
Billy Baggett (B)	22	Los Angeles Rams
1952		
George Tarasovic (C)	2	Pittsburgh Steelers
Jim Roshto (B)	12	Detroit Lions
Ray Potter (T)	13	Washington Redskins
Rudy Yeater (T)	13	San Francisco 49ers
Jess Yates (E)	20	San Francisco 49ers
Chet Freeman (B)	23	Dallas Texans
1953		
Paul Miller (T)	6	Los Angeles Rams
LeRoy Labat (B)	18	Baltimore Colts

Name (Position)	Round	Team
Ralph McCleod (E)	27	San Francisco 49ers
1954		
Charles Oakley (B)	23	Chicago Cardinals
William Harris (T)	24	New York Giants
Jerry Marchand (B)	25	Chicago Cardinals
1955		
Sid Fournet (T)	2	New York Giants (traded to Los Angeles Rams)
Gary Dildy (C)	21	New York Giants
Al Doggett (B)	22	New York Giants
Elton Shaw (T)	23	Green Bay Packers
1956		
Robert Nunnery (T)	12	Detroit Lions
O. K. Ferguson (B)	13	Detroit Lions
Vince Gonzales (B)	20	Washington Redskins
1957		
Earl Leggett (T)	1	Chicago Bears
Tommy Davis (B)	11	San Francisco 49ers
Lou Deutschmann (B)	16	New York Giants
Jerry Janes (E)	21	Chicago Bears
1958		
Jim Taylor (B)	2	Green Bay Packers
1959		
J. W. "Red" Broadnax (B)	15	Pittsburgh Steelers
1960 NFL		
Billy Cannon (B)	1	Los Angeles Rams
Johnny Robinson (HB)	1	Detroit Lions
Warren Rabb (QB)	2	Detroit Lions
Max Fugler (C)	8	San Francisco 49ers
Mel Branch (E)	10	San Francisco 49ers
1960 AFL		
Billy Cannon (HB)		Houston Oilers
Mel Branch (T/G)		Denver Broncos
Max Fugler (C)		Boston Patriots
Warren Rabb (QB)		Dallas Texans
Johnny Robinson (HB)		Dallas Texans
1961 NFL		
Charles "Bo" Strange (C)	2	Philadelphia Eagles
Bobby Richards (T)	15	Philadelphia Eagles
1961 AFL		
Charles "Bo" Strange (C)	3	Denver Broncos
1962 NFL		
Earl Gros (B)	1	Green Bay Packers
Wendell Harris (B)	1	Baltimore Colts
Roy "Moonie" Winston (G)	4	Minnesota Vikings
Fred Miller (T)	7	Baltimore Colts
Billy Joe Booth (T)	13	New York Giants
Jimmy Field (B)	16	Green Bay Packers
Tommy Neck (B)	18	Chicago Bears
1962 AFL		
Earl Gros (FB)	2	Oklers
Roy "Moonie" Winston (G)	6	San Diego Chargers
Wendell Harris (HB)	7	San Diego Chargers
Tommy Neck (HB)	20	Boston Patriots
Jimmy Field (QB)	26	Boston Patriots
Bob Richards (T)	32	Oakland Raiders
1963 NFL		
Jerry Stovall (B)	1	St. Louis Cardinals

Name (Position)	Round	Team
Don Estes (T)	4	St. Louis Cardinals
Dennis Gaubatz (LB)	8	Detroit Lions
Gene Sykes (B)	8	Philadelphia Eagles
Buddy Soefker (B)	18	Los Angeles Rams
1963 AFL		
Jerry Stovall (HB)	1	New York Jets
Don Estes (T)	2	Houston Oilers
Gene Sykes (E)	19	Buffalo Bills
Buddy Soefker (LB)	20	San Diego Chargers
Dennis Gaubatz (G)	25	Boston Patriots
1964 NFL		
Billy Truax (DE)	2	Cleveland Browns
Remi Prudhomme (T)	3	St. Louis Cardinals
Mike Morgan (E)	17	Philadelphia Eagles
Willis Langley (T)	18	Detroit Lions
1964 AFL		
Billy Truax (DE)	2	Houston Oilers
Remi Prudhomme (T)	14	Buffalo Bills
1965 NFL		
Dave McCormick (T)	5	San Francisco 49ers
Pat Screen (B)	10	Cleveland Browns
1965 AFL		
Dave McCormick (T)	1 (RS)	Boston Patriots
Mickey Cox (T)	4 (RS)	Oakland Raiders
Billy Ezell (DB)	6 (RS)	Boston Patriots
Beau Colle (DB)	8 (RS)	Boston Patriots
Pat Screen (QB)	12 (RS)	New York Jets
White Graves (DB)	17	Boston Patriots
1966 NFL		
George Rice (T)	1	Chicago Bears
1966 AFL		
George Rice (T)	3	Houston Oilers
Joe Labruzzo (HB)	11	Oakland Raiders
Doug Moreau (TE)	19	Miami Dolphins
1967		
77 Billy Masters (TE)	3	Kansas City Chiefs
152 John DeMarie (DE)	6	Cleveland Browns
206 Tom Fussell (DT)	8	Boston Patriots
Earl Leggett (DT)	EXP	New Orleans Saints
1968		
47 John Garlington (LB)	2	Cleveland Browns
184 Sammy Grezaffi (DB)	7	Kansas City Chiefs
349 James Dousay (RB)	13	Houston Oilers
White Graves (DB)	EXP	Cincinnati Bengals
1969		
136 Ken Newfield (RB)	6	Oakland Raiders
154 Bill Fortier (T)	6	Baltimore Colts
206 Maurice LeBlanc (DB)	8	Kansas City Chiefs
267 Tommy Morel (FL)	11	New Orleans Saints
1970		
83 Eddie Ray (DB)	4	Boston Patriots
286 Godfrey Zaunbrecher (C)	11	Minnesota Vikings
421 George Bevan (DB)	17	Buffalo Bills
1971		
167 Buddy Lee (QB)	7	Chicago Bears
216 Mike Anderson (LB)	9	Pittsburgh Steelers
420 John Sage (LB)	17	Philadelphia Eagles

Name (Position)	Round	Team
1972		
29 Tommy Casanova (DB)	2	Cincinnati Bengals
97 Andy Hamilton (WR)	4	Kansas City Chiefs
186 Ronnie Estay (DT/LB)	8	Denver Broncos
367 Ken Kavanaugh, Jr. (TE)	15	New York Giants
1973		
2 Bert Jones (QB)	1	Baltimore Colts
70 John Wood (DT)	3	Denver Broncos
1974		
264 Norm Hodgins (DB)	11	Chicago Bears
429 Collis Temple	17	Detroit Lions
1975		
22 Mike Williams (DB)	1	San Diego Chargers
77 Bo Harris (LB)	3	Cincinnati Bengals
163 Steve Rogers(RB)	7	New Orleans Saints
211 Brad Davis (RB)	9	Atlanta Falcons
250 Brad Boyd (TE)	10	Detroit Lions
308 Ben Jones (WR)	12	St. Louis Cardinals
1976		
149 Ken Bordelon (DE)	5	Los Angeles Rams
189 Steve Cassidy (DT)	7	Cleveland Browns
210 Larry Shipp (WR)	8	Seattle Seahawks
479 Allen Misher (WR)	17	Houston Oilers
1977		
13 A. J. Duhe (DT)	1	Miami Dolphins
200 Dan Alexander (DT)	8	New York Jets
223 Terry Robiskie (RB)	8	Oakland Raiders
1978		
248 Blake Whitlatch (LB)	9	San Diego Chargers
325 Lew Sibley (LB)	12	Chicago Bears
1979		
12 Charles Alexander (RB)	1	Cincinnati Bengals
151 Clinton Burrell (DB)	6	Cleveland Browns
269 Al Green (DB)	10	San Diego Chargers
1980		
30 Willie Teal (DB)	2	Minnesota Vikings
114 Carlos Carson (WR)	5	Kansas City Chiefs
126 John Adams (LB)	5	Oakland Raiders
214 David Woodley (QB)	8	Miami Dolphins
1981		
49 Chris Williams (DB)	2	Buffalo Bills
54 Lyman White (LB)	2	Atlanta Falcons
82 Greg LaFleur (TE)	3	Philadelphia Eagles
99 Tracy Porter (WR)	4	Detroit Lions
249 Hokie Gajan (RB)	10	New Orleans Saints
1982		
50 Orlando McDaniel (WR)	2	Denver Broncos
289 Willie Turner (WR)	11	Los Angeles Raiders
1983		
37 Leonard Marshall (DT)	2	New York Giants
43 James Britt (DB)	2	Atlanta Falcons
58 Tim Joiner (LB)	3	Houston Oilers
71 Ramsey Dardar (DT)	3	St. Louis Cardinals
124 Malcolm Scott (TE)	5	New York Giants
192 Bill Elko (DT)	7	San Diego Chargers
1984		
94 Rydell Malancon (LB)	4	Atlanta Falcons
205 Eugene Daniel (DB)	8	Indianapolis Colts

Name (Position)	Round	Team
298 Gene Lang (RB)	11	Denver Broncos
1985		
55 Jeffrey Dale (DB)	2	San Diego Chargers
72 Lance Smith (OT)	3	St. Louis Cardinals
74 Liffort Hobley (DB)	3	Pittsburgh Steelers
179 Eric Martin (WR)	7	New Orleans Saints
272 Gregg Dubroc (LB)	10	New York Giants
1986		
31 Dalton Hilliard (RB)	2	New Orleans Saints
99 Garry James (RB)	2	Detroit Lions
274 Jeff Wickersham (QB)	10	Miami Dolphins
1987		
59 Karl Wilson (DE)	3	San Diego Chargers
72 Henry Thomas (NT)	3	Minnesota Vikings
83 Michael Brooks (LB)	3	Denver Broncos
158 Toby Caston (LB)	6	Houston Oilers
183 Roland Barbay (DT)	7	Seattle Seahawks
335 Norman Jefferson (DB)	12	Green Bay Packers
1988		
27 Wendell Davis (WR)	1	Chicago Bears
79 Kevin Guidry (CB)	3	Denver Broncos
97 Sammy Martin (WR/RB)	4	New England Patriots
111 Eric Andolsek (OG)	5	Detroit Lions
243 Rogie Magee (WR)	9	Chicago Bears
331 Chris Carrier (S)	12	Phoenix Cardinals
333 Brian Kinchen (TE)	12	Miami Dolphins
1989		
10 Eric Hill (LB)	1	Phoenix Cardinals
38 Ralph Norwood (OT)	2	Atlanta Falcons
78 Greg Jackson (DB)	3	New York Giants
106 Mike Mayes (DB)	4	New Orleans Saints
171 Ron Sancho (LB)	7	Kansas City Chiefs
252 Rudy Harmon (LB)	9	San Francisco 49ers
1990		
43 Kenny Davidson (DT)	2	Pittsburgh Steelers
59 Tommy Hodson (QB)	3	New England Patriots
88 Tony Moss (WR)	4	Chicago Bears
100 Eddie Fuller (RB)	4	Buffalo Bills
164 Ronnie Haliburton (TE)	4	Denver Broncos
209 Karl Dunbar (DT)	8	Pittsburgh Steelers
246 Clint James (DT)	9	New York Giants
1991		
21 Harvey Williams (RB)	1	Kansas City Chiefs
168 Blake Miller (C)	7	New England Patriots
285 Slip Watkins WR)	11	Detroit Lions
1992		
60 Todd Kinchen (WR)	3	Los Angeles Rams
63 Marc Boutte (DT)	3	Los Angeles Rams
1994		
36 Kevin Mawae (C)	2	Seattle Seahawks
69 Harold Bishop (TE)	3	Tampa Bay Buccaneers
1995		
85 Rodney Young (S)	3	New York Giants
172 Marcus Price (OT)	6	Jacksonville Jaguars
1996		
18 Eddie Kennison (WR)	1	St. Louis Rams
44 Tory James (CB)	2	Denver Broncos
53 Gabe Northern (DE)	2	Buffalo Bills

Name (Position)	Round	Team		Name (Position)	Round	Team
1997				50 Devery Henderson (WR)	2	New Orleans Saints
22 David LaFleur (TE)	1	Dallas Cowboys		63 Marquise Hill (DE)	2	New England Patriots
75 Denard Walker (CB)	3	Tennessee Oilers		83 Stephen Peterman (OG)	3	Dallas Cowboys
165 Nicky Savoie (TE)	6	New Orleans Saints		142 Chad Lavalais (DT)	5	Atlanta Falcons
1998				224 Donnie Jones (P)	7	Seattle Seahawks
26 Alan Faneca (OL)	1	Pittsburgh Steelers		225 Matt Mauck (QB)	7	Denver Broncos
49 Kenny Mixon (DL)	2	Miami Dolphins		**2005**		
62 Chuck Wiley (DL)	3	Carolina Panthers		20 Marcus Spears (DE)	1	Dallas Cowboys
1999				43 Corey Webster (CB)	2	New York Giants
15 Anthony McFarland (NG)	1	Tampa Bay Buccaneers		104 Travis Daniels (CB)	4	Miami Dolphins
46 Kevin Faulk (TB)	2	New England Patriots		**2006**		
236 Todd McClure (C)	7	Atlanta Falcons		30 Joseph Addai (RB)	1	Indianapolis Colts
2000				55 Andrew Whitworth (OT)	2	Cincinnati Bengals
34 Mark Roman (DB)	2	Cincinnati Bengals		68 Claude Wroten (DT)	3	St. Louis Rams
252 Rondell Mealey (RB)	7	Green Bay Packers		125 Skyler Green (WR)	4	Dallas Cowboys
2001				134 Kyle Williams (DT)	5	Buffalo Bills
164 Brandon Winey (OL)	6	Miami Dolphins		197 Melvin Oliver (DE)	6	San Francisco 49ers
172 Josh Booty (QB)	6	Seattle Seahawks		231 Bennie Brazell (WR)	7	Cincinnati Bengals
211 Louis Williams (OL)	7	Carolina Panthers		**2007**		
2002				1 JaMarcus Russell (QB)	1	Oakland Raiders
35 Josh Reed (WR)	2	Buffalo Bills		6 LaRon Landry (FS)	1	Washington Redskins
117 Rohan Davey (QB)	4	New England Patriots		23 Dwayne Bowe (WR)	1	Kansas City Chiefs
126 Jarvis Green (DE)	4	New England Patriots		30 Craig Davis (WR)	1	San Diego Chargers
160 Robert Royal (TE)	5	Washington Redskins		213 Chase Pittman (DE)	7	Cleveland Browns
190 Howard Green (DT)	6	Houston Texans		**2008**		
2003				5 Glenn Dorsey (DT)	1	Kansas City Chiefs
101 Domanick Davis (RB)	4	Houston Texans		68 Chevis Jackson (CB)	3	Atlanta Falcons
103 Bradie James (LB)	4	Dallas Cowboys		69 Jacob Hester (FB)	3	San Diego Chargers
132 LaBrandon Toefield (RB)	4	Jacksonville Jaguars		81 Early Doucet (WR)	3	Arizona Cardinals
244 Norman LeJeune (DB)	7	Philadelphia Eagles		120 Craiz Stelz (SS)	4	Chicago Bears
2004				209 Matt Flynn (QB)	7	Green Bay Packers
15 Michael Clayton (WR)	1	Tampa Bay Buccaneers		232 Keith Zinger (TE)	7	Atlanta Falcons

National Award Winners

Heisman Trophy
Billy Cannon, halfback, 1959

Walter Camp Trophy (best player)
Billy Cannon, halfback, 1959
Jerry Stovall, halfback, 1962

Biletnikoff Award (best receiver)
Josh Reed, 2001

Rimington Award (best center)
Ben Wilkerson, 2004

Draddy Trophy (best football student-athlete)
Rudy Niswanger, center, 2005

Wuerffel Trophy (athletic, academic, and community service)
Rudy Niswanger, center, 2005

Manning Award (best quarterback)
JaMarcus Russell, 2006

National Coach of the Year
Paul Dietzel, 1959 (AFCA)
Charles McClendon, 1970 (AFCA)
Jerry Stovall, 1982 (Walter Camp Football Foundation)
Nick Saban, 2003 (AP, Bear Bryant, Eddie Robinson)

College Football Hall of Fame
Dana X. Bible, coach (inducted 1951)
Lawrence "Biff" Jones, coach (inducted 1954)
Gaynell "Gus" Tinsley, end (inducted 1956)
Ken Kavanaugh, end (inducted 1963)
Abe Mickal, halfback (inducted 1967)
G. E. "Doc" Fenton, quarterback (inducted 1971)
Charles McClendon, coach (inducted 1986)
Tommy Casanova, safety (inducted 1995)

Pro Football Hall of Fame
Steve Van Buren, halfback (inducted 1965)
Y. A. Tittle, quarterback (inducted 1971)
Jimmy Taylor, fullback (inducted 1976)

INDEX

—